Beacons in the Darkness

Beacons
in the
Darkness

Hope and
Transformation
Among America's
Community
Newspapers

Dave Hoekstra

A MIDWAY BOOK

AGATE

CHICAGO

First printed in October 2022

Printed in the United States of America

10 9 8 7 6 5 4 3 2 1   22 23 24 25 26

Cover design by Morgan Krehbiel

Author photo by Wendy Love/Pivot Photography

Library of Congress Cataloging-in-Publication Data

Names: Hoekstra, Dave, author.
Title: Beacons in the darkness : hope and transformation among America's
   community newspapers / Dave Hoekstra.
Description: Chicago : Agate, 2022. | "A Midway book".
Identifiers: LCCN 2022019158 (print) | LCCN 2022019159 (ebook) | ISBN
   9781572843165 (trade paperback) | ISBN 9781572848672 (ebook)
Subjects: LCSH: Community newspapers--United States--History--21st century.
   | Newspaper publishing--United States--History--21st century. |
   Publishers and publishing--United States--History--21st century.
Classification: LCC PN4888.C594 H64 2022 (print) | LCC PN4888.C594
   (ebook) | DDC 071/.3--dc23/eng/20220511
LC record available at https://lccn.loc.gov/2022019158
LC ebook record available at https://lccn.loc.gov/2022019159

Midway Books is an imprint of Agate Publishing. Agate books are available in bulk at discount prices. For more information, visit agatepublishing.com.

For Lon Grahnke and Dr. Marilyn Hollman

Contents

Foreword

by Ron Rapoport

First, a confession.

I have always envied Dave Hoekstra.

Back when Dave and I were working at the *Chicago Sun-Times*, I was a sports columnist chasing after Michael Jordan's Bulls, Mike Ditka's Bears, and various drearily anonymous Cubs teams.

This was good duty, no question about that, but it had the disadvantage of being tied to the calendar. October, World Series; February, Super Bowl; April, the Masters. And so on.

Which is why whenever Dave had a piece in the paper, I read it with a sense of wistfulness. While my sportswriting buddies and I were practicing group journalism at its finest, Dave was out there by himself, often in a small Midwestern town I'd never heard of, talking to somebody interesting about music or food or life on the road or something equally fascinating.

Occasionally, Dave would light out for the territory and report back from Biloxi or Houston or Key West, always coming up with a great story and always making me feel a sense of longing. Sometimes, Dave would leave the country altogether and wind up eating rabbit on the top of a 10,300-foot mountain in Colombia, talking to Fidel Castro's former cigar maker in the Bahamas, or hunting for sea turtles in Guatemala. Every time, I'd read one of Dave's great stories and I'd ask myself two questions: How did he find them, and why couldn't I have been there with him?

Occasionally, Dave would wander into my territory and, again, make it all his own. When the *Sun-Times* emptied the office to cover the Bears in the 1986 Super Bowl, Dave was the guy who gave a sense of the city, writing about voodoo doctors and Jim McMahon's wanderings through New Orleans. Dave also had such a great love for minor league baseball and the characters who populated it that he wrote a book about it. And when he discovered Ted "Double Duty" Radcliffe, a former Negro Leaguer who had a ton of great stories to tell—some of which might even have been true—I had to put his story about him in a collection of Chicago sportswriters I was editing.

The books Dave has written before this one provide another example of the wide range of topics that capture his fancy. A history of supper clubs, how soul food helped fuel the civil rights movement, and camping across America, a tale of the country in motion.

And now we are presented with Dave's latest book—a history of small family-owned newspapers and their fight for survival in a digital age—and what a beauty it is. Who but Dave would travel to Eldon, Missouri, and Carroll, Iowa? To Madison, Indiana, and Hillsboro, Illinois? To Charleston, South Carolina; Marfa, Texas; and Bakersfield, California?

Nobody, that's who.

It was no surprise to me that as Dave told the story of small-town newspapers and their efforts to survive in the modern age, he would come across a gathering of fascinating people with great stories to tell.

Doug Burns, the son of the general manager of the *Carroll Times Herald*, told him how as many as fifty presidential candidates had visited Carroll over the years because it was a regular stop on the Iowa caucuses trail.

Curt Jacobs, former publisher of the *Madison Courier* in Indiana, told him how riverboats used to dock in the town, pick up papers, and deliver them to customers downstream.

Walter Hussman Jr., owner of the *Arkansas Democrat-Gazette*, told him how he created an all-iPad edition of the paper, and when older readers balked at the newfangled gizmo, he gave them free iPads and taught them how to use them.

And wherever he went, Dave found a spirit of resilience and strength of will that keeps America's small-town newspapers going against all odds.

"The newspaper is like the family farm," John Galer, who started out as a delivery boy for the Hillsboro *Journal-News* in Illinois and ended up owning the place, told Dave.

"We're kind of like the last Comanches that haven't been dragged onto the reservation," Doug Burns told him.

It doesn't take a lot of imagination to understand why Dave loves the people who tell him stories like this. Or to understand why writers like me are so envious of the places he goes, the people he meets, and the stories he writes.

Ron Rapoport is a sportswriter and author who lives in Santa Monica, California. He was a sports columnist for the Chicago Sun-Times *and the* Los Angeles Daily News *and was sports commentator for NPR's* Weekend Edition Saturday. *He is the recipient of the Ring Lardner Award for Excellence in Sports Journalism and has written a number of books about sports and show business. His latest book is* Let's Play Two: The Legend of Mr. Cub, the Life of Ernie Banks.

Introduction

When people walk through the front door of the Hillsboro *Journal-News* office in Hillsboro, Illinois, if they look down to their right, they will see a series of cardboard file folders. The folders are inscribed with "Weddings" and "Anniversaries," and they are usually empty. "We want to paint the image that if it is important, it has to be in the newspaper," *Journal-News* publisher Mike Plunkett said. "If people don't submit those [announcements], a lot of times we know about it through Facebook. We reach out to them and say, 'Make sure you send us a picture when you get married. We want that in the newspaper.'"

To understand a community newspaper like the *Journal-News*, you need to understand the meaning of community, and the idea that the sense of place these publications are trying to foster is becoming more distant in modern America. This is not just a book about journalism. It is not another account of the miseries of the newspaper industry. It is a book about a vanishing terrain of community ties and dedication to the common good. It is a celebration of the potential of the newspaper model when it embraces and understands neighbors and possibilities.

I began research on this book in June 2019. I traveled around America, interviewing multigenerational family newspaper publishers, reporters, readers, and community figures. I went to Bakersfield, California; Eureka Springs, Arkansas; Memphis, Tennessee; Carroll, Iowa; Dixon, Illinois; and Eldon, Missouri; and I dipped into the unique family history behind the *Chicago*

Reader alternative weekly in my own backyard.

But my North Star was the town of Hillsboro in central-southern Illinois. The ties that fifth-generation *Journal-News* owner John Galer had with his rural community were inspiring and unbending. He was fatherly and gently spiritual, and I found his optimism a rare commodity in cynical times.

I did more than fifty interviews for this book. Throughout these conversations I tried to draw from the characteristics I saw in Hillsboro:

- Dedication to the meaning of community
- Respect for history
- Humility
- Isolation—physical or social
- Empathy

Empathy is birthed from the richness of a community. The unselfish energy of independent family newspapers creates a light that, when at its brightest, can shine on everyone. The multigenerational family-newspaper owners I met had visions far greater than their own self-interest. A family newspaper is the connective thread of a community, its hopes and dreams, its past and its present. I tried to respect the hopes of these journalists and share the beauty of their collective history.

They are beacons in the darkness.

Sometimes, while I was researching this book, people asked me, "Who is going to read a book about family newspapers?" And that question even came from a couple of older journalists. But this book does not just describe the struggles independent family operators face today; it also profiles the steadfast family members that create identity and conscience in a community.

The newspaper helps you understand where you are and what that means. This is untapped territory in a country that is so divided. "When a newspaper dies in America, it is not simply that a commercial enterprise has failed; a sense of place has failed." That's what Richard Rodriguez wrote in the cover story for the November 2009 issue of *Harper's Magazine*.

A continuous five-generation newspaper in any American city in 2019 was an amazing thing. I wondered how the core values of commitment and community evolved through generations at family newspapers. Were America's "ghost" newspapers (defined by diminished staff and ambitions) even relevant? If both family-run and community newspapers went away, where would truthful, organic news come from? In November 2019, PEN America released a comprehensive report that concluded the local news-gathering process was broken. "That first draft of history is not being written—it has completely disappeared," said Suzanne Nossel, chief executive of PEN America. The group also reported that since 2004, more than 1,800 local print outlets had closed in the United States and at least two hundred counties had no newspapers at all.

And then, in January 2020, all bets were off.

The first American case of COVID-19 was identified on January 20, 2020. In March, Americans were told to shelter in place. By the end of the year, there were 20 million cases of COVID-19 and over 350,000 confirmed deaths in America. Every aspect of American life had changed. Businesses and restaurants closed. All sports stopped. And started. And stopped.

America's newspapers, already in critical condition, were hit hard from a loss of advertising. Some papers stopped print editions and pivoted to digital. Others completely closed.

More than once during in-person interviews, I witnessed newspaper staffers and community members become emotional about their connection with their newspaper. A couple of family publishers were near tears. These newspapers were not about hedge funds and stockholders, here today and gone tomorrow. These newspapers were about life itself, an ethic as entrenched as a century-old oak tree. And as I circled back with my sources during the pandemic, I became inspired by characteristics that had emerged from pure necessity. Perhaps I did not recognize them before. No one gave up. Newspaper people chase down every story, even when they don't know how it ends.

The pandemic cut to the core of what I set out to chronicle: the meaning of community. American life was broken down into bits and pieces. There were no big concerts, gatherings at movie theaters, or large congregations at church. It was easy to transfer this more intimate thinking to newspapers, and I did witness that in my research. Smaller, rural newspapers were generally positive and forward-thinking.

On one hand, Americans were told to practice social distancing. On the other hand, Americans were told that they were all in "it" together, even though everyone certainly had a different definition of "it." The optimum result, of course, would be an enriched community. In the March 25, 2020, *New York Times*, Harvard political professor Michael Sandel defined the meaning of the common good for columnist Thomas Friedman. Sandel said, "The common good is about how we live together in community . . . the benefits and burdens we share, the sacrifices we make for one another. It's about the lessons we learn from one another about how to live a good and decent life."

—

My newspaper career started in 1972 at the midsized *Aurora Beacon-News*, a daily about fifty miles west of Chicago. I was a junior in high school. I bobbed and weaved through suburban Chicago journalism before landing at the *Chicago Sun-Times* in February 1985. A year earlier, half-brothers Marshall Field V and Ted Field had sold the paper to tabloid king Rupert Murdoch. The *Sun-Times* never became as sensational as Murdoch's *New York Post*, and Murdoch had deep pockets to cover the news. I was one of several reporters who were dispatched to New Orleans to cover the Chicago Bears' 1986 appearance in the Super Bowl. The newspaper rented an office at the Hyatt hotel, adjacent to the Superdome. I was in New Orleans for six days. You never see this extreme devotion to news today.

Murdoch dumped the *Sun-Times* in 1986 so he could buy WFLD-TV in Chicago as part of his emerging Fox network. A series of dream weavers and grifters followed, including Canadian press baron Conrad Black, a worse version of Murdoch. Black and his vice president David Radler were indicted for skimming money from their own company.

During their tenure our offices were on the fourth floor of a building at 401 N. Wabash (ironically razed to make way for Trump Tower), and we were told the escalators were shut off to "conserve energy." The money was going into our owners' pockets. If newspapers do reflect community, these colorful days of the *Sun-Times* certainly mirrored the long, crooked history of Chicago and Illinois.

By 2014 I'd had enough. I was in the features department and our news holes were shrinking. Morale was crippled. Digital was not translating in presentation, nor was advertising amounting to increased revenue. Chicago-area tech entrepreneur Michael W. Ferro Jr. was in charge with his new company "Wrapports" (the rapport of new technology and the wrapping of a newspaper). Trouble was, Ferro had no passion for newspapers. He did install a Pop-A-Shot machine adjacent to our break room. Ferro sold out in 2017 and moved over to the *Chicago Tribune*. He helped ruin that paper as well by selling his 25 percent share in Tribune Publishing to Alden Global Capital. I took a buyout. Frankly, I was encouraged to take a buyout.

I wrote books, produced a music documentary, continued to write stories for my website, and somehow always came back to the idea of sense of place. As I grew even older, I thought about cycles of life. I remembered the tight sense of community around the smaller papers I worked at when I was coming up in Chicago-area journalism: the *Aurora Beacon-News*, the *Barrington Courier-Review*, and the *Suburban Sun-Times*, next to the Vegas-style Navarro Ballroom in Elk Grove Village, Illinois.

As I visited small family-run and community newspapers for this book, I saw how some journalists' roles in their community often became blurred. I didn't remember things that way. Trevor Vernon is the third-generation publisher of the *Eldon Advertiser* in Eldon, Missouri. In June 2020, he was elected mayor of Eldon just before his fortieth birthday. Doug Burns, vice president of news for the Herald Publishing Company in rural Carroll, Iowa, used his outside community-related businesses to keep the family newspaper alive. I continuously checked in on these people. I wound up caring about them. During a Mother's Day conversation in the midst of the COVID-19 pandemic, Burns was frustrated and tired. He told me he had considered suicide. He told me to go ahead and print that. And I'll never forget my visit to Bakersfield, California, to learn how a family publisher green-lighted an in-depth investigation into her own family's sordid background of murder cases and pedophilia.

John Galer and his family welcomed me into their offices and community for several visits to Hillsboro. I learned about the challenges of running their business, I heard about personal family tribulations, and I learned a lot about Hillsboro, a small town with daring dreams. By the fall of 2021, the

Smithsonian Institution had picked Hillsboro to be featured in a traveling exhibit about innovation in rural America when many towns are confronting globalism and the closing of manufacturing corridors.

There were long shadows down the home stretch of this book, and the year 2020 was turning into a fast-moving kaleidoscope of tragedy. By Memorial Day weekend 2020, the pandemic had been pushed aside by the murder of George Floyd in Minneapolis. But I still witnessed streams of hope and a spirit of independence. I could not stop asking questions. I will still be asking questions after this book comes out because, really, is a journalist's work ever done?

I was concerned about post-publication timeliness. I thought about how fast the newspaper industry was changing and how my reporting would have settled when my book came out. Doug Burns had shared some of his deepest secrets with me, so I shared my concerns with him.

"I see your book being incredibly relevant in two ways," Burns said in August 2020. "Either it will be an instruction manual or inspirational book that will have ideas that have helped preserve or resurrect newspapers. It could be a big part in saving journalism. Or, even if we get to the point where coronavirus ravages the nation even more and the for-profit journalism model is largely done, your book will be like chronicling the last Comanches: those of us who are still independent and family owned. It's almost surprising when you see one of us. 'Whoa, you're still covering county supervisors?' 'Whoa, you're still covering state government?' 'Whoa, you still print a newspaper?' We're at that point where if a lot of us are gone, even me gone, you will have literally written a book about the last stand."

Rest easy.

The heart of a newspaper will continue to beat across America. Community newspapers will fight on and innovate. Readers will continue to clip articles about their neighbors and scan death notices and police reports. The hyper-local history of small, family-operated newspapers has successfully been adapted by digital sites like the nonprofit *Block Club Chicago*, where reporters deliver local news from Chicago's diverse neighborhoods.

The nonprofit Outlier Media in Detroit, Michigan, takes neighborhood identity one step further under the theory of building news from the ground up. For example, Outlier will text residents with advice on how to pay bills. During the height of the pandemic, they helped residents navigate vaccine information and sign-up on the web.

This kind of empathy strengthens trust with an audience. It can bring new voices to the table. The compassionate spirit is what connects small, independent news operations. Empathy toward our fellow man is why we all got into this business.

Dave Hoekstra, 2022

Chapter 1

The Commitment

Commitment in the world of community newspapers is the ability of editors, publishers, and employees to stand tall against the strong winds of declining revenue, skeptical readers, and herky-jerky online news. For family-run paper owners, the newspaper is your name. You are there for all to see.

Such commitment is evident in Hillsboro, Illinois. In a world that moves so fast, the Formica-and-pine counter in the downtown office of the Hillsboro *Journal-News* has been in the same place since 1950. Thousands of southern Illinois readers have dropped off birth notices and obituaries, complained, paid bills, and tried to see eye to eye at this counter. It has been a runway for the elements of a good newspaper: advocacy, empathy, interpretation, and sense of community.

Papers like the *Journal-News* are rare in America. The history of this family-run newspaper spans five generations. Founded in 1886 as the *Hillsboro Journal*, the paper merged in 2004 with the *Montgomery County News* to become today's *Journal-News*. Their credo is to report on every angle of community, and in Montgomery County that means reporting on swirling themes of family, faith, tradition, and innovative visons of the future. Located about sixty miles north of St. Louis, Missouri, the community's legacy is coal mining and agriculture. Hillsboro (pop. 6,037) is the county seat. The *Journal-News* also covers Litchfield (pop. 6,800), nine miles west along old Route 66.

I first visited Hillsboro's *Journal-News* in the spring of 2019. It was an emotional, throwback experience that I did not anticipate. There were four staff members in the quiet office. It was around lunchtime and no one was on their cell phone or iPad. Instead, they talked in hushed tones as they wrote stories. It appeared as if they should have been writing on typewriters and their world was all black and white. A middle-aged woman greeted me at the front desk.

It reminded me of my first journalism job—fifty years ago. In 1972 I was a high school stringer for the *Aurora Beacon-News*, a daily newspaper about fifty miles west of Chicago. The *Beacon-News* had a bureau in downtown Naperville, where I grew up. The four-person bureau was on the first floor of a historic 1854 blacksmith's home in downtown Naperville. It was filled with grizzly characters such as Naperville city reporter Bill Tuite. Before writing on deadline, Tuite walked over to the Elbow Room cocktail lounge in the bowling alley next door. "I'm going out looking for a lede," he would say to no one in particular. Even as a kid, I was impressed with the old soul of a small operation.

Like in Hillsboro, anyone who walked through the *Beacon-News* front door would be greeted by a middle-aged woman ready to take an ad, a complaint, or a wedding notice.

I later moved to the main operation in Aurora. The everlasting gift was that I did everything. During the week I covered the school board. On Friday nights I covered high school sports. I wrote features, including the obligatory story about Squiggy the Water-Skiing Squirrel. On rotating Saturday mornings I took reports from the Aurora Police Department. I brought them back to the office and typed them up on triplicate sheets of paper that embraced the smoke of the newsroom. Nearby, Aurora city reporter and columnist Charlie Ward would be shaving at his desk, looking into a pocket mirror with a face covered in shaving cream. Today, that kind of eccentric behavior would get you shipped to HR.

The *Beacon-News* was a family newspaper. It was owned and operated by Helen Copley of the Copley Press chain based in La Jolla, California. After Helen died in 2004, the chain began selling off properties. At one time Copley owned the *State Journal-Register* in Springfield, Illinois, only forty-five minutes from Hillsboro, and the *Courier-News* in Elgin, only about thirty miles from Aurora. Ironically, Copley sold to Hollinger International, which was the parent company of the *Chicago Sun-Times*, where I was a staff writer between 1985 and 2014.

The John Galer family never sold.

They publish seven small newspapers in a county that includes Litchfield, the VFW in Panama, and the Skyview Drive-In, the last original Route 66 drive-in in Illinois. Heading into Hillsboro from the west, you drive by 66 Truck Repair and a Hillsboro welcome sign that promises "Pride, Progress and Prosperity."

Most newspaper families and independents are racing to the exit sign. "It's a lot," said Phil Murray, former partner of the Dirks, Van Essen, Murray & April newspaper brokerage group in two interviews: December 2019 and July 2020 during the COVID-19 crisis. His firm's report said 154 daily newspapers changed hands in 2019 in thirty separate transactions worth $1.33 billion. That set a newspaper industry post-recession record for transaction volume.

For example, MediaNews Group, the Denver-based newspaper group owned by Alden Global Capital, acquired the 151-year-old *Reading Eagle* (Reading, Pennsylvania) through a U.S. bankruptcy court proceeding. The *Eagle* had been owned by the same family since its founding in 1868. "With revenue declining, and you own a single newspaper in a small or midsized town, it is becoming increasingly difficult to keep it profitable," said Murray, whose firm mostly represents sellers. "Because you don't have the same opportunities as a larger company to consolidate back-office functions like business office and graphics. All those things that are invisible to readers and advertisers but make a difference in the ability to keep the newspaper profitable."

In November 2019, Gannett (*USA Today* owner) and the New Media Investment Group (formerly GateHouse Media) merged. They were the nation's top two newspaper owners as measured by circulation. The Gannett/New Media deal accounted for more than 70 percent of all dailies sold in 2019 and nearly 90 percent of the dollar volume.

"There's been very little activity in 2020 because of the pandemic," Murray said in late July 2020. "It's a combination of sellers pulling back because they don't want to sell in the middle of terrible numbers and buyers unwilling to make a bet on newspapers until we see what it is going to look like on the other side." Before the Gannett merger in 2019, GateHouse published 144 daily newspapers and 684 community publications. "GateHouse drove a lot of deal making the last three or four years," Murray said. "It also makes a difference with them on the sidelines."

Tom Latonis is editor of the Taylorville *Breeze-Courier* and former managing editor of the *Pana News-Palladium*. Pana and Taylorville are about thirty miles north of John Galer's Hillsboro. "Back in the heyday of community newspapers and the Illinois Press Association, my father-in-law and John were good friends," Latonis said. "The Joneses over in Virden [the *Virden Recorder*], he was great friends with them. They had twin sons. My father-in-law was big in the Navy Reserves. He got those two to enlist. It was a family atmosphere. Plus, the Southern Illinois Editorial Association [SIEA, based in Carbondale] was a family organization. We had a spring convention where wives and kids all went to Carbondale at the Giant City State Park. It was just a big family of newspaper people. I was president of SIEA one year. You could see the family newspapers dwindling and the corporations coming in. The old-timers were retiring. Community newspapers, the biweekly, the once-weekly, I think John is the last owner north of I-70. You go south of I-70, they're all corporate run.

"There's nobody there."

But in the places where you still find commitment, you also find hope.

———

I was a child of local print.

My father would often bring four daily newspapers to our suburban home from his commute back and forth to downtown Chicago on the old Burlington Northern Railroad. The *Chicago Sun-Times* and the *Tribune* were the morning papers, the *Chicago American* (later the *Chicago Today*) and the *Chicago Daily News* were the afternoon papers. I grew up reading columnists like Mike Royko, magnificent feature writers like M. W. "Bill" Newman (who wrote the front page *Daily News* obit when it ceased publication), film critic Roger Ebert, and sports columnists like Ray Sons and *Chicago Today*'s Rick Talley, who actually sent me a hopeful letter in response to one I wrote him as a high school student wondering about my future in journalism.

Newspaper print was a rough, sepia-soaked window into a colorful community. On Sundays, family dynamics came into play as the bulky newspaper was broken down in our house. Dad grabbed the news section and real estate. Mom would take the arts and entertainment section and the magazine. Yes, there was a glossy Sunday magazine in the *Tribune* and the *Sun-Times*. My brother and I liked the sports section. And everyone loved the comics.

Newspapers were in my blood. As an adult, I bought the hefty Sunday edition of the *Chicago Tribune* on Saturday afternoon. On Sunday I bought the *Chicago Sun-Times*. It is a habit I still can't break, even though the Sunday size of each newspaper is half of what it used to be—and still costs more than it used to.

Reading a physical newspaper still holds a sense of adventure for me. I wander around the word jungle looking for items just as I do in a physical bookstore or record store. It stings when that physical ritual goes away. For example, the award-winning *Carroll Daily Times Herald* in rural Iowa published a print edition five days a week until April 2019, when they cut print editions to twice a week. The *Daily Times Herald* was rebranded as the *Carroll Times Herald*. "That was an extraordinarily painful decision," said Doug Burns, co-owner and vice president of news for the Herald Publishing Company in Carroll, about seventy miles west of Ames, Iowa. "We took an absolute fucking beating for that. The good thing about running a community newspaper is that I've always felt we're just temporary stewards of the newspaper. The community really owns the newspaper."

His mother, Ann Wilson, is publisher of the four-generation operation. Burns explained, "Mom and I have always operated under the philosophy of, 'Let's make a good living. Not into the six figures, but a good five-figure living and invest back into the newspaper.' Over our collective twenty-three years of running it together, we could have made a hell of a lot more money. But we always had the largest staff possible and covered the broadest area."

Burns had just celebrated his fiftieth birthday when I spoke to him in early 2020. He figured the next twenty years of his newspaper career should be his best. "But we're having to build the airplane as we fly it to keep the newspaper in the sky," he said. "We don't have the time to do the things we're good at. This is my whole identity; my whole life is tied to the newspaper. I spend seventy to eighty hours a week here over the last fifteen years. Before that it was about fifty hours. I'm not married. I've had girlfriends through the years. I don't know. . . ."

He stopped as his mother listened from behind her desk. She said nothing. And then he continued, "Being in the newspaper business is probably a big reason I'm not married. And choosing to live in a rural area where you combine the pressures and the hours of the job. There's a limited dating pool here. You put that in a blender and you end up fifty and single with your whole life tied to this newspaper. Mom and I have given too much to the paper and didn't build enough of a life outside of it. We've stuck around longer than it makes sense financially to do so, if you want the God's honest truth. The commitment? It's a sacrifice. Sometimes it's your own health and well-being. A sacrifice is emotional and financial. I've cut my own salary to $32,000 a year in the last year and a half."

—

The population of Dixon, Illinois, is about fifteen thousand people. Dixon was one hundred miles west of Chicago. Most people in the Chicago area know Dixon as the boyhood home of President Ronald Reagan. "Dutch" was born in nearby Tampico and moved to Dixon at the age of nine.

Many people in the Chicago area do not know Dixon was the original headquarters of Shaw Media, the third-oldest continuously owned and operated family newspaper company in America, according to the newspaper brokerage firm Dirks, Van Essen, Murray & April. Shaw Media is rolling into its sixth generation. During a 2019 interview in his Dixon office, forty-one-year-old trustee John Peter Shaw smiled and said, "One paper older than us is the newspaper owned by the Mormon Church. They're sort of the one we call the 'cheaters.' It's a family-owned newspaper, but it's a church."

As of this writing, the Shaw Media holdings cover eighty-two titles in print, magazines, and websites, employing in the neighborhood of three hundred journalists. Shaw Media also publishes the popular *Pro Football Weekly* and *Starved Rock Country* leisure magazine. In 2019 the Poynter Institute had Shaw Media listed as America's eighth-largest newspaper company by title. The first issue of the *Dixon Telegraph and Herald* was printed in 1851 in Dixon. Benjamin Flower "B. F." Shaw was the editor and owner at age twenty. He was one of the founders of the Illinois Republican Party along with Abraham Lincoln. The Shaw family has continuously owned the newspaper since then.

Shaw Media's corporate headquarters are in the Northwest Herald building in Crystal Lake, a suburb of Chicago. But the deep history can be found at the *Telegraph* (a.k.a. Sauk Valley Media) building in downtown Dixon. As visitors walk in, they are greeted with a wall that features the First Amendment: "Congress shall make no law respecting an establishment of religion, or prohibiting the free exercise thereof; or abridging the freedom of speech, or of the press; or the right of the people peaceably to assemble, and to petition the Government for a redress of grievances." The First Amendment also appears on the editorial page of the flagship *Telegraph* newspaper.

On the eastern end of the rotund reception area there is a small Shaw Media museum. Featuring more than one hundred pieces, the museum is anchored by a hand-operated Washington printing press, the same kind of press that printed the first single-sheet edition of the *Telegraph*. There are photographs of President Reagan reading his hometown newspaper and a black-and-white photograph of more than forty *Telegraph* newsboys with food baskets they collected for the needy in the early 1950s. Preserved under glass is the largest paper ever printed in Dixon, published in 1951 for the one hundredth anniversary of the *Telegraph*. The newspaper weighed in at 272 pages and sixteen sections. It was so large the Dixon National Guard had to be deployed to assemble the sections for delivery.

The leader at the helm for much of this *Telegraph* history was Mabel Shaw, who was publisher during the first half of the twentieth century and eventually established the Mabel Shaw Trust for her three sons. John Peter (known just as Peter) Shaw is her great-grandson and was the trustee until he resigned on June 3, 2021, to pursue another opportunity in local media. He would not elaborate at the time. In January 2022, Shaw said, "At this point in time I am an industry agnostic. I want a local organization that I believe in and wants to grow with me. If this opportunity presented to work with an organization that is in local media, I wouldn't rule it out offhand, but it isn't my focus."

After Shaw left, the majority of income beneficiaries hired a firm called

Trustee Services Group (TSG) in Colorado Springs, Colorado, to replace him. His brother, Tom Shaw, continues to lead the chain's digital transformation as vice president of content. He remains as one of four family members on the board of directors.

TSG is considered a "boutique" trust office. "I don't know that there were other family members positioned or interested," Peter said in August 2021. "But with end-of-trust planning considerations on the horizon, having an experienced firm involved makes sense."

Peter Shaw was born in Dixon and graduated from Northside Christian School in St. Petersburg, Florida, in 1996. He worked part time in the *Telegraph* mail room and was a photographer-reporter at the *Sterling Gazette*, near Dixon.

Dixon is another world off the Reagan Memorial Tollway (I-88) that flies between Chicago and Iowa. Visitors cross Bloody Gulch Road as they exit the toll road and pass signs for the historic site where John Deere created the first commercially successful steel plow. The newspaper was birthed a couple blocks away from the current location. The *Telegraph* moved into its present location in the 1940s.

"For the life of the majority of the residents, this has always been the *Telegraph* building," Peter said.

Jamie Hogan was a *Telegraph* reporter in the late 1970s. "The business of the paper seemed hustling and thriving," she recalled in 2021. "Even so, everything about the place was a little bedraggled. Inside, our offices and desks were in a style best described as 'old government issued.' We worked on VDTs [video display terminals] that blinked with green lights, the precursor to modern word processing. The *Telegraph* building exterior was stuck in an era of mid-century that decades later achieved some level of cool."

Peter said, "We still have heavy traffic of people coming in talking circulation, classified. Mostly coming in because they didn't get their paper and they wanted to yell at somebody. When everything is working right, you don't typically hear from people.

"A newspaper and its community is one of the strangest but most important relationships. My dad [retired Shaw Media CEO Tom Shaw] was talking about how it's almost like a medieval royalty setup. It's like a duke or somebody who is in charge of this area, but the people never have a say about who that is. I listen to people come in here and complain about the paper. You hear it everywhere you are. Somebody hears the word 'Shaw' and they go, 'Are you one of those Shaws?' Well, if you mean the newspaper, yeah. And they'll start talking about whatever they want to talk about."

These small towns are places where one can feel off the grid and talk face to face. People take time to listen. These were more reasons they spoke to my heart. In 2009, the Nobel Prize–winning songwriter Bob Dylan talked to Bill Flanagan about growing up in rural Minnesota. "Mass media had no overwhelming reach, so I was drawn to the traveling performers passing through," he said. "The side-show performers, bluegrass singers, the black cowboy with chaps and a lariat doing rope tricks . . . the deformed and bent . . . I learned about dignity from them. Freedom too. Civil rights, human rights. How to stay within yourself.

"The stuff off the main road was where force of reality was."

—

On a spring day in 2019, *Journal-News* owner John Galer took a break from working on cardboard subscription cards at his cluttered desk in downtown Hillsboro. He finished a meeting with longtime *Journal-News* publisher Mike Plunkett. Galer and his wife, Susie, adjourned to the expansive rear kitchen to meet with me. Galer carried no pretense. Kindness was etched into his face with the detail of a rare gem. "I am proud of what newspapers mean to a community," said Galer, who was sixty-six at the time. "Day-to-day living." He looked at his newspaper photo of twenty-eight students from the Rising Sun Martial Arts School in Hillsboro. He smiled and said, "Half the moms who have kids in that picture are going to cut it out and put it on the refrigerator. Or it's going to be in church. Or in school."

When my beloved *Chicago Sun-Times* was struggling, I joked that the newspaper's sports department should resurrect its bowling column. Old-school bowling spoke to the neighborhood identity of the newspaper. Suddenly, while reading a 2019 edition of the *Journal-News*, I saw a large box at the bottom of the sports page with the area's "Bowling League Standings." The action in the Wednesday Night League at Hillsboro Bowl saw the Rednecks in first place with a 33–11 record, while the Pin Pals were in sixth and last place at 17–27.

In a separate conversation Plunkett said, "It's important to let your readers define what news is. So if somebody walks through our door and says, 'Look at the size of this mushroom I just found,' that may not be news to me, but if they care enough to drive into town and bring that in, that is news to them. And I guarantee you the next day there's gonna be people saying, 'Did you see the size of that mushroom in the newspaper?' When somebody calls and asks if we saw the flock of swans out by the lake, we go take a picture of that. Because somebody cared enough to call and by golly, it's going to be in the newspaper."

There aren't many newspapers with this kind of commitment left in America. Looking back on the arc of my newspaper career, I saw that the level of newsroom cynicism often grew in relation to the size of the publication. Commitment takes time, understanding, and even a bit of levity.

In the late summer of 2019, the Pew Research Center released its annual report on American news media. Newspaper circulation was at its lowest point since 1940. Then, in 2020, the Knight Foundation and the University of North Carolina found that since 2004, the United States had lost one-fourth (2,100) of its newspapers. That included 70 dailies and more than 2,000 weeklies.

—

P. J. (Pamela Jo) Browning started at the daily *Post and Courier* in Charleston, South Carolina, in 2012. In 2019, *Editor & Publisher* magazine named Browning "Publisher of the Year." She was honored in part for the paper's digital initiative and for winning a 2015 Pulitzer Prize for Public Service for the *Post and Courier*'s series on domestic violence, "Till Death Do Us Part."

Browning has worked for newspapers in Fort Collins, Colorado; Grand Rapids, Michigan; and Asheville, North Carolina. Her first job as publisher was with the *Sentinel* in Carlisle, Pennsylvania. Just before coming to Charleston, she had been publisher at the *Sun News* in Myrtle Beach, South Carolina. The *Post and Courier* was the first family-owned newspaper she had worked at.

Browning comes from a family-owned industrial tools and supplies business in Springfield, Missouri. "My father and I used to get into good discussions about the differences between family businesses and publicly held companies," she said. "It's fun to be here and see the differences. My father and I are very creative, and we love running businesses. We always felt a privately held company provided for more creativity and less of a playbook, where everyone gets to the same end by the same means. Creativity enables sparks of energy and new ways of looking at things. It's an opportunity to try new things with fail-fast mentality, but don't be afraid to try. Publicly held companies are more of a top-down approach with little opportunity to try new things and certainly less of an appetite for failures, which is where we grow and learn."

Her parents, Forrest and Barbara Hutton, still run the family HK&W Supply company in Springfield. It is a block from the *News-Leader*, the Gannett newspaper where she started her career. Browning's first newspaper job was taking classified ads over the phone at the *News-Leader* while studying marketing at Southwest Missouri State (now Missouri State University) in Springfield. Browning was born in Kansas in 1964 and lived in Springfield from the time she was five until the age of twenty-six.

"I worked for Gannett and McClatchy for a while," Browning said. "Gannett had a playbook. Everything was driven by numbers. It was great training. But here, and what I've always loved, is the ability to be creative. We're able to experiment more. There's less red tape. Your systems are different. There's times I wish this was a little more organized, but all in all you're able to have a little more freedom to try new things.

"Before, at the corporates, it was not unusual to get a call when we were coming up on a quarter. I remember the calls. 'Can you cut a million dollars out of the quarter?' It really wasn't 'can you,' it was 'I need you to do this.' And so you did. You knew your numbers inside and out: If I dropped a page of newsprint. If I needed to lay this person off. If I needed to combine this job. There were so many numbers that you always, always, always had a contingency plan. Today, you can get to whatever number you want from a profit standpoint. But there's hard decisions that have to be made."

In November 2019, after Gannett and New Media Investment Group announced their merger, a *New York Times* report said that researchers from the University of North Carolina concluded that one in five daily newspapers in the United States has the same owner, under the Gannett name.

Also in November 2019, a PEN America report stated that corporate consolidation "devastated" the media in Denver, Colorado. In 2009, two legacy newspapers—the *Rocky Mountain News* and the *Denver Post*—had more than five hundred working journalists on staff. In 2019, Denver had one legacy newspaper (the *Post*) with fewer than seventy journalists on staff.

The New York–based hedge fund Alden Global Capital was founded in 2007. Its subsidiary MediaNews Group/Digital First Media owns about two hundred newspapers, including the *Orange County Register* and the *Denver Post*, and in 2019, MediaNews laid off nearly a third of the *Denver Post* staff.

In November 2019, Alden acquired 32 percent of Tribune Publishing Company shares (the *Chicago Tribune*, the largest daily newspaper in Illinois, the *Baltimore Sun*, the *Hartford Courant,* and more). Alden again began implementing severe staff cuts. On January 13, 2020, staffers at Tribune Publishing were offered buyouts. The *Chicago Tribune* editorial staff was gutted between buyouts, layoffs, pay cuts, and three weeks of furloughs—all during a time when America was going through social unrest and a pandemic. In a January 21, 2020, *New York Times* op-ed piece, *Chicago Tribune* investigative reporters David Jackson and Gary Marx wrote in part, "The *Tribune* does not just safeguard the city; by devoting coverage to every aspect of daily life, it creates a sense of community." Jackson, a Pulitzer Prize–winning reporter, left the *Tribune* in June 2020 after a twenty-nine-year run.

By February 2021, Alden had acquired the rest of Tribune Publishing for $630 million. A flurry of buyouts and layoffs followed. As predicted, the *Chicago Tribune* was devastated. It became a ghost of iconic publisher Colonel Robert McCormick's dream. According to a July 2021 Poynter report, the *Chicago Tribune* weathered a 21 percent decline in jobs. (From 111 full-time News Guild members down to 87 full-time members.)

In addition to the *Chicago Tribune*, in August 2021, Tribune Publishing owned the *Baltimore Sun*; the *Hartford Courant*; the *Orlando Sentinel*; the *South Florida Sun Sentinel*; the *New York Daily News*; the *Capital Gazette* in Annapolis, Maryland; the *Morning Call* in Allentown, Pennsylvania; the *Daily Press* in Newport News, Virginia; and the *Virginian-Pilot* in Norfolk, Virginia. That adds up to a lot of folks in the fading trenches. The acquisitions made Alden the nation's second-largest newspaper publisher by circulation. Gannett is the largest.

Randy Smith (born 1942) is the founder and chief of investments at Alden Global Capital. Many people do not know his brother Russ (born 1955) cofounded the *Baltimore City Paper* in 1977 and the *Washington (DC) City Paper* in 1981. Both newspapers became models for the alternative newspaper industry.

Nancy Lane is CEO at the Local Media Association (LMA), a group of more than three thousand media companies that network and discover sustainable business models. "There's a lot of doom and gloom at the big papers," she said. "The ownership structure is miserable. It's a shame because there's great journalists who are doing fantastic work at those organizations. And they're not happy about ownership structure. It's a real problem in the industry. The family owners don't have that to deal with. They're in it for the right reason. Profits are probably not their top priority in life."

Browning agreed. "From a family-owned perspective, journalism is a great place," she said. "You see how Gannett and McClatchy and others are hurting because everybody realizes that content is what you need to be able to perform online. There's so many different things. Without content providers, that's hard. Newspapers now are stumbling as they're trying to figure out how to bring back content providers. It is a different world from the family side. I've always felt from the family side, content is very important to the community. And it is the basis of what the newspaper is built on."

Mike Jenner is a professor and faculty chair of Journalism Professions at the University of Missouri in Columbia. Before returning to his native state, he was the longtime editor of the family-owned *Bakersfield Californian*. Between 1978 and 1982 he worked at the family-owned *Columbia Daily Tribune* and later at the family-owned *Hattiesburg American* (Mississippi) and the *Coffeyville Journal* (Kansas). On the flip side, he worked for the *Philadelphia Inquirer*, then owned by Knight Ridder, and then the *Hartford Courant*, which at the time was a Times-Mirror newspaper.

"When you look at the world we're in right now, newspapers seem to do better under a benevolent single-owner proprietor than they have under publicly traded organizations that have no commitment to the community but have a significant commitment to their shareholders," Jenner said in a July 2020 interview. "Their first priority is to raise the price of stock and make money. It doesn't matter if it is a newspaper, soup company, or a shoe factory. I don't mean to be unkind, but for many of these companies their first order of business is not shining a light on the community conversation. And for a community publisher who gets yelled at when he or she is standing in the checkout line at the grocery store over something they published or didn't publish, the whole attitude is different. Because you're living in the community. Your kids are going to the schools. I've had some real good experiences working for family-owned newspapers. I have a lot of respect for those publishers who took it as far as they could take it before they had to sell for whatever reason. I've worked for chains too. Some good, some not so good. They're not all bad, but I do have a bias on behalf of family-owned newspapers."

Robert Halpern is the former co-owner of the award-winning *Big Bend Sentinel* in tiny Marfa, Texas. Robert and his wife, Rosario, sold the paper in 2019 after a successful twenty-five-year run. Halpern had a nice job as assistant city editor at the *El Paso Times* when Gannett entered the west Texas picture. He worked part time at the *Times* while he was getting his journalism degree at the University of Texas at El Paso (UTEP).

"In hindsight it was the beginning of mega-mergers," he said. "It started feeling like it wasn't the *El Paso Times* anymore as much as it was the *Gannett El Paso Times*. Directions were coming out of Washington [DC], where Gannett was based at the time. Stories could only be 350 words. 'News to Use.' 'Gotta have a breakout bar.' All these little things. But we were writers, basically. I get that stuff, but if a story calls for two thousand words and you even have to break it up over two weeks . . . it just became one size fits all with Gannett. Like what became of *USA Today*. It became disheartening."

So Halpern quit to take a job at the *Sentinel*, which is located near his hometown of Alpine, Texas. "The opportunity presented itself to return to our roots and we did," he said. "We bought the paper four years after we worked for the previous owners, but after we took over, we turned it over little by little. No one told me lengths, what photos to use. It was cool. We could do what we wanted to do. We just continued that. We designed the coverage, whether it be on immigration issues or whatever."

—

Walter Hussman Jr. is the chairman of WEHCO (an acronym for Walter E. Hussman Company, pronounced "way-co"), which operates ten daily newspapers in Arkansas, including the flagship *Arkansas Democrat-Gazette*. He points to three major communication transitions in the course of human history. "The transitions came from a conversation I had with Alex Jones," Hussman said. Alex S. Jones worked at the *New York Times* and won a 1987 Pulitzer Prize in Specialized Reporting for "The Fall of the House of Bingham" about the Bingham family newspaper wars in Louisville, Kentucky. Jones also wrote the 2009 book *Losing the News: The Future of the News That Feeds Democracy*.

"Alex mentioned the first transition was 3000 BC in Mesopotamia," Hussman said. "At that time all human communication was verbal. Someone came up with a brilliant idea of 'Why don't we take what we're saying and revisit it on paper? Or even stones?' The great thing about that transformation is that you could take what people say and transport it over distances. Or, you could transport it over time—five years. And see what people talked about five years earlier."

The second transformation in history was in 1440 when German metalworker Johannes Gutenberg invented the printing press. Prior to that, the text was hand copied or pressed with wood blocks one letter at a time. Gutenberg also printed the first mass-produced version of the Bible.

Hussman continued, "The third transformation was in the early 1990s with the creation of the World Wide Web because [it] allowed everyone to get on the internet and communicate with anyone. And there's the economic advantages of digital versus print. There's no arguing with the economics of that. It's been unbelievable to see the drop of ad revenue throughout America. I went to the *Boston Globe* and talked to Linda Henry, whose family owns it, and she said, 'If we can't get a dollar a day for all the value we provide to our subscribers, we essentially don't have a business.' That makes a lot of sense.

"Why should we do all this if we can't get a dollar a day for our product?"

The commitment to truth and evocative storytelling is what keeps a newspaper viable. The payoff is a deeper understanding of where we live. But the sharing of common pride and spirit are the real riches of a small-town newspaper.

—

The *Journal-News* comes out on Monday and Thursday mornings in Hillsboro. Since the *Journal-News* still has its own press, it is printing at around midnight the morning of publication. It has a competing paper, the smaller *Litchfield News-Herald*, a five-days-a-week newspaper owned by the John Hanafin family. The *News-Herald*, founded in 1856, has been in the Hanafin family since 1928.

In 2020 the *Journal-News* had a circulation of five thousand. Galer said that was a saturation rate of around 50 percent. "We cover Litchfield, Hillsboro, Raymond, and Nokomis," he said. (Hall of Fame baseball players Jim Bottomley and Red Ruffing were raised in Nokomis.) "We've been the dominant county paper for a long time. The Litchfield and Hillsboro communities' populations are very close. They shop together, there's a lot of interactions socially. The city governments are not real close. You have little communities, but this is one pretty-good-sized region. There's thirty thousand people in Montgomery County. We stretch our editorial staff pretty hard. We have about seven people who actively write, which is a ton for a small newspaper. The challenge is keeping all these people on board."

Galer's wife, Susie, said, "It's hard to get young people in any role. Our daughter married our sports editor. It is truly a family affair." She explained that their daughter dropped down to part time to care for their special-needs daughter, then added, "Well, she still works full time, but at least she doesn't work sixty hours a week."

Between October 2020 and October 2022, John Galer served as vice chairman of the National Newspaper Association. In a separate interview, he said, "Years ago, my grandfather, my dad, and me, you were able to dedicate your whole life to what you're doing. But now there's so many family responsibilities. But we got the same old family newspaper thing about the community, and you want to do it the right way. Some of these newspapers just wait for stuff to come in. Nobody is out trying to dig up news. People will always want to know about community events. We have a regular page on agriculture. Our paper was the official newspaper of the Montgomery County Farm Bureau until 2006. All the bureau members bought subscriptions. It got too pricey for them. They had to cut costs, too. I'd say half or two-thirds of the bureau are still subscribers. We are the last paper on earth that doesn't charge for obituaries. I just don't believe in it. When my dad died my mom was adamant it had to be in the state paper. It was like $800. Crazy. It went all over central Illinois, but it was obscene."

The Galers and Shaws will never be confused with newspaper barons like Jeff Bezos or Rupert Murdoch. Although Bezos has increased staff at his *Washington Post*, the commitment to the spirit of community over the stark reality of profit is consistently evident at smaller papers and even struggling alternative newspapers like the *Chicago Reader*.

Tracy Baim is publisher of the *Reader*, established in 1971 and one of the oldest alternative newspapers in America. In 2000, she became owner of the acclaimed Chicago LGBTQ newspaper *Windy City Times*. She has been writing about the Chicago LGBTQ community since 1985. Her career has been defined by commitment to the community over commercial profit. "My thirty-four years of running newspapers, I never made a dime," Baim said in a 2020 interview. "My average salary was $25,000. I was never in this for that. I was grateful and lucky to get a ton of people who gave money to *Windy City Times* over the years. But they never made a nickel. One friend of mine gave over $200,000 over those thirty years. She never got anything."

Galer said, "Every business has to make money to stay in business. This is true in any business; if you get away from the core and you want to expand and bring people in for the money end, you get money managers. If it is just for the bucks, you're missing the point. For us it is about community. Hospitals, sports, city government, community groups, kid groups. We're the only thing that tries to tie it all together as one place. My folks never had tons of money. We've never had tons of money. But you make it work.

"Truthfully, if we have a penny left at the end of the year, we're doing good."

If you could put a price on commitment, newspapers would still be a rich part of America's daily routine. But commitment is costly. Many editors, writers, photographers, and designers go without a long vacation or a fancy car. But the reward is found within the daily truths of community.

Chapter 2

The Price of Community

Regardless of a family-run paper's commitment to community over share-holders, money is inevitably a universal theme of newspapers big and small.

The rich crossroads of community and neighborhood don't always pay for salaries and newsprint. A newspaper also requires a commitment from the reader. A defunct newspaper benefits no one. Can a family newspaper serve the community adequately and make money?

"There's the question," said former Champaign *News-Gazette* publisher John Reed as he passed his hand across a long desk in his office. "I can wax philosophical on that forever. What newspapers do is really important to society at large. The fundamental rub is that as a profit motive, I'm not sure how it continues."

From his home in Dixon, Illinois, Tom Shaw, the retired longtime CEO of Shaw Media, said, "It's the chicken or the egg. Serving the community is hugely important. The quality of the life of the community can be directly affected by the level of involvement by the newspaper. That's one of the sad things about so many newspapers being sold to Wall Street. Local influence and leadership is gone. We've tried to be community advocates, and not only geographical communities but various people communities within our markets. To do that you have to be profitable. You've got reinvestment, wage increases; in our case we had debt. We had to make money to meet our obligations and that's not all bad."

The *Eureka Springs Independent* in Arkansas covers community news under the subhead "Locally Owned Hometown Free Newspaper." In 2019, the weekly circulation was four thousand, incorporating other small towns and a few outposts in Bentonville, Arkansas (pop. 49,000), the headquarters of the Walmart retail chain. Editor Mary Pat Boian writes a regular column, "ISawArkansas." She is an economic yet colorful writer with sharp wit.

In the July 3, 2019, edition of the *Independent*, Boian commemorated the newspaper's seventh anniversary. She told readers, in part, "Our business model has always been the same—nonexistent. We started doing this despite knowing newspapers are an endangered species. We're not doing this for any reason other than we enjoy it, and yes, of course, we hate being yelled at and not having a retirement plan. So we're careful. We're wrong at times, but it's not because we were lazy or uninformed or mean-spirited. It's because, well, we were wrong."

Marfa, Texas, could be a freethinking, mystical sister city of Eureka Springs. The predominately Hispanic community of 1,700 with a hipster facade sits about 180 miles southeast of El Paso. In 1971, minimalist artist Donald Judd moved from New York to Marfa. The Lannan Foundation hosts a writers-in-residency program in Marfa. New York poet Eileen Myles bought a home in Marfa. The 1956 James Dean film *Giant* was filmed here.

The *Big Bend Sentinel*, established in 1926, is Marfa's weekly newspaper. Under the umbrella of the West Texan Media Group, the *Sentinel* also publishes the smaller bilingual newspaper *Presidio International*. *Sentinel* husband-and-wife owners Robert and Rosario Halpern retired in 2019.

"Community is a shared sense of fellowship, a shared sense of culture, a shared sense of the environment we live in," said Robert, who was sixty-four when he retired. "There's circles within circles and that's how we covered it. It's also about the land, the proximity to Mexico; we live in the only mountainous area of Texas, so we're defined by our environment. Twenty-five to thirty years ago you said good morning to everybody or waved at everybody. Not so much anymore. The real sense of community is that you look each other in the eye. You may need someone one day. If you have a flat tire in the middle of the road here in west Texas, you may need someone to come help you. We all live in this place, the natives, the newcomers, the art guy and girl, the ecotourists.

"All these circles define community."

Robert grew up in the family of a Jewish dry goods merchant in Alpine, Texas. His mother, Flo, and father, Bob, were business partners with his aunt and uncle. Before earning a journalism degree from the University of Texas at El Paso (UTEP), he helped with advertising for the Alpine newspaper and wrote copy for the local radio station. "That's how I drifted to this career," he said.

Robert and Rosario sold the newspapers to Max Kabat and his wife, Maisie Crow, a young couple who moved to Marfa from Brooklyn, New York. Their debut issue was July 4, 2020, almost eight years to the day that the *Eureka Springs Independent* was born. Newspapers are not dead if they share the spirit of experimental thinking with the community. Not so long ago, next door to the Big Bend newspaper office was Padre's, an empty bar in a century-old adobe. Kabat and Crow reimagined the dive bar into The Sentinel—a restaurant, bar, and coffee shop.

"Everybody went to Padre's," Robert said. "It was the happening place for a while—except for some locals whose dearly departed loved ones were in repose in the building because it used to be a funeral home. They said it creeped them out. I used to feel spirits dancing in the shadows, actually, but I didn't have departed loved ones there."

Newspapers have always delivered news to the community. Through The Sentinel cafe, the *Big Bend Sentinel* was now bringing the community to the newspaper. "This model we came up with takes advantage of what exists here," Kabat said. "It has a fantastic support system of people that are super engaged."

The Sentinel cafe opens at seven thirty a.m. daily with coffee and pastries. Tacos are served for lunch and dinner. The Sentinel covers about 4,500 square feet indoors with a 2,000-square-foot outdoor space. The newspaper's offices are just 450 square feet. "You get people who walk up to the barista to order a latte," Kabat explained. "Then the next person in line says, 'Here's my subscription money.' They're paying in cash. It's not worth it to tell that person to walk around the corner into the newspaper office. There's writers that have gotten leads from people that hang out in the coffee shop.

"Everything we do is about community. We view our whole business, newspaper, media company space as one holistic brand. Any extensions have to be true to what we are and what we stand for. Our coffee roaster sources beans from co-ops and farmers that go beyond fair-trade standards. We serve our drinks in pottery thrown by a woman-owned business based out of Terlingua, Texas, and Santa Fe, New Mexico. The retail items in our shop, from our MiiR-branded mugs to items we bought on travels to Mexico, all come from community-minded endeavors." There are also edgy "Support Your Local Newspaper" tote bags and vintage paperboy T-shirts for sale.

"Newspaper day, Thursday, is the best," Kabat said. "From the newspaper regulars that come to the back door at six a.m., to the coffee regulars, folks dropping in for lunch, people doing work, visitors starting to come in for the weekend. It's not our busiest day. And we have most of that happen every day of the week. But it's my favorite day when it all comes together [with the Thursday publication]."

The goal for these young owners is to frame their intentions and personalities around the newspaper's reason for being. "How do we continue to invest time, money, energy, and resources to getting people more of what they want?" Kabat asked. "The investment for us and the consumer might be a bit more costly, but it's about executing a long-term vision and building a business built for a marathon and not a sprint."

For example, by January 2022, the *Sentinel*'s staff consisted of two full-time reporters and a managing editor that also does reporting. They all receive benefits. "The model is working," Kabat said. "It's more staff than there was when we took over the paper."

Robert's wife, Rosario, is from the neighboring border town of Presidio, Texas. "The border has always been an hour and a half away," Robert said. "My wife is Mexican American. My high school classmates were 50, 60 percent Mexican American. Even though I'm Jewish, I consider myself semi-Anglo. I always had an affinity for the border. My parents honeymooned there. You have your ear to the ground; this is the prevailing culture. We started looking at it from that point of view."

Robert and Rosario bought the *Sentinel* and *International* in 1993 after Robert was a reporter-photographer-editor at the two papers for four years. As co-owners, Robert ran the editorial side and Rosario ran the business side. "When we took over, we tried as much as we could to have the staff reflect the demographics of our coverage area," Robert said. "If you're born here, you have an inherent leg up if you're writing the first take of your area. Mexico, and now Central America, has always been a focus of our attention because it defines the community. It's 70 percent Hispanic in Marfa, but it doesn't look like it. Because the 2 percent hipster makes the news. But the rank and file are Hispanic. Presidio is 80 percent Hispanic. If you're producing a community weekly, this is what you have with your ear to the ground. We're writing about ourselves, whether it is all Hispanic, biracial families, it's the demographic. And it was a joy to do that."

Robert and Rosario dug deep into hard news. In 2001, Rosario wrote about a Presidio man who was wrongly arrested in Mexico for the murder of a reporter across the Rio Grande in Ojinaga, Chihuahua. He was freed because of the coverage from the *Presidio International*. "We didn't shy away from anything," Robert said. "In a small town, the sensitivity in which you have to approach certain critical stories is a defining benchmark. You do see the people in the grocery store the next day. If you want to be a Pulitzer Prize–winning journalist, you gotta work at a weekly. Because the words have to be precise. If someone is charged with a sex crime, of course you write about the crime, but not just about the victim—everybody involved. There's a precision of writing in a community weekly."

For example, Robert insisted his reporters use the term "undocumented migrant" instead of "illegal alien." When writing about people of a community, he had his staff call them "residents" instead of "citizens," because no one knew who had citizenship. But everyone deserved dignity.

Small things matter in small-town journalism. *Texas Monthly* writer Sterry Butcher worked at the *Big Bend Sentinel*. In an October 2019 profile on Robert and Rosario, she wrote, "The paper noticed the small things. The Halperns allowed us, encouraged us, to notice." *New York Times* Sunday magazine editor Jake Silverstein worked at the *Sentinel* for a year. "Even more recently, Sarah Vasquez, a young Hispanic woman, brings a sensibility of writing about her culture," Robert said. "Young journalists do come to the 'Marfa Mystique.'" Just in the matter of two months in late 2019, Vasquez wrote about a Texas man who came through Big Bend on a 992-mile walk along the U.S.–Mexico border and a sci-fi and fantasy bookstore that opened inside a former school bus in Marfa.

After buying the *Sentinel*, Kabat and Crow began researching the economic health of cities and small towns and how that relates to local journalism. Crow taught as an adjunct professor at the Columbia University Graduate School of Journalism and the CUNY (City University of New York) Graduate School of Journalism. She received an Emmy for her 2016 documentary *Jackson* (Mississippi), which examined reproductive health care through residents in the Deep South.

"We started realizing the demise of our democracy might be contributed by the vacuum of local voices across America," Kabat explained. "There's nobody to explain things to locals and make national and global issues pertain to them. How else are they supposed to not feel forgotten? Or angry? If Ivy League–educated people can't understand the gamesmanship that's done on the local and national basis, how is everyone else supposed to understand? We understood this was a big challenge that needed to be solved in some way, shape, or form."

A similar outside-the-box marriage of newspaper and community took off in late 2021 and early 2022 when the *Tennessee Tribune* opened two stores in the bustling Nashville International Airport. Headquartered in Nashville, the *Tennessee Tribune* is the state's largest minority-owned newspaper with a circulation of more than 150,000.

Besides selling copies of the *Tribune*, the stores carry items from nearly forty minority vendors. It's a brilliant concept. Not only does the *Tribune* have access to a new audience passing through the airport, but there's also local empowerment when travelers buy coffee, popcorn, clothing, purses, and books from a small Black-owned business based in Tennessee.

The outreach is the brainchild of the newspaper's iconic founder, Rosetta Miller-Perry, who was a spry eighty-six years old in March 2022. "I always come up with crazy ideas," said Miller-Perry, who worked closely with Dr. Martin Luther King Jr. and the SCLC (Southern Christian Leadership Conference) during the 1960s in Memphis. "It's difficult for Black newspapers. It's difficult to get advertising. The hip-hop generation doesn't read newspapers. Many of my readers are non-Black. So you have to have something else. You can't depend on your newspaper for income.

"And there's nowhere to put anything for Black folks in Nashville. A lot of people come through that airport. Lots of Black organizations. Black fraternities and sororities. We sell sweatshirts from Black colleges like Fisk [University] and American Baptist College. The other gift shops were only carrying Vanderbilt. But now they're carrying Fisk and others. You see?"

The *Tribune* comes out every Wednesday. The paper also has an online platform. Miller-Perry launched the *Tribune* in 1991 in an effort to reach an underserved Black audience, especially in the areas of education and voter registration. In the early 1960s, Miller-Perry received her bachelors of science degree in chemistry from the University of Memphis, becoming one of the first Black students to graduate from the school.

—

Just like the vision of Miller-Perry, a well-reported story reveals universal themes. The lasting reward in community journalism is the humanity these stories reveal: people's frailties, honor, and struggles. The payoff is immeasurable: a greater understanding of who we are. This is where the cost of community becomes priceless.

Mary Herschelman, managing editor of the *Journal-News* in Hillsboro, revels in this kind of community journalism. She is the Galers' outgoing and poised daughter, the fifth generation to enter the newspaper business. She is married to Kyle Herschelman, the *Journal-News* sports editor. Mary was born in 1980. "I like good news and I do a lot of the news," she said. "The building next to the [downtown movie] theater burned. The gentleman that lived there operated a taekwondo studio underneath it. He was a track coach. His name is Son [Clayton]. The coaches at the high school had a 'Run for Son' and they raised $500. I would print that kind of news every day. Now when you get mad at your mom, you set your house on fire, and they tase you in the front yard, that's also news."

Mary returned to Hillsboro in 2004 after attending college. "I've built a lot of relationships," she said. "Teachers in Litchfield [nine miles west of Hillsboro] texted me about how they just walked their principal [Doug Hoster] out. I emailed the superintendent and said, 'I heard the principal is on leave, can you confirm that?' She wouldn't. She told me it was personnel.

She stonewalled me at every turn."

Herschelman would not take no for an answer. She believed that taxpayers had a right to know what transpired. Herschelman contacted Principal Hoster. He came to the *Journal-News* office and met with Mary and her husband for several hours. "The superintendent was trying to get rid of him," she said. Hoster, who has since retired, was reinstated a month after he was placed on leave. "It is not my forte," Herschelman said, "but it is important to be a watchdog."

Family newspapers know that when editorial staffs are cut, there is an increased failure to hold public and corporate officials accountable. Peter Shaw cited a 2019 Poynter Institute report. He said, "In communities that don't have newspaper coverage, the cost of city government goes up 40 percent and road projects go up 25 percent. It's a real issue. There has been so much wealth zapped out of rural America. Dixon has a strong sense of self-identity. We're the town of Ronald Reagan and a lot of good and notable people have come out of here. A lot of my generation is returning. But a lot of other rural markets have become the 1980s urban ghetto. All you're left with is a Walmart and a meth problem."

Shaw was vice president of the local United Way board and did fundraising with the Dixon Family YMCA board. He learned how charity had to come in greater increments from smaller sources as opposed to a couple of large benefactors. "With retail going away, there's less business owners that would be able to contribute," he said. "I'm not trying to rail against Walmart, but it is the reality of what has happened digitally. Local companies put out that many less journalists."

The fabric of community is essential in an America that has become so fragmented. It doesn't matter if it is a small town or a big city. Community is defined by the spirits of connection and hope. When Tracy Baim became publisher of the *Chicago Reader* in December 2018, one of her first tasks was to ask the community of readers of the legacy alternative newspaper to donate as little as a dollar to help keep the *Reader* alive. In a pitch letter, she cited the pre-pandemic closings of the alternatives the *Village Voice* in New York City, the *Missoula Independent* in Montana, and *VUE Weekly* in Edmonton, Alberta. Baim wrote, "This is an experiment in whether a community-focused independent newspaper can survive in this environment."

In a span of six weeks, the *Reader* raised more than $130,000.

The effort reflected the Chicago community. "People are still passionate about the *Reader*," Baim said in a January 2020 interview at the *Reader* offices in the historic Bronzeville neighborhood. "Over 2,500 people gave an average of forty-something dollars. But quite a few people sent in a dollar, because we said, 'Do you give a buck?' And the way they gave that buck to us was unbelievable. Some people walked in here. Some people went to the trouble to make a dollar money order, put a stamp on it, and mail it to us. That meant as much as a couple people who gave a thousand dollars. I realized right then there's a passionate following in saving the *Reader* and it did help us bridge some costs."

The *Reader* hosted three public community events in 2019: "Yes We Cann: Cannabis Market & Symposium," the newspaper's first-ever "Pride Block Party," and its annual "Best of Chicago" party that celebrates the paper's biggest issue of the year. Baim reflects, "All three of those events were very diverse racially and age-wise. At the cannabis event in particular, because I was standing at the table most of the day, the people that came up to me were every kind of person. But the people who were most emotional that the *Reader* was still around were older African American women. Our editor is a middle-aged African American woman. They have been reading the *Reader* since they were teenagers or twentysomethings."

The longtime *Reader* readers told Baim it was important for them to feel connected to Chicago. She also heard positive feedback from people who had only lived in Chicago for five or ten years. "Now, we don't need every single person in Chicago to read the paper," she said. "We need fifty-four thousand people to pick it up and as many as want to online. The *Tribune* doesn't reach everybody, nobody does. We're at the critical mass of where we can be at this point in history. And it is a significant pivot point in the city, where the *Reader* still is for some people what it was then. It's not for everybody."

Throughout its history, the *Reader* was stereotypically viewed as a "North Side" paper in racially fragmented Chicago. Baim said, "There are many people who still think it is white, male, North Side. I took the job because that was not true. Maybe that stereotype was true about 90 percent of the content. But what wasn't true is that it wasn't reflected in the readers. An outside audit firm says our audience demographics are basically similar to the city of Chicago in terms of race. Age and income are all over the place. It really is a microcosm of the city's community. The difference, mainly with the *Tribune*, is that a lot of people who read the *Tribune* are suburban. They go out, but they maybe go out once a week or twice a month. Our people are going out all the time, regardless of age and income. They're doing things. They want to know what's new, what's now, and what's next."

In the emerging nonprofit model, news organizations embed themselves into community. The *Sahan Journal* in Minnesota is one of the only independent digital outlets producing daily news for and by immigrant communities in Minnesota. In May 2021 when reporting on the permanent closing of a charter school that predominately served East African families, education reporter Becky Z. Dernbach discovered that parents weren't even aware of the closing. Dernbach had come to the nonprofit *Journal* as a corps member in Report for America, a national service program that places journalists to write under-covered stories in local newspapers. The *Journal* eventually partnered with a local Somali television station to host a live event with community members and school representatives to confront the issue.

"The *Journal* was founded by a Somali American man who felt like his community in particular and immigrants in general weren't being adequately represented by mainstream media in Minnesota," said Jonathan Kealing, chief network officer for the Institute for Nonprofit News (INN). "A lot of large organizations make a big deal about telling stories about a particular community, but many nonprofits like the *Sahan Journal*, *Cicero Independiente* [Illinois], and Outliers in Detroit are really telling stories *for* that community. It is not journalism *about* a community."

—

What does community mean to Peter Shaw?

"That is a great question," he answered. "If you find a community with a strong self-identity, you're going to find a strong newspaper there. And how do you get the community voice in the paper that's not the paper telling the community that's the voice? We have the editorial board, and we live in the community, so there's that."

Ethel Sengstacke moved from Chicago to Memphis, Tennessee, when her late uncle, *Chicago Defender* owner John Sengstacke, transferred her father to Memphis to become general manager of the sister publication *Tri-State Defender*. The Black-owned *Defender* immediately became a voice for the Black community. Ethel described community this way: "You're aware of what's going on. You uplift the community. People don't realize the history and how great this [Memphis] community is. And that bothers me."

Carroll Times Herald co-owner Doug Burns cited the essence of community often delivered by former Iowa governor Terry Branstad. A native of Leland, Iowa, Branstad was Iowa's governor between 1983 and 1999 and again between 2011 and 2017. He is the longest-tenured governor in American history. Branstad told Burns that what separates a great community from an average community is the presence of a locally owned bank and a strong, locally owned newspaper. Burns said, "And Branstad, who is certainly no liberal—he's Donald Trump's ambassador to China, and he ran Trump's campaign in Iowa—he loves newspapers as much as any political figure I've worked with. So many small communities in a state that he loves are being devastated by financial consolidation and media consolidation. By the standards set by arguably the most successful conservative politician in the history of Iowa, small towns are set up to lose two ingredients [banks and newspapers] he identifies as being most [important] to their success."

Community is best witnessed as a place where everyone works together. The newspaper is often such a place.

Shaw Media employs around three hundred journalists. What is the value the company places on editorial personnel? "I am not part of the budgeting process," former trustee Peter Shaw answered. "But the budget, the expense budget, is being reduced each year to match the revenue that is going down. Top leadership has said, 'Look, we need to cut X million dollars and it cannot come from content producers.' There might be other functions inside of editorial we need to consolidate, but it cannot be reporters. I would say we highly value, as much as we can afford to, what we consider our core competencies. And that is content generation, which is primarily journalism, and the marketing, the sales reps. It was a no-brainer to outsource printing. If we could outsource circulation here, we would. We're now in a place where we not only have to manage this downward slope but transform it to something different going forward. The operational leaders have never *not* been working on solutions with transition to digital subscriptions and memberships. It is that direct relationship with consumers that has to be the whole focus of it."

The Hillsboro *Journal-News*'s Mary Herschelman looked at the customers next door. She said, "Community is caring about your neighbors. The world would be a better place if we were all just kind."

Herschelman half-bowed her head as she looked at the November 18, 2019, edition of the *Journal-News*. There were two main stories above the fold. One was a large picture with the headline "Community Group Rakes Leaves for Locals," with a cutline about volunteers who rake leaves for the elderly and veterans. The second story was about a head-on collision on Route 185 near Hillsboro. "I saw posts on Facebook today," Herschelman said. "The four people that died in this collision were in one van. The accident was caused by a seventeen-year-old kid in a truck who crossed the center line. Remember, he's a kid. Don't say negative things. We live in a world where we're mean. Maybe it's always been that way and social media allows it to be more known. But what if that was your teenage kid that crossed the line and caused this accident? Would you want people to say that about your kid? Would you say that about your kid?

"We're a small rural area and we don't get a lot of grant money for things. But we have a community that's invested. They built a dog park just off of donations. You build up trust over the years. I wish the world was a kinder place. I wish we would think twice before some of the things we say sometimes. Maybe we will get there someday."

Sandy Leitheiser has been the Montgomery County clerk in Hillsboro since December 1998. She was born in 1958 and has read the *Journal-News* for more than forty years. Leitheiser grew up on a family farm in Witt, outside of Nokomis, which is about twenty miles from Hillsboro.

Leitheiser remembers the excitement when her parents, Dale and Marilyn Houck, received the *Journal-News*. "It was mailed to the house and eagerly awaited," she said. "Everybody took their turn. Dad got priority. He went to the front page and the letters to the editor. My mother was born and raised in Hillsboro. Hillsboro covered Nokomis, and at the time there was also the Nokomis *Free Press-Progress*." The Nokomis paper still publishes every Wednesday with no online presence.

"But the *Journal-News* has become the county newspaper. They have good, broad coverage of the county and what's going on in terms of meetings and public bodies. Sports. Family events. I'm finding the smaller the community, the more important the newspaper is. It offers that tie to each other and that glue that we're going to stick together in a crisis."

Leitheiser has a public relations degree from the University of Illinois Springfield. Her family receives the twice-a-week hard copies of the *Journal-News*, but she also reads the paper's digital edition. "More recently they clamped down on some free items, which I understand," she said. "You have to make money like any other business. On a Monday or Thursday morning, I'm logging in and reading it the best I can to catch the main points. They're very community-minded. The employees and family are trustworthy and that speaks volumes. What you read is coming from a community member that knows a neighbor—somebody that goes to church with you. You saw them at the grocery store. If they're printing it, it is coming from a trusted source. Sadly, that's something you can't say about a lot of media.

"On the challenging side they may need to go more in depth with social media to stay relevant to the younger generation. I'd like to see them editorialize at times when we have controversial topics. They don't offer opinions much. I guess there's a reason. Part of their trustworthiness is the noncontroversial approach they take."

During the late 1980s, Leitheiser and her husband, Kevin, were members of Rusty Halo, a five-piece country-pop band that played around St. Louis and central Illinois. In the late 1970s, they also owned Rainbow Records on the courthouse square in Hillsboro. "When we had a gig coming up, we made sure it hit the newspaper," said Leitheiser, who sang and played keyboards. "And after the gig there would be mention of the band in the newspaper, and we got great publicity out of that."

Hillsboro was founded in 1823. Visitors enter town from the west on the two-lane Illinois Route 16 and approach a couple of rolling hills that are out of character for the flatlands of south-central Illinois. The village got its name from the hills that were created from drainage of the nearby Shoal Creek watershed. The town is off the grid. It is not adjacent to a major highway, and the buses and trains left a long time ago.

The efforts to preserve the forward spirit of community in rural America were not lost on the Smithsonian Institution. In September 2021, the Smithsonian announced that Hillsboro was chosen to be featured in the traveling exhibit *Spark! Places of Innovation.* The exhibit highlights innovation as a response to the closing of manufacturing systems and globalization. The stories will be told from the perspective of the residents. The exhibit will run from 2023 to 2026 and will travel to at least twenty-five states.

Hillsboro is a featured city for the entire run, according to Hillsboro community and economic planner Jonathan Weyer. *Spark!* will be hosted in Hillsboro in 2023, the city's bicentennial year. The *Journal-News* will be involved in curating information, interviews, and history. It is big news for this small town in the middle of America.

Hillsboro contains only eight square miles, and it feels even more condensed than that.

Brian Lee is a musician and a force behind Gold Pan Records in downtown Hillsboro. Lee explained, "We lived in East Nashville, [Tenessee] in 2011. I thought that was a close community, but living here, it's like, 'What the heck is this?' There's no other way to have this much face-to-face. In architecture and design, they always say when you put people together in public places, it's safer. You can't cheat on your spouse or whatever. Anything you do, you're gonna get caught.

"We're all right here."

His Gold Pan business partner, Matt Sands, added, "There seems to be a culture among the residents here that want to see it succeed."

Lee said, "The difference between Hillsboro and all the towns around—besides Greenville and some of Litchfield—they're just the normal Midwest towns that are dying. I moved here about seven years ago with my wife. We bought this huge building down at the end of the [Main] street with my father-in-law. We built our house into the back of that, so we have this loft apartment kind of house. I started a blog about five years ago about everything that is happening. It feels not as important because it's real now. This was before whatever Facebook did to change the reach of their stuff. Everybody's aunt, mom, was 'Look what's happening in our town.' And the local government is supportive, too. Everybody wants a building downtown now."

Quaint downtown Hillsboro appealed to the manufacturer Atlas 46, which opened a plant in Hillsboro in July 2020. Atlas 46 makes vests, motorcycle bags, and equipment products for military, law enforcement agencies, and homeland security. The manufacturer also opened a boutique store called Hardcore Hammers, selling hammers and axes next door to Gold Pan Records.

"They wanted to expand, and within a couple years they're going to have two hundred people working here," Galer said in the spring of 2019. "They came here because the owner [John Carver] likes the look of Hillsboro. He wants an old-town kind of feel."

Journal-News publisher Mike Plunkett wore an Atlas 46 baseball cap in a separate conversation at a downtown Hillsboro coffee shop. He wondered, "Maybe people want to be a part of something that is bigger than them, but not so big that they are a tiny speck." He looked upward towards his cap and said, "The guy who is putting this here employs a hundred people in Fenton [Missouri] and nobody cares. He employs a hundred people in Hillsboro and he's changing lives." The newspaper is a cheerleader for the new businesses coming to their small community.

Matt Sands described neighboring Litchfield as four separate towns: businesses off I-55 between Chicago and St. Louis, a shopping mall that surrounds a Walmart on the near north side of town, a modest downtown area, and old Route 66 that snakes through town. Lee said, "It's a Walmart town that got shredded by Walmart. It's pole barn [buildings with no foundation] development. It seems like people don't know each other so much in Litchfield. Everyone knows each other in Hillsboro. Me and my wife have three kids. When there's nothing to do we just walk down the street and talk to people. We know everyone that's walking down the street." The Hillsboro newspaper follows in those footsteps.

—

Good fortune comes to the stranger who hangs around long enough to become part of a family community.

That's the legacy of Doug Ray.

Ray is chairman, publisher, and CEO of Paddock Publications in Arlington Heights, a northwest suburb of Chicago. Paddock's *Daily Herald* is the third-largest newspaper in Illinois with a daily circulation of ninety-four thousand in 2020. The *Daily Herald* is specifically focused on the six counties that ring Chicago. The Daily Herald Media Group includes various niche publications, commercial printing for publishers, and two dozen weekly newspapers in central and southern Illinois. Ray was born and raised in the southern Illinois town of Effingham (pop. 12,300), which may be best known for "The Cross at the Crossroads." The two-hundred-foot-tall steel cross at the intersection of I-57 and I-70 is the second-tallest cross in the United States.

Ray graduated from Effingham High School and took off 120 miles down the road to attend Southern Illinois University (SIU) in Carbondale. He earned his journalism degree from SIU in 1969 and landed his first job as a reporter in 1970 for the suburban *Daily Herald*, owned by the Stuart Paddock family.

He never left.

Ray said in a June 2020 interview, as he was commemorating his fiftieth year at the company, "My first beat was [suburban] Rolling Meadows in 1970. The smallest beat at the paper. I don't think they thought I could handle that from southern Illinois, a little bit of an accent. Someone asked how I went from that to CEO. I said, 'I've been around all these years and everyone else quit.'" Ray has clearly not given up his folksy Midwestern wit.

In September 2018, Robert Y. Paddock Jr. and Stuart R. Paddock III sold their interests in the company to the newspaper's employees. It ended 120 years and four generations of family ownership. The newspaper was founded by Hosea C. Paddock when he bought the *Palatine Enterprise* for $175 in the fields thirty miles outside of Chicago. Hosea's motto still appears on the front page of the *Daily Herald*: "To fear God, tell the truth and make money." Robert Jr. and Stuart III are Hosea's great-grandsons. In February 2020, Robert Jr. retired from daily responsibilities as the company's executive vice president but remained on the board of directors. He declined my request for comment on his family newspaper. In March 2022, while I was fact-checking this book, Doug Ray said through an email that he had "no further comment."

I asked Ray what it was like to work as an outsider for a family-owned newspaper. "It depends on the family," he said. "The Paddock family has been one of the best newspaper owners in my experience. I've sat on the NNA [National Newspaper Association] board with the family members of the *New York Times*. I was the little guy. The GateHouse CEO was there. I got a lot of exposure to others over the last fifteen years or so." Ray treasured the autonomy he was given throughout the years.

Ray had thoughts of being an English teacher while growing up. His father, Harold, was a bookkeeper, his mother, Twila, was a homemaker and the manager of a Spiegel catalog store in downtown Effingham. His sister, Tamara, still lives in Effingham. "I studied journalism in Carbondale," he said. "Anyway, that's not very interesting."

It is interesting how Ray worked his way up the Paddock chain. In 1972, he was named city editor. From 1976 to 1983 he was managing editor. He was appointed *Daily Herald* editor in 1991 and was named senior vice president/editor in 1996. Ray said he was left alone in all his years as an editor. "Stu Paddock [Jr.] never . . . never asked me to put anything in the paper," Ray declared. "And he never asked me to leave anything out. Not many editors can say that. The editor of the *Chicago Tribune* couldn't say that. They couldn't say it honestly. I can."

The *Daily Herald* has done a good job of making a paper that covers the crescent northwest and west suburbs of Chicago feel like a community newspaper. "People [staff] go to the Rotary Club," Ray said. "You see our people. It's not like the old days when people would come in the office through a revolving door, work here eighteen months, then they'd go do something else. People have been here a long time. We write for the community; we don't write for the officialdom. Papers that are successful are the ones that write for people like 'me.' That's the secret. If the newspaper is written for 'me,' they will embrace it."

Dann Gire is the celebrated semi-retired film critic at the *Daily Herald*. He started at the paper in 1975 as a local government reporter and became a critic in 1978 when the *Herald* became a daily. He took a buyout in 2017 but continues to freelance for the newspaper.

"As the DH [*Daily Herald*] began its evolution to the third-largest daily in Illinois, we still practiced weird stuff," Gire said in a 2021 interview. "Our policy was to address men by last name on second reference. Women on second reference had to be addressed as 'Mrs.' or 'Miss.' My twenty-two-year-old self rebelled at this nonsense, not just because it rattled my Helen Reddy sensitivities, but that it took longer to confirm the marital statuses than it did to write the stories. I finally stopped the practice on my own and nothing happened. Covering an expanding number of murders and related crimes as the suburbs grew denser was never boring. But I remember locals talking about how people from the city were coming into the suburbs and they weren't happy."

The connection between the reader and the newspaper is more intimate in small towns. When reading a small- or midsized-town paper, I'm reminded of my lifelong love of minor league baseball, where fans are always closer to the players. In Gire's long tenure with the *Daily Herald*, he compared notes with reporters from the "big city" newspapers.

Gire won ten Peter Lisagor Awards for Exemplary Journalism in Arts Criticism and created the Chicago Critics Film Festival, the only festival of its kind curated by professional film critics. "None of this would have happened if I had gone for the money and bailed for the 'prestige' of the metros," Gire wrote in an email. "The opportunities to work a government beat, a crime beat, a metro desk beat, and a Chicago movie critic beat in the span of three years could never happen on a metro. Never. The Paddocks ran their newspapers as a family enterprise, supportive and nurturing, but able to build the paper into the third-largest daily in Illinois. The now employee-owned paper grew as the Chicago suburbs expanded. I was along for this amazing ride.

"Did I have discussions with other journalists about benefits and drawbacks of working at a family-owned newspaper? All the time. I would generally characterize that most of the *Herald* grads were happy with the time they spent at the *Herald*, but never considered it a life career. I was experiencing such an amazing journalistic dream, I never considered anyplace else."

Twenty-three miles from the *Daily Herald* headquarters in Arlington Heights, former trustee Peter Shaw said his company Shaw Media had looked at regional expansion but not in recent years. He pointed to Shaw's 2012 acquisition of twenty-two suburban Chicago weekly newspapers from GateHouse. "We were one of the first companies to make a newspaper acquisition coming out of the 2008–09 nonexistent newspaper market," Shaw said in a July 2020 interview.

Shaw Media places strong emphasis on local government and high school sports, which can get territorial. The chain covers more than one hundred high schools, bundling that coverage into a digital channel called "Friday Night Drive." In 2019, "Friday Night Drive" won *Editor & Publisher*'s Best Sports Website (with under one million unique monthly visitors) in its first year of existence. Some print features get published out of the digital content. Football, in particular, hits home.

The ear is closer to the ground in family-run newspapers. Papers become more responsive to what is heard, be it rumblings about sports, education, or other issues. Evanston, Illinois, is an increasingly gentrified Chicago suburb about 260 miles north of Hillsboro. In 2021, Evanston became the first city in the nation to approve reparations to Black residents, partly funded by marijuana sales tax revenues. There are differences between rural Hillsboro and Evanston, which lives next to Chicago and Lake Michigan. Education is the driving gear of the *Evanston RoundTable*, an award-winning news service that transitioned from print to digital in 2020.

What is it that makes their community rich?

"I viewed the paper where I would cover education all the time," said *RoundTable* writer and former senior editor Larry Gavin. "The achievement gap in Evanston has stayed the same as the rest of the country for twenty years. We have not made a dent in that even though Evanston has more resources than Chicago and more than most places, in terms of money and people who are interested in trying to solve it. Another thing is affordable housing. Back when we started the paper, we badgered the city they needed somebody to take a look at housing and they never did. We had an idea that the government was okay with gentrification, and that's happened. A lot of people are getting priced out of the market. And property taxes are miserable. Two market forces that are impossible to stop."

Former *RoundTable* publisher and manager Mary Helt Gavin is married to Larry. She added, "The way city council is compensated is so minimal. And what they're asked to do is so much. The pool of people who can run for office is very small. It's like our newspaper.

"If you can afford to work with us, we can buy you coffee."

Please note how Mary said "with us" and not "for us."

Hillsboro's Galer reflected, "As with any operation, to have a newspaper go over several generations is a real challenge. But the biggest challenge is economics. You're probably okay as long as your town is still fairly vibrant. But if your town has troubles, you're going to have real troubles to keep the wheels turning on a newspaper. When the economics of your town changes drastically, that will eventually affect who and how many people live here. If the number really dwindles, it will hurt in total subscribers, and it will also hurt the community economically as many of your smaller stores will not be able to survive."

Overall, more subscribers means a bigger audience and more readers of the product—print or online. But the reality is that advertising carries most of the cash-flow load and in essence determines a newspaper's survivability.

Galer explained, "On the business level, to keep the world running takes a ton of brainpower. You almost have to be an MBA. And you have to have that desire to want to do it. Desire has been my goal the whole time. I like what I do, but for us it has never been about the family. I like being what we are.

"It has been about the community."

Chapter 3

Serving History

Families rooted in a community for generations have a greater stake in serving that community. It is in their DNA. They want to continue building where others are selling. There is a Native American belief that the past, present, and future are forever linked. One cannot exist without the others. In the same vein, long-standing family newspapers are serving history as much as they are serving readers.

For example, as a stubborn nod to customers' desires, the *Journal-News* offices remain open on Saturday mornings in Hillsboro. Customers wander in to pay subscriptions, take out advertisements, or just ask questions at the old office, which, after World War II, was the popular Barnes Supper Club.

"Most of the time downtown Hillsboro isn't busy on Saturday mornings," said John Galer. "There used to be a bank across the street. People used to come to town to do their banking on a Saturday morning. That whole world has changed with the internet. When you think about it, ever since the iPhone in 2007, this world has changed massively. I'm not sure totally for the better."

Galer said, "Until 2004 there were two independently owned family newspapers here. Both [the *Hillsboro Journal*, est. 1886, and the *Litchfield News-Herald*] were in operation over a hundred years. That's what makes this town really special. The only other town I can think of is Carlinville [Illinois], and that once had two independent weeklies over a hundred years."

The 1939 *WPA Guide to Illinois* does not mention Hillsboro. It calls nearby Litchfield an "old mining town, center of a coal field that underlies parts of six counties." And it adds, "Litchfield, incorporated in 1859, was the scene of the first commercial oil production in Illinois, in 1882; the small pocket then tapped has long since been exhausted."

Schram City (pop. 557) is just two and a half miles from Hillsboro in Montgomery County. In 1907 the Schram Glass Manufacturing Company began producing fruit jars in Schram City. "We had coal, we had water, we had two rail lines," Galer said. The Ball Brothers of Muncie, Indiana, took over the plant in 1925. Ball Brothers was the world's largest fruit jar company.

In October 1961, Hiram Walker purchased the plant and began producing liquor bottles under the name of Hillsboro Glass. The plant ceased operations on September 14, 1997. "That was a big part of our world here for a long time," Galer said. "You had a lot of blue-collar jobs. It was the type of job where a guy graduated high school and you could put kids through college. It was the typical blue-collar job we don't have anymore. The change from a blue-collar environment to a different structure is the biggest change I have seen in the past thirty years. We've been hit hard on the economic end."

Mike Plunkett observed, "I was born in 1965 and grew up in Hillsboro in the '70s and '80s. The blue-collar jobs are gone. Now, it seems like you graduate from Hillsboro High School, go to college, and don't come back—or if you stay here you work at Hardee's or Walmart in Litchfield. Or in my graduating class of 150 [if you said], 'Raise your hand if you live on a farm,' about a third would raise their hands. Now if you say, 'Raise your hand if you live on a farm,' it's probably four people. We're still growing more corn, but it is fewer and fewer farm families that are doing that."

Galer offered a seen-it-all sigh and said, "I see struggles in small towns. Obviously if you're a small-town newspaper, you are tied to the community dead on. So you're going to have the same kind of struggles."

—

Of course, some papers, and some towns, struggle less than others. The *Post and Courier* of Charleston, South Carolina, is the oldest daily newspaper in the South. It was founded in 1803 as the *Charleston Courier*. The *Evening*

Post in Charleston was founded in 1894 but ran into rough financial waters, and Charleston rice planter Arthur Manigault bought the paper in 1896. It has remained in the Manigault family since then. The *Courier* (then called the *News-Courier*) and the *Evening Post* merged in 1991 as a single morning paper.

Pierre Manigault is the fourth-generation chairman of the board of Evening Post Industries. But the paper is run by professional managers: John Barnwell was the president and CEO who retired in October 2021. And P. J. Browning is publisher after spending thirty years with Gannett, Knight Ridder, and McClatchy chains.

"Heritage and tradition is a big part of the makeup of our culture in Charleston," Manigault said in a 2019 interview. "Families stay here a long time. There's been a desire for the paper to stay in the family. Secondly, it has been very profitable for generations. It has allowed us to expand into television and other businesses. Today's company is vastly different than one newspaper. But it has been the engine that has allowed us to build when others are selling. We believe in our commitment to the community. It's a very tight community made up of a lot of people that have been here for a very long time. Our family has been here since the late 1600s. So we have a real stake in this. We're all becoming more aware as newspapers struggle, the importance of the newspaper to any community. Without the newspaper, the community would suffer. This newspaper has been the most recognized, trusted voice in this community for a very long time. We still have that, but it is very fragile."

Manigault left Charleston in the 1980s. He is a graduate of Southern Methodist University in Dallas and in 1987 was a photographer and editor of television news at the NBC affiliate in Colorado Springs, Colorado. He next joined the National Geographic Society as a film editor in the television division. Manigault returned to Charleston in 1994.

"It's funny, I never really thought I would go into family business," he said. "I wanted to go into documentary filmmaking. I worked at one of our [Evening Post] television stations in Colorado to learn about camera work and editing. I really wanted to be a documentary filmmaker at National Geographic. But I decided documentary filmmaking wouldn't be realistic for me. And that I could make a difference in an area I really cared about, which was this part of South Carolina. I talked to my dad and told him I was interested in the newspaper business after all. He told me it was a grand idea, but that I needed to go get some experience." His father, Peter, was chairman of the board for the *Post and Courier*. He had replaced his father, Edward Manigault.

Pierre landed at the *Washington Post*—not a bad first gig. He started on the bottom as a copy aide, then became a writer and copy editor. "I was there three or four years and came back to the paper," he said. Pierre rebooted in 1994 as an editorial writer at the *Post and Courier*. In 1998, he spent a year in the business office before assuming the role of president of Evening Post Community Publications Group, overseeing the operations of twelve subsidiary newspapers.

In August 2004, Pierre was elected chairman of the board of Evening Post Publishing Co. He was forty-two years old. He replaced his father, Peter, who died in June 2004 at age seventy-seven. Then–Charleston mayor Joseph P. Riley said Peter Manigault helped shape today's historic hipster Charleston vibe that has attracted residents such as actor Bill Murray (who is a co-owner of the Charleston RiverDogs Minor League Baseball team), Charleston-area native Stephen Colbert, and acclaimed chef Sean Brock. Riley said Peter "provided the leadership for the newspapers to make preservation issues important news. He gave ink, he gave space, he gave coverage. Without all that, Charleston would have been a very different place."

Pierre added, "Two of the main pillars of the editorial portion of the newspaper, certainly for three generations, have been historic preservation and natural resource conservation and land conservation. We're one of the leaders on the East Coast of the nation in land that has been saved and preserved—forever."

—

The *News-Gazette* in Champaign, Illinois, is a long exit ramp away from Charleston. The newspaper's struggles magnified in August 2019 when it was sold to the family-owned Champaign Multimedia Group, LLC, in West Frankfort, Illinois. The *News-Gazette* then filed for bankruptcy as part of the sale process. In November 2019, the company laid off thirty-four people in Champaign. The paper estimated its assets at $1 million to $10 million and its liabilities (in particular, pension obligations) at between $10 million and $50 million.

This is how the legacies of some grand family newspapers end.

Marajen Stevick Chinigo was a larger-than-life figure around Champaign -Urbana. She owned the *News-Gazette* from 1967 until her death in 2002. Marajen was an Italian contessa by marriage. She had poodles named Popcorn, Aria, and Lucia and homes in Rancho Mirage, California, on the Amalfi Coast in Italy, and in Champaign.

She was the Hearst of the Heartland.

Marajen was married five times. Her last husband, Michael Chinigo, was a former United Press war correspondent and an Italian count. He died of a self-inflicted gunshot wound in Rome in 1974. Marajen died of complications from a stroke in 2002 in an Urbana hospital at the age of ninety. She had been at the newspaper two days before her death.

She had no survivors.

Locals were surprised at the modest turnout for her funeral mass at St. Patrick's Church in Urbana. Marajen didn't have many contemporaries left in Champaign-Urbana and the services were two days after Christmas. Fewer than one hundred people were in attendance. Veteran *News-Gazette* reporters Tom Kacich and Mary Schenk spoke at her mass. They are keepers of a flame from a prosperous and proud era that seems too long ago.

They were sitting in Marajen's former office when I spoke to them on a mid-March day in 2020. A portion of the penthouse office overlooked downtown Main Street; another portion overlooked the front entryway of the newspaper building. A greenhouse had since been added. Marajen's chair lift was still in place at the bottom of a fifteen-step stairway. The chair would take her from the first floor to her office. The chair was now as empty as a corner news box.

As part of the *News-Gazette* sale, the newspaper staff would leave their legacy Stevick Building, formerly home to a JCPenney department store before the *News-Gazette* moved into the building in 1984. For the previous seventy years the offices had been two blocks away in a former harness factory.

Why the 1984 move? "Life was good," Schenk answered. Now, one floor below her was a mostly empty newsroom.

The Stevick Building contained the *News-Gazette*'s principal editorial, advertising, circulation, and business offices as well as the three radio stations the company owned. Visitors entered a stunning three-story glass atrium, accented by a glass-and-metal spiral stairway. Marajen's elegant and spacious office has since been lost to the ages.

Upon Marajen's death, *News-Gazette* editor and future publisher John Foreman told the *Chicago Tribune* that her passing was "the end of an era, when strong families really controlled all of the newspapers in Illinois."

Kacich said it was ironic that Marajen would pass away in 2002, the 150th anniversary of the founding of the newspaper. "We had a big celebration that year," he said. "There was a book. She was grand marshal of the Fourth of July parade. I drove the convertible. It was fun. That's when we had lots of money.

"She was eccentric."

Marajen's father, David W. Stevick, founded the *Champaign Daily News* in 1915. He bought the *Champaign Daily Gazette* in 1919 and merged them. He was a stickler for detail. Marajen once recalled how he would retrieve the newspaper from their front lawn when he returned home from work and adjourn to the home library. Stevick would spread out the *Daily Gazette* and after a couple glances, without pencil or paper, was able to determine, based on its advertising content, whether the paper made a profit for the day. Stevick suffered a fatal heart attack in 1935 while driving from Florida to Illinois. He was forty-eight years old. His wife, Helen, took over. When she died in 1967, Marajen reprinted what her mother had written on the front page after her husband passed away: "My daughter, Marajen, and myself have implicit faith in the loyal, progressive employees of an organization which has endeared itself to our hearts."

According to a December 23, 2002, *News-Gazette* story, Marajen's favorite childhood memory was riding on her father's shoulders through downtown Champaign at the celebration following the end of World War I. She also remembered him taking her on visits through the various departments at the newspaper. "I grew up sharing his desk, and he yearned to teach me all that he had learned," she once said. Marajen also said the best advice she ever heard was delivered from her father: "Baby, two things you must remember—never spend more money than you earn, and know there is no one so important you cannot live without them."

During Helen Stevick's 1935–1967 tenure, the *News-Gazette's* circulation grew from 13,138 readers to nearly 35,000 in 1967, according to *News-Gazette* stories. Also, while Helen was in charge in 1949, the *News-Gazette* opened its radio station WDWS-AM (standing for David W. Stevick). It was the first commercial radio station in Champaign. Later, WHMS-FM was named as a tribute to Helen. After Helen's death in 1967, her only child, Marajen, assumed control of the company.

Schenk said, "Eccentric only begins to cover Marajen. She had a villa in Italy to which certain members of management were invited from time to time. Then when they would go on their vacations, they had to take turns paying for a night of dinner. She usually invited like a dozen guests. I know this because one of my best buddies' wife was in management and they got invited. Imagine their surprise when [she] said, 'Okay, you have to pay for dinner for these fifteen people tonight.'" Marajen also liked to raise lemons and olives at her Italian villa, a restored twelfth-century monastery on a mountain crest overlooking Salerno Bay. She painted landscapes of hillsides filled with lemon and olive trees, and many of her works were on display at the *News-Gazette* headquarters. Jacqueline Kennedy visited the Stevick compound in Italy.

"At her home in California she hobnobbed with some Hollywood types," Schenk said. "Bob Hope, but less famous people like Larry Storch, Mary Pickford, and Loretta Young." Peter Marshall, the host of the television show *Hollywood Squares* and father of former Cubs first baseman Pete La-Cock, was another friend.

The late Pulitzer Prize–winning film critic Roger Ebert began his career at the *News-Gazette*. As a teenager, Marajen married B. H. Rogers, the brother of actor Buddy "America's Sweetheart" Rogers. In the *News-Gazette* obituary for Marajen, Ebert told writer Paul Wood, "One time I was on a talk show with Buddy Rogers and he turned to me and said, 'I think Marajen mentioned you used to be at her paper.' She knew all these people. She was very social."

Marajen's mother is believed to be the first Champaign County woman to fly in an airplane. Marajen often boasted that she had applied to make the first commercial space flight.

"She was interesting," Schenk said. "Not a lot of employees felt comfortable approaching her or talking to her."

Former *News-Gazette* publisher John Reed said, "Now, I didn't even arrive here until six years after she passed, but my sense of it was that she was never really an operator. She was an owner. Back in the day, it supported her lifestyle. She always had professionals to operate this." Ebert told the *News-Gazette*, "She rejected any offers from big chains and continued to supply Champaign-Urbana with an independent, locally owned voice."

But with homes in Italy and California, Marajen didn't spend a lot of time at the newspaper. Once in a while she would meddle. "One time [opera singer Luciano] Pavarotti was at the Krannert Center," Kacich recalled, referencing an October 1980 performance in Urbana. "Our reviewer panned it. And that poor guy got canned because Pavarotti knew Mrs. C or something. It would happen once every two years. She didn't exercise power much outside of the newspaper. She didn't call politicians or ask them to call upon her. She was beyond that."

Marajen's father was a different breed. He had the spirit of a circus promoter. When Stevick launched the first local Sunday paper, as a stunt he had newspapers delivered by air to nearby Rantoul and Tuscola. He allowed University of Illinois journalism students to produce one edition of the *News-Gazette* every spring. A staunch Republican, he still promoted the idea of a birthday party for Franklin Delano Roosevelt to raise funds to combat polio. "He wrote front-page editorials," Kacich said. "He was into the journalism, he was into the community. I would have loved to have known him."

Kacich cited the late 1970s *Lou Grant* television show based on a fictional Los Angeles newspaper. The newspaper's publisher, Margaret Jones Pynchon, was based on a blend of powerful actual newspaper publishers Dorothy Chandler of the *Los Angeles Times* and Katharine Graham of the *Washington Post*. "Marajen was not Pynchon," he said. Schenk added, "And if she was, we were insulated. John Foreman, our late publisher, deflected her from us."

Reed, though a self-described "relative newbie," claimed, "Everybody you meet in town has a Marajen Chinigo story."

"She always brought her little yippin' dogs around," Schenk said. "We were always on alert to clean up [workspaces]."

Kacich added, "Everybody would either leave, or [be] like Fred Kroner, who would take all the shit from his desk and put it in the trunk of his car when she was in town. Once she left, he would take it out of the trunk of his car and bring it back in."

The nearby Esquire Lounge is the newspaper watering hole. (Try the homemade pineapple tequila.) "We treated her there," Kacich recalled. "She had a Coors Light with ice. Before I got here in 1975, when the paper was barely getting by, they had a Christmas party in the newsroom. Everybody was making $10 a week or whatever it was at that time. They all chipped in a buck or two and bought her an engraved something. She was so moved by it, she wrote about it in the paper. . . . It just touched her for the rest of her life."

—

Roger Ebert developed an affinity for these larger-than-life Hollywood stories while growing up in small-town Urbana. His family lived in east Urbana, and in his memoir, *Life Itself*, the *Chicago Sun-Times* journalist called his white stucco childhood home "the center of the universe." The Eberts were next-door neighbors of *News-Gazette* city editor Harold Holmes, who hired Kacich. Holmes also hired Ebert. In 1959, Ebert got his first front-page byline at age seventeen for covering the *News-Gazette*'s all-state football banquet. "Roger loved working here," Kacich said. "He hated the politics of the *News-Gazette*, but it didn't matter. He was in high school and he was writing the Urbana game stories that appeared Saturday morning. The *News-Gazette* was proud of him for the rest of his life."

Schenk is a native of downstate Alton, Illinois, and obtained a bachelor of science degree in journalism from the University of Illinois at Urbana-Champaign in 1980. Upon graduation she immediately began work as a news reporter and anchor at Marajen's radio station. Schenk moved to the *News-Gazette* in November 1983. "I didn't read newspapers much before college," she said. "I liked to read in the summers, mostly Nancy Drew mysteries."

According to Schenk, Marajen spent more time at the radio station than at the newspaper. Marajen was comfortable in smaller settings. Schenk recalled, "The assistant radio station manager was a woman, which was rare in those days. She kind of kowtowed to Mrs. C and kept the rest of us in line. When Mrs. C would come to town, we were all put on our best behavior. 'Make sure you dress up this day.' 'Make sure your desk is clean.' This was the early 1980s and we all dressed nicer than we do now anyway."

Marajen would have lunch with employees in a room named The Vito Lounge. "I've lived through multiple renovations of this company," Schenk said. "They added an addition that about doubled the size in the three years I was there. She liked being there. It had the same [Italian classic] flourishes we have here. This is a lovely building, and it has been a great place to work. I remember distinctly her saying to me that if your employees don't have nice toilets to use, they're not going to be happy. And we have lovely bathrooms. Talk about Maslow's hierarchy [of needs]."

The walls of the WDWS radio station were decorated with pictures of Marajen and her friends. One of her husbands was Lieutenant Colonel William Dyess (1916–1943), a survivor of the Bataan Death March after the Japanese attacked Pearl Harbor. After being released as a POW, he was promoted to lieutenant colonel and resumed flying on December 22, 1943. He was killed that day attempting an emergency landing in Burbank, California. Schenk said, "There were huge printed copies of the newspapers framed at the radio station: 'Japatrocities Told!' One time I'm interviewing some Japanese Rotarians, and I took those down and put them in the closet. They had translators with them.

"[Marajen] was born with a silver spoon in her mouth."

Reed said, "She never really had an appreciation for what her dad and mom did to keep it going. By the time she got it, the thing was a license to print money for a meaningful chunk of her life. My predecessor, John Foreman, talked often about her. Even though she wasn't involved in the day-to-day, she didn't sit on the editorial board, she didn't participate in making endorsements. But she was deeply committed to keeping the media company independent and local. Which goes to the whole structure of how it would be architected after her death."

Marajen was adamant that the newspaper and radio stations remain locally owned and operated. After her death, ownership was transferred to a private foundation that was named the Marajen Stevick Foundation. (The paper, however, is not nonprofit.) In recent years the foundation awarded grants to support the literacy program of Urbana Neighborhood Connections Center, which assists children with after-school homework, and the Memory Connection project, which offers resources to people diagnosed with dementia and to their families. She wrote a check to help finance the new Illinois Press

Association headquarters in Springfield, and she helped underwrite one of Roger Ebert's first film festivals in Champaign.

"She really viewed the paper as an important community asset," Reed said. "As an employee of the company and just as an outside observer, that's the biggest chunk of her legacy that is important. She had multiple opportunities to sell this. She'd get rattled by the Shaw folks [in Dixon] who made several overtures. And this was back in the time when women business owners were not the norm. So when the Shaw people would call the attorney and the deal would be half-done before she found out about it, she'd blow a gasket and the lawyers would back off.

"She wanted it to be independent and local."

The *News-Gazette* stood for a profound sense of pride in Champaign-Urbana. During the 1980s, a newsroom employee printed T-shirts that read "*News-Gazette* . . . The Miracle on Main Street." It was a salute to the journalists, printers, ad reps, bundle haulers, and others who published three editions a day with a circulation of more than fifty thousand.

A bronze statue of a paperboy stands alone at the corner of Walnut and Main Streets outside the old Stevick Building. The statue is dedicated to David Stevick and "all of the boys and girls of all ages who have brought Champaign-Urbana its news since 1852."

David Stevick's last signed editorial ran on September 1, 1935, three months before his death. He reflected on the day, twenty years earlier, when he assumed control of the *Champaign Daily News*. He wrote, "Twenty years in the life of a healthy, rugged newspaper is but a wave of time. A conscientious, sincere, well-managed newspaper should live and does live, generation after generation. If honesty, integrity, fearlessness for the right, with good business management are molded as one—its heart—a newspaper will live on and on and on. For it, there will be no end."

On April 20, 2020, the *News-Gazette* left the Stevick Building for good.

In August 2020, an auction was held to sell the building and hundreds of items trapped inside. The initial bid was set at $900,000. Proceeds from the auction were used to pay back creditors. Then, in September 2020, University of Illinois graduate Laura Kalman bought the old newspaper building for nearly $1.2 million. She is founder of the CS+X Foundation in

Champaign and president and CEO of Studio Helix, a health and wellness center in downtown Champaign. Kalman reopened the building in February 2021 with plans for an innovation museum and technology center.

Chapter 4

Stop the Presses! Technology Has Come to Town

Rural newspapers cannot escape the advances of technology. Cell phones and social media have made distant news immediate and personal. Where journalists once got tips at the local diner or tavern, they now harvest leads on Facebook, Twitter, and Instagram. Just because family tradition anchors small papers doesn't mean they are resistant to change.

John Wright knows more about changing technology than most. On a sunny afternoon in mid-June 2019, John and his wife, Kendra, were hard at work restoring the vacant Red Rooster Inn just off Main Street in downtown Hillsboro. Like the *News-Gazette* building, the historic Rooster had been a focal point for the community. The local Rotary club met for more than sixty years in a hotel conference room. The endgame was for the Wrights to rebirth the nearly century-old Rooster as a twelve-room hotel with two apartments, a craft brewery, and a tavern.

John Wright changed the world.

Now he is changing his small community.

Wright led the Apple team that invented the iPhone. He retired in 2016 at age forty-three. After leaving Apple, he and Kendra, along with their three children, moved from San Francisco back to their rural Illinois roots. John is from St. Joseph, Illinois (pop. 3,900), about two hours northeast of Hillsboro. Kendra is from Raymond (pop. 995), just outside of Hillsboro. The Wrights built a home on Glenn Shoals Lake, a large lake connected to Lake Hillsboro.

"I'm from Montgomery County," Kendra said. "Even when we lived in California we came back here almost every summer. It's a fun place for the kids. We camped at Glenn Shoals all the time when I was a kid."

The spirit of communication runs through the Wright family DNA. For the past thirty years, Kendra's father, Mike Niehaus, has been sales manager at the family-run country music/adult contemporary WSMI-AM (1540) in neighboring Litchfield. Two of their sons help with computers for the *Journal-News*. John smiled and said, "They get the biggest kick of seeing their pictures in the newspaper."

People see their timeless reflections in small-town newspapers.

Journal-News owner John Galer said, "Their son [Oliver] has been doing computers for us. We're trying to speed some things up. They need to be cleaned every year, blowing all the dust out. He's been doing that. We have some software we want to upgrade. He's a wonderful kid. Right above us for years and years was computer heaven. Used computers. At one time we had forty to fifty computers up there. His brother [Griffin] heard about it."

The teenaged Oliver and Griffin asked if they could visit the inventory at the *Journal-News*. They wanted to take a few items home to tinker with. "I figured they'd be a half hour, forty-five minutes to get what they wanted," Galer said. "Three hours later they were still upstairs, just having a ball going through old computers. They found some old software. Their grandmother let them have the second floor of her house. So they take it all there, take it all apart, and make things work again. It's a blessing to have them here. They both know what they're doing. It's probably a good experience for them too, to be part of our world."

In a separate interview, John Wright took a break from working on new gutter pipes at the Rooster. He said, "The ironic part is that I really don't like phones. I don't like talking on a phone. I don't like carrying a phone." He was not keeping time on his Apple Watch because he was working at the Red Rooster and he didn't want to break it. Kendra said, "He leaves it at home when he comes here. I had one and I couldn't stand it. It was too big."

John picked up his smartphone. It was shut off. He continued, "But I like this because then I can message people or email. I don't have to talk on a phone.

It's funny, living in California, you read Yahoo! news, Apple, or whatever. You come back to Hillsboro, and you want to know what's going on locally. It's either what is in the local paper or what's on local radio. They're talking about what people are interested in. Things about your neighbors. Where you get into the big cities and even the suburbs, it's all about political stuff. I don't need to go that extra mile to find that information. In California, we never considered picking up the newspaper. I still read my news on the phone in the morning but read the [print *Journal-News*] on Monday and Thursday."

Kendra smiled and said, "The paper has to be read. It doesn't take seven hours to read it. It's an okay commitment. If you pick up the *New York Times*, you can't commit to that twice a week. In Litchfield, there's still a paperboy that comes around on his bicycle every afternoon. We have this joke because we have insane amounts of technology in our house, but we have this tiny radio that sits up in the kitchen window and that's where we listen to WSMI in the morning. We don't have satellite radio. Our youngest, she listens to iHeartRadio and a couple of those apps. We notice there's a big difference between our oldest [Oliver, nineteen years old in 2020]. He spends a lot of time without any kind of iPhone or iPad in his hand. By the time you get our seventeen-year-old [Griffin] and thirteen-year-old, they don't remember life without those things."

The Wrights' youngest child, Anabelle, was born in 2007. The first iPhone debuted June 29, 2007. "She's always had stuff around like that," John said. "When we were working on the iPad, she must have been two or three. She climbed up on the couch and said, 'Daddy, you're working.' I had my laptop and she started touching the screen. I thought, 'That's all these kids are ever going to know.'"

Everyone around Hillsboro knows John Wright as "the guy who invented the iPhone."

John laughed and said, "I get that a lot. I was one of many people who worked on the first one." (Although he was team leader.) Kendra added, "Probably the only one from Illinois."

Journal-News publisher Mike Plunkett said, "Their story is fascinating. I've known John since they came back to town. One of his kids is in my son's class. John is quiet and unassuming. But whether you're holding the iPhone or an Android device to your head and John comes by, it's 'There's the guy who came up with that.'"

Journal-News editor Mary Herschelman said, "It is an amazing story. It is hard to tell some of those stories here. He doesn't want to be a celebrity."

In a 2019 International News Media Association (INMA) report, Dietmar Schantin, founder and CEO of the Institute for Media Strategies, declared, "The introduction of the iPhone in 2007 revolutionized the way people interact with technology. For most news websites today, mobile phones are the number one device people use to visit a site, and the share is still growing."

—

John and Kendra Wright met at the University of Illinois at Urbana-Champaign. Kendra was an economics major. John started as a business major and switched to computer science. His father, Henry Wright, was a University of Illinois electrician, and his mother, Lucille, was a U of I secretary. John worked for the university's computer labs before he graduated. John and Kendra married during their final semester of college. After graduation the Wrights moved to Portland, Oregon, where John worked for Sequent Computer Systems (now part of IBM), which manufactured large mainframe–style computers.

John Wright found parallels between restoring the downtown Red Rooster and developing the iPhone. The project began with demolition at the historic hotel in December 2017. The Red Rooster was slated to open in the summer of 2022. "Thousand balls in the air," he said. "And lots of challenges. In old buildings like this, you go, 'How has this ever held up?' They tried to build it the right way. You have to hold up the old structure and build the new structure underneath it. People ask us all the time, 'Are you sick of it or surprised?' No, I knew it would be difficult. Surprises come with the territory."

The Rooster had spiraled downhill so much that it was the subject of drug calls to the police about squatters cooking meth. The Wrights evicted the transient residents. The Rooster is next door to St. Paul's Lutheran Church, founded in 1832, and it is across the street from the Courthouse Pub. "It was a bad situation for being right next to downtown," John Wright said. "But we wanted to do something that changes the needle a little bit. And the Red Rooster would be a big game changer for downtown."

In a separate conversation, Mike Plunkett nodded down Main Street toward the Red Rooster. "It's unbelievable. The building is over a hundred years old. He's doing something," he said, in reference to Wright. "Without them everyone said, 'Aw, that Red Rooster is going to hell. It's gone.' None of us can print money. This guy comes in and he can do something about it. And he does it. It's rare for a town this size to see all these young entrepreneurs. And it has fueled more interest."

Wright turned around to look at a large wall board that listed to-do jobs for the Red Rooster. Kendra served as project manager for the restoration while Wright was more hands-on with restoration tasks. "She's the boss," he said. "She's the one who writes the checks." A row of tattoos filled Wright's left arm. An iPhone remained silent on the Red Rooster office floor. Wright was asked just how much he thinks the phone has changed the world. It is a heavy question.

"It is a changing force," Wright answered. "Most of it is for good because people have access to more information. Some of it is negative. My team and I would go out after work and eight people would be sitting around a table. They'd all be on their phones. I'm like, 'Put your phones away. This is actually time to talk to each other.' It can be an addiction for some people to the point it is not healthy. We have rules with our kids about not using your phone at the table, the phones and iPads go up before you go to sleep. Read a book or whatever.

"I don't want people to be so far into technology that they miss out on life."

—

The iPhone radically changed the way news is delivered through remote Hillsboro and the world. Anyone with an iPhone is an instant witness to history. News is now immediate. Traditional newspaper deadlines are out the window and filed stories are fluid, as stories are constantly updated. But facts should never succumb to speed.

On May 25, 2020, George Floyd, a Black man, was killed in Minneapolis, Minnesota, during an arrest for allegedly using a counterfeit bill. A video of his death was made on an iPhone by seventeen-year-old Darnella Frazier. She posted the video and her footage rapidly stoked emotions across the world. In 2021, Frazier won a Pulitzer Prize in the Special Citation category.

By early June 2020, Black Lives Matter protests were being held throughout predominately white and rural central and southern Illinois communities, including Hillsboro.

These towns had never seen such activism from young people.

"What happened in Minneapolis is immediately resonating in Hillsboro," said Matt Sands, the thirty-four-year-old co-owner of the Gold Pan record store and recording studio in downtown Hillsboro. "A small town that has a very small minority population." Sands co-organized a June 7, 2020, rally in Hillsboro in support of Black Lives Matter. "Taylorville [pop. 10,000] had a large [BLM] protest the day before we had ours. Vandalia [pop. 6,700] had one the afternoon we had ours. Greenville [pop. 6,400] had one. It spread because of the iPhone. When you don't see it, you don't think you need it."

Mike Jenner, University of Missouri School of Journalism professor and faculty group chair of Journalism Professions, observed, "Our connection to an event through the power of technology makes the connection to the event stronger. A lot of the old-school borders that separated Hillsboro, Mount Vernon, or some other town in southern Illinois from Chicago, Palo Alto, or Minneapolis are being dissolved. That's a game changer for our society and for journalism."

After Matt Sands saw the Floyd video, he felt the need to do something. Empathy runs in the family. His father, Randy Sands, is pastor of the Hillsboro Free Methodist Church. About a week after the Floyd incident, Matt noticed a Facebook post of a single white teenager protesting in Flora, Illinois, about seventy-five miles southeast of Hillsboro. Matt was born in Flora. The girl stood alone on a street corner holding a large hand-scrawled sign that read "Black Lives Matter." The teenager requested anonymity, but she told the *Clay County Advocate-Press* that "it only takes one" for change to begin.

That's what Rosa Parks did on December 1, 1955, by refusing to give up her seat to a white man on a city bus in Montgomery, Alabama.

On the evening of June 3, 2020, Matt posted the Flora girl's picture on Facebook. He wrote a companion note that mentioned how he was born in a Flora hospital but that it was never his hometown. Matt did not know who the girl was but wrote that he was proud of her courage. And then Matt continued, "Her bravery has also convinced me because I've been afraid in the past to speak out and to join any marches or protests. I've been afraid of the reaction I would get. I've been afraid of offending anyone. I've been afraid of potential violence. All of the things Black people fear every day for just being Black. I'd like to change that, so does anyone know of anything planned in Hillsboro?"

A flood of Facebook comments came in that Matt should organize something.

So he did.

At the time, Devin Moroney owned the building that houses the Gold Pan record store. He lived above the record store with his wife, Emilie, before relocating to St. Louis in late 2020. Moroney saw the post and texted Matt that they wanted to help. "I said, 'You're going to help because I don't know what I'm doing,'" Matt explained. "And they have an adopted son that is African American. So it's very personal."

Matt, Devin, and Emilie met up on June 4, 2020. After talking to the city and local clergy, they held the rally three days later at Lincoln Plaza in downtown Hillsboro. "It all happened through social media," Matt said. "It was the convenience of the iPhone that made it simple to plan during all hours of the day. And through some of our Facebook posts, people understood a little better what the term Black Lives Matter means. We were not saying they matter more or that white people's lives don't matter. We were saying they feel they have mattered less. When people are hurting and feel hurt, let's share in their hurt and let them know we're here for them."

Journal-News publisher Mike Plunkett covered the BLM rally. Nearly two hundred young and old people showed up to gather in silence for eight minutes and forty-six seconds—the amount of time that Floyd had a foot pressed against his neck by a Minneapolis police officer until he died. "The rally was dignified, and it was quiet," Plunkett said in a mid-July 2020 interview in the *Journal-News* offices. "It was over in ten minutes. What really moved me was it was the same shadow of twenty-five years ago where the Ku Klux Klan had a demonstration at our courthouse steps."

Hillsboro is the home of a historic neon sign that flickers "The World Needs God." The sign was installed on the Montgomery County Courthouse in October 1940 by a Sunday school teacher who was looking for ways to drive bootleggers out of Hillsboro. In 1992, the ACLU (American Civil Liberties Union) demanded that Montgomery County remove the sign or face a lawsuit. Today, the restored sign is on the north side of the nondenominational World Harvest Church in downtown Hillsboro.

Journal-News owner John Galer covered the May 14, 1994, Klan rally in Hillsboro.

"The 'World Needs God' was a big thing, so the Ku Klux Klan wanted to milk that," Galer said. "The Klan was people not from here choosing our spot and using it. The Black Lives Matter was on Lincoln Plaza, where the [Abraham] Lincoln statue is. The Ku Klux Klan was on the steps of the [nearby] courthouse. They put a fence and metal detector all across the front of Main Street. There were highway barricades all around the courthouse. Maybe fifty Klan members showed up. Back in those days there was a chapter down in Fosterburg [Illinois]. It was way over the top. We had a little girl that set type for us on Saturday mornings. Her mom said she couldn't come to work that morning because it was too dangerous. I had to laugh, we had six hundred state cops, sheriff's deputies from twenty counties. This was the safest place on earth on that Saturday morning in Hillsboro, Illinois.

"We didn't do a huge story on it. We didn't quote them much, just the fact they were supporting the sign. That's all we do. We don't try to make it a bigger story than it should be." Galer wrote, in part, "Speakers spoke in defense of 'Christian' rights and rights of citizens, but their 'White Unity White Power' banner urged another theme."

The only words spoken at the 2020 Black Lives Matter rally in Hillsboro came from Reverend James Hayes, who led a prayer of unity. Hayes was the pastor of St. James Baptist Church in Hillsboro. Matt said, "St. James is the Black church in town with thirty, forty members." Hayes, who is Black, was born in Hillsboro in 1954. He became a deacon at St. James Baptist Church in April 1994—a month before the Klan rally—and was ordained church pastor in June 2006.

"We wanted the church to be involved," Matt said as he leaned against his record store counter with a rare copy of Nina Simone's *Pastel Blues* LP. "We didn't want to make it political. We didn't want to put the burden on the Black people in town to make it about them if they didn't want to be involved. I called Reverend Hayes before we did it and he was totally on board and supportive."

Trevor Vernon, publisher of the rural *Eldon Advertiser* in Missouri, said, "I will tell you as far as social unrest, this one [BLM] is more rural than I've ever seen, if that makes sense. Normally we're pretty isolated. If someone wants to get involved they have to drive two and a half hours to Kansas City, Springfield, or St. Louis. This one has hit way closer to home. More people are talking about it."

Galer said, "In some ways the iPhone has taken us out of the little clique of being here in the borough and this rural area. There's a sense of urgency to all types of news, and the phone definitely makes that urgency even greater. That's the conflict you get with journalism. It takes time to do a good story. You don't want to just blow out something. You want to research it and get factual information out there. The first thing out the door isn't always the truth. That's one of the problems with the phone." *Journal-News* editor Mary Herschelman said people still drop or send physical press releases to the newspaper, but in many other markets, reporters now find story leads on Facebook and Twitter feeds.

The University of Missouri's Jenner observed, "There's still a place for the curated story, the story that is vetted and stories that are common to a shared narrative or shared set of facts. That's an important thing we used to be able to count on. Now it's been exploded by the fact there's billions of voices. The battle for attention is incredible. That old way of looking at things doesn't work so well anymore. There is some benefit to some of the new technology that will tear down some of the geographic barriers you see around these little towns—the East Coast from middle America, the North from the South, the West Coast from middle America."

In February 2020, the *Carroll Times Herald* became the smallest newspaper in North America to participate in the Facebook Journalism Project Accelerator. The program worked with more than one thousand global participants to strengthen business strategies on and off Facebook through a blend of one-on-one coaching and pre-pandemic personal gatherings. "They accepted us," Doug Burns said. "We're in it with the *L.A. Times*, the *Salt Lake Tribune*. They're helping us try to boost digital subscriptions. We have a video virtual call every Friday for an hour. We got a $75,000 grant. We'll be using that money to boost our digital subscriptions."

In 2018, Facebook launched the initiative for mostly metropolitan-based news organizations to gain more digital subscribers. Publishers also participated in weekly training sessions about digital subscription marketing. Burns observed, "The *New York Times* has four million digital subscribers. The problem is when you move things online, you just can't scale it in a rural area. When people bash the media and root for newspapers to fail, websites and other forms of information crop up in cities. This [Carroll, Iowa] could be a news desert. If you don't have a newspaper here, somebody might start an online newspaper. But who is going to sit in the zoning board meetings? Who is going to sit through a four-hour school board meeting when two and a half hours of it is on curriculum development? The internet can handle Trump nonsense, celebrity news, and titillating stuff. What it can't handle is the production of the good, solid, day-to-day, lock-stock journalism.

"Digital is definitely the way forward, but there are a lot of our larger advertisers that are with us specifically because they want to be in print. My separate [company] Mercury Boost Media Marketing Solutions is where if somebody doesn't want to buy print, we sell them Facebook or mobile ads. But in terms of reaching rural and hitting elderly people, there's a lot of areas around here that do not have good internet service. Older readers want their paper. It's just more real. If a member of your family dies, seeing that obit in the newspaper means something." His brother and *Times Herald* co-owner Tom Burns added, "And recall is higher. A lot of people can't remember anything now because it was on their screen. The newspaper registers more in your brain."

At the *Eldon Advertiser*, Vernon said, "We're still heavily print. We dabble in digital. We've had a website for twelve-plus years. Smaller communities like ours aren't heavily into the digital world, but it is coming."

The absence of stockholders has given Vernon ample room to explore and evolve with his company. "I only have to answer to myself and my wife," said Vernon, the third-generation publisher of the company. "It allows me to take bigger chances. Fail and pick up the pieces quickly, then try something else. If we have a year where we only make 1 percent profit or no profit, I don't sweat it."

Vernon cited the Vernon Publishing Interactive (VPI) experiment. He said, "We call it 'The Harry Potter Newspaper.' You go over a picture in the newspaper with an app on your phone and the picture moves, talks, and turns into a video. It's cool. We've had it about a year and a half and made a little bit of money with it from advertisers. But it hasn't caught on like I thought it would, and part of that is because our market is not ready for it.

"But you have to think outside the box. Something will stick somewhere. It may not be your initial thought. We will branch out and do things like golf course signs that show drone video of the hole before you play it. Museums could use VPI to talk about artifacts. With one of the smaller papers, I'm not buying them cameras anymore. I'm buying iPads for them to take out in the field and use. It's an experiment.

"I try to have a really open mind with my staff, and sometimes we go to crazy places."

Hillsboro's Galer said, "Print to me is still everything. We're out of business without print. We have a lovely website. Probably five hundred or six hundred people use it all the time. We don't have a paywall, but it is coming." In fact, it arrived in February 2022. Galer continued, "We can monetize it to cover hosting fees and to cover the cost of uploading the stuff, but I don't know how you get the basic cost of this operation, the news gathering, what we do in the office; we don't generate enough income off the internet. The information we have you can't get anywhere else. We are one hundred percent local. We don't have room for crossword puzzles or comics. Everything we do is locally driven and locally written. We certainly are hyper-local."

Small-paper owners have had to get creative and take chances to leverage technology to help keep their enterprises afloat. In early 2019, Doug Burns launched his digital marketing company called Mercury Boost (Media Marketing Solutions). The money he is bringing in from Mercury Boost is helping keep his rural newspaper afloat.

"But I just turned fifty years old," he said in a February 2020 interview. "I can't run around eighty hours a week trying to run two for-profits and support this one. At some point, if I don't get the support, I'll have to say to the community, 'If the ad money is not here and you'd rather live your life on Facebook and shop on Amazon, the newspaper won't be here, and a lot of small stores won't be here. And eventually a lot of people won't be here because we're one of the organizations that ties the community together and gives the community a sense of identity and self.' We're still the best way to get people to shop local. All of a sudden our really strong schools don't have money for the arts program. Or they can't build a new building. People start looking at us and say, 'Well, why do I want to live in a small town with limited opportunities? I want to go to the sprawling suburbs of Des Moines.' That's where we're headed if people continue to put convenience over community and comfort over truth. It may depopulate rural Iowa to a point where you may come out here in twenty years and see buffalo roaming through town.'"

—

Through technology, the *Arkansas Democrat-Gazette* brought life and community into some of the most remote areas of the state.

The most successful innovation from Walter Hussman Jr., chairman of the *Democrat-Gazette*'s parent company, WEHCO, was a 2019 initiative coded as "To save the paper—give up the paper." The *Democrat-Gazette* is a daily newspaper headquartered in Little Rock that serves all seventy-five counties in the state.

"Arkansas is a community," Hussman said. "Every state is somewhat of a community. But we don't have any giant metropolitan areas like Dallas or Houston. Little Rock is the biggest place and we're only several hundred thousand people. So everybody in Arkansas is interested in what is going on in Arkansas."

Hussman was born in 1947 and is a third-generation newspaperperson. His father, Walter Hussman Sr., was publisher of the *Camden News* out of Texas and his grandfather, Clyde E. Palmer, was publisher of the *Texarkana Gazette*. In 1974, Hussman persuaded his father to buy the *Arkansas Democrat*, the afternoon daily newspaper in Little Rock. The *Democrat* merged with the *Gazette* in 1991, creating the *Arkansas Democrat-Gazette*.

The *Democrat-Gazette* profit began declining every year starting in 2008. And in 2018, for the first time in twenty years, the *Democrat-Gazette* lost money. "Most family-owned newspapers had been sold by the end of 2017, while there were still buyers," Hussman said. "Many newspapers became unprofitable, with hundreds of newspapers closing. Back in 2000, newspapers still got 22 percent of all the ad revenue spent in the United States. But by 2017, it was down to under 5 percent."

Advertisers have moved from mass media advertising to targeted advertising.

"Americans have surrendered their privacy for the convenience of services offered by Google and Facebook," Hussman said. "These two companies can target individuals with far greater accuracy and effectiveness than any newspaper company, including the *New York Times*."

For a statewide publication the knee-jerk reaction would have been to cut back on unprofitable circulation in the remote areas of the state. "But newspapers are not just a business, but a public trust vital to our democracy," Hussman wrote in a May 18, 2019, letter to subscribers. "We tried to determine some way we could continue to be a statewide newspaper delivered to all seventy-five counties."

Hussman knew that his newspaper was still being read on iPads. Why not try to eliminate the print edition altogether in favor of the iPad?

For the iPad experiment, the *Democrat-Gazette* targeted Blytheville, Arkansas, a community of sixteen thousand people about 190 miles east of Little Rock. Blytheville is a blue-collar community that is the birthplace of late soul singer Dee Clark and soul saxophonist Junior Walker. Blytheville was selected for the test run because it was expensive and unprofitable to deliver the printed edition to two hundred subscribers in an area with about five thousand households. "Blytheville is about as far away from Little Rock as you can get," Hussman said. "It used to be the largest cotton-producing county in America. Now it's the second-largest steel-producing county in America. It's gone through a lot of changes. But we picked it because of how remote it was from Little Rock."

At first, *Democrat-Gazette* circulation salespeople went door to door to all two hundred Blytheville subscribers to introduce the iPad. The subscribers weren't impressed. The *Democrat-Gazette* returned a couple months later and told readers they could no longer afford to deliver the paper to Blytheville. "This was a seminal moment in our history because we always delivered to all seventy-five counties in Arkansas," Hussman said. "But the good news is, if you take your cell phone to AT&T and get a new phone, which you're going to have to do eventually, they will sell you a $350 iPad for $99. It is better than a phone. It is better than a laptop, it is more portable. And we're going to sweeten the deal by giving you a check for $50 after you've downloaded the fiftieth edition. Our idea was that after fifty editions, they may get used to it and might like it. So now your iPad only cost you $49. Wow! What a deal!

"Four people took it."

Hussman laughed. Two trips back and forth between Little Rock and Blytheville and two failures.

Undeterred, the *Democrat-Gazette* returned a third time.

"This time we said, 'We will GIVE you an iPad,'" Hussman declared. "This time we're not going to ask you to turn in your phones. We gave them the big $800 iPad. If you hold it sideways, it is the same width as the newspaper. We said they could keep their iPad as long as they kept their subscription. There was no contract to sign."

Many subscribers had never used an iPad.

So, the *Democrat-Gazette* rented conference rooms at the Blytheville Holiday Inn. They dispatched ten customer service representatives to Blytheville and sat down with all two hundred subscribers at the hotel, gave them their iPad, and then did one-on-one tutorials on how to use it. "Our plan was to smother these people with customer service, the likes of which they hadn't seen in years," Hussman said. "That intensive customer support may have made the difference. People are bewildered and impressed with the level of customer service we're offering. These days most people are used to 'Dial one for this. Dial two for that.' We actually had human beings sitting down and talking to them."

And this time the experiment worked.

The newspaper's customer service representatives also loved the engagement with loyal readers. Hussman reflected, "It is so interesting, you send out a job description: 'You're going to get in a car, drive 183 miles, and check into a Holiday Inn and spend a week there. You're going to get up every morning, not go outside, and sit in a ballroom and show people how to use the device and do it over and over.' These people make about $40,000 a year. But they love their jobs. We have almost no turnover. All day long all these people do is help other people. One of the most gratifying things you can do in life is to help people. At first people were depressed when they weren't going to get their newspaper anymore. But then they used the iPad a couple weeks and they liked it better.

"One ninety-three-year-old man had never used a cell phone. We said, 'You don't need to use a cell phone.' He said, 'I've never used a computer. And I don't know what an iPad is. But I've read your paper for over sixty years, so you tell me what I need to do.' So we sat down and showed him everything." The gentleman was excited and returned home only to find his iPad did not work like it had at the Holiday Inn.

He had no internet connection at his house.

"Then he asked, 'What's internet service?'" Hussman said. "There are rural places in Arkansas that don't have any cell phone signals. Not a lot, but there we advise people to drive into town, go to the public library where they have Wi-Fi. And download your newspaper there."

When the deal rolled out, subscribers paid exactly what they were paying for the print edition: $36 a month for the distant regions of Arkansas and $34 a month everywhere else. "We realized we were on the low end," Hussman said. "Other papers were charging $50, $63 a month."

More than 70 percent of the subscribers converted from the print edition to the iPad. They could keep the free iPad if their subscription stayed active. If subscriptions were canceled, the iPad had to be returned. If the iPad wasn't returned, the device would be disabled. "We did a survey later and we found more subscribers were reading the iPad as frequently as the print edition," Hussman said. The survey revealed that subscribers appreciated the following:

- Readers have the ability to enlarge the type, just by touching the screen.
- Articles can be shared with friends or family through email, Facebook, and Twitter.
- News items can be read aloud to you from your iPad. That's good for the sixty-seven-mile one-way drive down I-55 between Blytheville and Memphis, Tennessee.

- The newspaper can be delivered and downloaded to the iPad anywhere (as long as there's an internet connection).
- The iPad edition contains later news. The *Democrat-Gazette*'s statewide print subscribers receive the city edition, almost always delivered before four a.m.
- A subscription to the iPad edition offers free access to the *Democrat-Gazette*'s archives.
- The clarity of type and photos on the iPad are much sharper than in print.

Throughout 2019 the *Democrat-Gazette* converted subscribers from print to an iPad in most of the counties in the state. In the summer of 2019, a 103-year-old man in Magnolia, Arkansas, was reading his iPad daily. The successful *Democrat-Gazette* experiment resulted in the elimination of production, newsprint, and delivery costs.

Profits returned.

And the most important payoff?

"We could do this without reducing any cost in our newsroom," Hussman said. "We didn't want to cut pages. We didn't want to cut the news staff. Today [May 2019] we have 106 staffers in our Little Rock newsroom compared to, for example, the *Denver Post* with 60."

The *Democrat-Gazette* also learned that many statewide subscribers preferred reading a print edition of the Sunday paper because the Sunday paper has more sections and more advertising circulars. Subscribers who converted to the iPad subscription received the digital replica and the Sunday print edition.

By the end of 2019, Hussman had stopped printing and delivering the daily edition of the *Arkansas Democrat-Gazette*. The Sunday print edition's advertising inserts account for about 40 percent of the newspaper's advertising revenue.

By February 2020, WEHCO had purchased close to fifty thousand iPads with an investment of nearly $14 million, according to Hussman. "So far we have implemented it in all but one of our newspapers," he said in early 2022. "We are currently converting the *Chattanooga Times Free Press*, which should be finished in summer of 2022. We finished Little Rock and most of the state in early 2020 and were expecting a great year. And then in March [2020], COVID hit. If that hadn't happened, it would have been a very good return on investment. It has generally taken newspapers that were cash flow negative and turned them into cash flow positive. It has allowed us to maintain the size of our newsrooms and actually increase the number of pages we offer our readers. We offer five full pages of COVID coverage with graphs, tables—not only for Arkansas but nationwide data. We also have AP [Associated Press] features that hardly anybody carries, maybe in the Sunday edition. But we carry them every day."

All iPad subscribers still get a Sunday print edition. "We do print a few thousand single copies daily, distributed at convenience stores and grocery stores in the county," Hussman said. "We don't print any home delivery Monday through Saturday."

Newspaper broker Phil Murray said, "Walter's got a vision. He's probably right. And he's going to see it through. I thought we'd see it by now, a lot of people publishing one or two or three days a week in print. And the rest of the time it's digital. You got to have paywalls. Hussman is an evangelist for that. And he has been for a long time, even when the mantra was that you need more eyeballs. Like it has to be free because you need the eyeballs. Now everyone realizes the eyeballs are worthless because you're always short of the eyeballs Google and Facebook get. Even in your local market. Even in a market like Madison, Indiana, the digital market share for Facebook and Google combined would be 90 percent. The newspaper website might be third at 8 percent. But you just can't give it away for free."

Carroll Times Herald co-owner Tom Burns (Doug Burns's younger brother) said, "Our readers are all over, but obviously they trend older. Digital was a decision that was forced on us. It's not what we wanted to do."

His mother, newspaper publisher Ann Wilson, added, "We had ransomware a few months before that. Recovering from that was very bad. Then some of the people I've known from when I was young . . ." She stopped to collect her thoughts. Then she continued, "They stopped taking the paper."

Doug Burns did not stop to collect his thoughts. He jumped in: "They just don't see the value of that integration of information. They just don't see community the way they used to. They live in narcissism pods. Place doesn't matter like it used to. Place used to be essential to identity. Now people have an online avatar that's almost more important to them than where their actual physical being is. So if you're in this narcissism pod where you have your Facebook friends, your Netflix queue, and your Amazon wish list, what the fuck does it matter whether you live in Carroll, Iowa, or Dubuque, Iowa? What's sad is watching this march of people to these soulless [Des Moines] suburbs like Waukee, Grimes, Ankeny. Every time I drive to Des Moines there's a new subdivision, a new store going up. Those places have no past and no future. They exist entirely in the present. They are purely consumer, commercial-driven monstrosities. Iowa is losing a lot of its character because of it. And that comes down to our business because people don't feel the same way about community things thanks to fucking Mark Zuckerberg."

In 2020, Doug Burns was named Carroll's Citizen of the Year, making him the third generation and fourth recipient in his family to receive the honor. His grandfather (James W. Wilson), his uncle (Jim Wilson), and his mother (Ann Wilson) are all previous recipients of the award. "We really put in the sweat and the equity," Burns said. "And we were Newspaper of the Year in Iowa not that long ago [2013], judged by over two hundred newspapers in Iowa by our peers. I was one of the last guys to let a full-time photographer go. . . . We have a news staff that is 75 percent larger than a city newspaper our size. We pay our reporters more than most newspapers of communities our size.

"We are a community newspaper. We cover the community whole cloth. We see everything and it is presented as integrated. What happens at Carroll High School, what happens at the police station."

Burns said he likes the physical newspaper for what he calls "surprise knowledge." He enjoys stumbling across a review of a new restaurant or a feature story on a community figure from the shadows. "When you're reading online, you just go where your own biases and interests take you," he said. "I'm fifty and I've been doing this for twenty-eight years. I worked on Capitol Hill for four years, but other than that I've been a working journalist. When I interviewed World War II veterans in the 1990s, the most common comment I would get in Carroll would be, 'I disagree with just about every one of your opinions; you're too progressive. But I'm glad you write them because they make me think.' And 'One out of ten times you changed my mind.' I would hear that *weekly* in the 1990s.

"I never hear it now."

—

Small papers have always faced changing technology and adapted. Part of the unique history of Indiana's *Madison Courier* includes the fact that in the 1980s, the *Courier* was among the first small-town newspapers in the nation to receive international news via satellite transmission. "I don't know much, but I know we had a large AP [Associated Press] satellite dish in our parking lot," said former sixth-generation *Courier* publisher Curt Jacobs, who was born in 1962. "That was pretty early for a small-town newspaper. It's funny. I have a sheet of paper from the Drake Hotel in Chicago and on the back my grandfather typed some milestones. One was, 'AP satellite installed February 1982.' It was in our parking lot until I had it taken down three or four years ago. It was big. If you stood beside it, it was taller than you."

The *Courier* is a charter member of the Associated Press. Before the satellite dish, national news was transmitted by wire service. "As a kid I remember the AP wire machine in the closet," Jacobs said. "I'm assuming the satellite dish replaced that. It would be like my grandfather to push that. He wasn't the kind of guy who said, 'Oh, we're just some small-town newspaper.' He'd be the guy that would be calling AP and say, 'Hey, I hear you're transmitting this stuff by satellite and what do we have to do to get a dish?' If they said we were some nine-thousand-circulation daily in some little town, he wouldn't let that stop him. I heard the speech a couple times: 'You hear about the *New York Times* and the *Wall Street Journal*, well, let me tell you, the most important paper to the people in Madison is the *Madison Courier*.' That's what he would have told these AP guys. You never know what you get when you say something like that. Some people might say you're crazy, other people will say, 'Let's try it.'"

Before selling the *Courier* in February 2020, Jacobs said small-town papers needed to move forward into digital delivery. "We haven't done that as quickly as we should," he confessed. "You don't need six days print anymore when you can deliver news online. We can't sit on the sidelines because somebody else will tell you about it, even in this small market. They'll tell you about it on Facebook, but they might not tell about it accurately. If you count on 'newspaper only' readers, you will be out of business before too long. It is just a slow march into the deep end of the pool."

Walter Hussman was named Publisher of the Year in 2008 by *Editor & Publisher* magazine. He was a member of the board of directors of the Associated Press from 2000 to 2009 and of C-SPAN from 1995 to 2003. Hussman serves as chief executive officer of WEHCO, which operates thirteen daily newspapers, eleven weekly newspapers, and thirteen cable television companies in Texas, Arkansas, Oklahoma, and Mississippi. Multimedia lessons did not come into play for the newspaper's iPad experiment. "We got out of radio and television around 2000," Hussman said. "We put a TV station [KCMC-TV, Shreveport, Louisiana] on the air in 1952." KCMC became KTAL-TV in 1960 when it began broadcasting from the second-tallest tower in the South. KTAL was also the first station in the Texarkana-Shreveport market to add color broadcasts. The Hussman family sold the station in 2000.

"Lessons learned from TV?" Hussman asked. "I've been doing this for almost fifty years now. One thing I've learned is to not give up. I just hate seeing all the family-owned newspapers in America give up. I'm not saying this in a critical way. I can't blame them. Maybe they've made a better financial decision than I've made. The value of newspapers have gone way down. I'm really concerned we're going to lose family journalism in America. We have to find some solution. If we don't, we're going to go down trying."

In his 1,500-word May 2019 iPad pitch letter to subscribers, Hussman wrote in part, "Many newspapers in America still confront enormous challenges. There has been a hostile takeover attempt for Gannett, the largest newspaper company in the country. Some investors are buying newspapers for short-term profits before they liquidate and close them. Other newspapers in some large markets, like the *Philadelphia Inquirer* and the *Salt Lake Tribune*, have been donated to 501(c)(3) charities, hoping to remain alive with philanthropy. We believe the most sustainable business model ever created was to have a company that is profitable. As long as business is profitable, someone will continue to operate and sustain it."

No newspaper had ever tried anything like the iPad experiment. Hussman said the people at Apple were mystified about his newspaper iPad plan. "But who is buying more iPads than us?" Hussman asked. "We've already placed eighteen thousand of them in the hands of people in eighteen months. I know when they sell them to doctor's offices, they sell forty to a clinic. People say, 'Apple must love you.' But they've been coy about it." Hussman also traveled to more than twenty-five Rotary clubs across Arkansas to explain the newspaper iPad. "Every town in Arkansas that had a population over 7,500 and a Rotary club," he said. "I went so they could ask me questions."

—

Another newspaper attempting to harness technology to remain profitable is the *Post and Courier* of Charleston, South Carolina. In 2018 the *Post and Courier* participated in the Poynter Institute's local news innovation program called Table Stakes. "Table stakes" is a poker term where players may bet no more money than they had on the table at the beginning of their hand. For newspapers, it was meant to illustrate the stakes needed to win.

Post and Courier publisher P. J. Browning explained, "Table stakes from the journalism perspective is not so different from poker. We have to change the way we do business as news organizations, and the stakes are high. If we don't play the right hand, make the right moves, newspapers and journalism don't have a future."

The *Post and Courier* was among twenty-one news organizations in the nine-month program, which focused on shaping newsrooms into audience-focused, digital-first enterprises. Newspapers, public radio stations, and digital news organizations applied for selection to Table Stakes. Program fees ranged from $1,500 (Sunday circulation of less than fifty thousand) to $4,500 (Sunday circulation exceeding one hundred thousand).

"It was really a cultural change meant to have a team focus on growing digitally and growing it culturally," Browning said. "It became more important than print. It was being able to tell stories in print and online and being able to train our journalists on how to tell stories different. Digital readers read stories differently than print readers. It's been a cool experience. At the end of the day, we say all our reporters want their stories read. That's why they write them. So we've learned how to write different for print and online. They've learned how to optimize our headlines. It was a culture change. I've been in the business thirty-six years today. It was one of the most frustrating conferences I attended. I went through all of the emotions, 'I don't know why we're going through this.' But to do it right we had to come back and change a lot of the ways in which we were doing business and the way we approached writing stories.

"Journalism is important, but we must meet readers where they want to read us, and they must be willing to pay for journalism online or our model is dead. So what type of stories resonate with readers are critically important."

Table Stakes actually used loose family dynamics.

Imagine the newspaper as the dining room table. Family members are gathered around, ready to share current news and topics of interest. Browning established mini-publisher groups around different topic areas. She said, "We looked at data on what readers were reading and we picked the top five topics to create these groups. For example, food is a popular topic. Charleston is a great food town. We created a cross-divisional team that explored everything about food and how to maximize readers, engagement, and revenue. This boiled down to content—events that were food-related, newsletters, and books. We did this for five topic areas, and we've seen good growth around food, real estate, and business. Today everybody understands what we mean by 'digital,' 'table stakes,' and 'mini-publisher groups.' All in all, it has been very successful for us. I can see where some newspapers may not take it as serious as they need to. I told the team, 'It's not a project, it's our future.'"

The *Post and Courier* had been hemorrhaging readers. In the fall of 2009, weekly paid print circulation was 86,084 daily and 94,940 on Sundays. The newspaper had already laid off twenty-five employees in February 2009. By the fourth quarter of 2015, paid circulation was 57,000 for daily and 68,400 for Sundays.

Evolve or repeat.

In the summer of 2020, the *Post and Courier* had over 10,800 digital subscribers. The newspaper's print circulation was 38,236. Browning said her newspaper comes to the digital market with a higher price. "For example, Gannett comes to market with a 99-cent start-out and then it goes to $9.99, $12 a month," Browning said. "Our goal has been more of a full-price approach. People are more likely to stay with us if they pay annual full price [$15.99 a month in July 2020]. We think that is a direct link to the journalism that we provide."

Through Table Stakes, the newspaper reduced story count by 44 percent, but monthly digital conversions were up 25 percent. The *Post and Courier* deemed conversions as more important than page views. Browning explained, "We found that we were printing stories in the paper that people didn't really care about, so we needed to redirect resources to what resonated with readers."

The *Post and Courier* has networked with the *Arkansas Democrat-Gazette*. "We are experimenting a little with what Walter Hussman has done," Browning said. "You look at our statewide presence, then you bring out regional, and then to your core market. Our focus statewide is definitely digital-only subscription: iPads and tablets."

—

By January 2020, John and Kendra Wright had taken on a second large-scale project in remote Hillsboro, Illinois. They restored a former public beach house on Lake Hillsboro into The Lakehouse, a year-round lakeside getaway with two separate units for nightly and weekly rentals. The beach house closed to the public in 2016. Despite COVID-19, in the first half of 2020 they had guests from Missouri, Minnesota, and Oklahoma. The rooms include access to kayaks and life vests and feature landscape art from local artist Taylor Meyers.

Maybe not so ironically, Wi-Fi connections are spotty by the remote lake.

John and Kendra spent four years in Portland, Oregon, before moving to North Carolina, where John was senior software engineer for a mini-computer firm. They spent a year in North Carolina. John looked at Kendra and explained, "She said, 'Next time you get a job, can you not move me across the country again?' I said, 'Sure.' And then I got the job in California. We moved there in 1999." He worked at a couple of Silicon Valley firms before being hired at Apple in August 2004. He spent twelve years there before retiring.

"After a couple years at Apple, they started the iPhone project," he said. "They asked me if we could work the operating system macro lab. I said yes, and they said, 'Here's your team, go do it.' We prototyped it. We went full throttle. I was in charge of the OS [operating system]. When you look at your phone, the operating system is everything you don't see. Software is all in layers. So it's not the app, but it is the power that runs the app, everything behind the scene. I was in charge of that for about eight years.

"The first one was pretty crazy. There was some competition between groups: the hardware, the operating system. Steve [Jobs] said, 'Go ahead and take anyone you want from the company. Don't tell them why and don't tell their managers why.' That was a little crazy and probably didn't make me a favorite amongst people until we shipped the software out. But that first round was a small team. I think I had about thirty people. We worked day and night. Steve said, 'Here is when we're going to ship it,' and it wasn't anywhere near ready. I think there was eight months in a row that we worked every day including Christmas Day—and I mean fourteen-hour days and ten or twelve hours on weekend days. It definitely was a death march."

John emphatically referred to Kendra as a single mother. She would bring blankets and pillows to work because John worked so late. "But I wouldn't trade it for the world," he said. "It was a once-in-a-lifetime opportunity."

What drove him?

"We knew it was going to change a lot of things," he said. "When they came to me with the project and the hardware specs, I looked at them overnight, came back the next day, and said, 'This is like a computer in a pocket.' That's how we started having discussions. Then I went off and did a couple special projects. One was the watch. The last project I had, the team was more than four hundred people. We were on a special project I can't talk about, but it was ramping up. We were hiring like crazy. It is still going on, but it was time for me to go in another direction."

Kendra pinpointed a different moment when she felt it was time to move on: "When you stopped shaving."

—

In the 2018 book *Them: Why We Hate Each Other—and How to Heal*, Senator Ben Sasse writes about "the evaporation of social capital" and the rewards of work and community. He discovered that in the last quarter of the twentieth century, the average number of times an American entertained at home declined by 50 percent. With the median American checking their smartphone every 4.3 minutes and nearly 40 percent of those aged 18 to 29 online constantly (according to a Pew survey), he concluded Americans are "parched for genuine community. . . . We do not know how to develop new habits of mind and heart."

A small town's down-easy vibe celebrates the very connection of mind and heart.

"Our kids were ecstatic about moving back here," Kendra said. "That's a hard move to make. But it's a different level of freedom for a kid. They can walk around uptown without any problems. Ride their bike down the street. All that kind of stuff in the city made you nervous." The Wrights lived in the Bernal Heights neighborhood of San Francisco, which offers a breathtaking view of the city skyline.

Kendra said, "The best part about being here is that our kids absolutely love being in the newspaper. Literally, at least once a month one of them is in the newspaper. It's, 'You're in the newspaper again!' Or, 'Look, there's your sister!' Between swimming, basketball, choir, and bands. They're on the junior board. All the stuff they do."

All that stuff shapes community.

Kendra continued, "Sometimes the DAR will do something and I'm in the paper. John is the one who is in the paper the least of all of us."

John was in the *Journal-News* for a fall 2018 "CEO—Creating Entrepreneurial Opportunities" class he taught to local high school seniors at the Free Methodist Church in Hillsboro. CEO chair Heather Hampton-Knodle introduced Wright with the line from the hit Broadway musical *Newsies*: "Give me a big life in a small town!"

John volunteered for CEO through the Imagine Hillsboro group. The community group formed in 2015 from a program facilitated by the Illinois Institute for Rural Affairs at Western Illinois University. John explained, "People got together and said, 'Imagine what we could do with Hillsboro.' They've organized festivals and summer concert series. They asked me about how to get more technology in the schools. I get a range of kids. A third are nerds; okay, they're going to get into computers somewhere. Then there's a third of the kids that don't really know what they're going to do, but when we exposed it to them, they got it. Then there's a third of the kids where their parents forced them to come, and they have no interest whatsoever. Which is fine. It's good for them to be exposed. It's important for them to take a look at these options. There's not as much computer influence here as there is in Silicon Valley. In Silicon Valley, computers would be a natural thing for every kid to look at."

Even the remote farm families around Hillsboro are plugging in. John observed, "The influence in the whole agricultural-farming community is that people are having less kids. And more and more farming is automated. You don't need ten kids to run the farm. You need big machines that have computers in them. And you need someone to program those computers. You can be an influence in the community by teaching those things. It's the same thing with the coal miners. Those jobs are dwindling, but you still need the machinery, and the machinery is automated. We talk a lot about that. What are the jobs you like in this community?"

—

The iPhone transported newspapers to places most publishers never imagined. I had a front-row seat on May 31, 2013, when the editors at the *Chicago Sun-Times* fired all twenty-eight of its photographers. Reporters and writers like myself were instructed to shoot pictures on our cell phones—with no bump in salary.

Many of the photographers were my friends. John White is a Pulitzer Prize winner who is extremely respected in the Black American community. He had been a *Sun-Times* photographer since 1978. John often accompanied me to stories where I covered the funerals of blues and gospel singers. He was greeted with smiles and hugs. The newspaper fired more than a photographer. The *Sun-Times* fired a connection to community.

The mass firing became national news. It is now included in journalist Luke Dormehl's blog *Today in Apple History*. Dormehl pointed out that in late 2012, a photo of Hurricane Sandy used on the cover of *Time* magazine was taken on an iPhone. On May 31, 2021, he wrote, "Combine the iPhone's popularity with the immediacy of online news and the decline of traditional print media, and you've got a recipe for a revolution."

By the time the layoffs occurred, the *Sun-Times* had moved from its mid-century location along the Chicago River to a sterile office building west of the Merchandise Mart. One of my memories of this period is standing on an escalator and passing by the managing editor who approved the photographer layoffs. His eyes were glued to his iPhone.

There was an unseen world around him.

Chapter 5

Migratory Paths and Connections

Advances in our nation's transportation technology, from waterways to railroads to interstates, have always helped carry the news, especially to and from family newspapers in rural America. When commuter lines were owned and operated by private railroads, many trains were used to deliver daily newspapers. In the early twentieth century, newspapers traveled by trucks and trains. But the road of communication was affected as the routes slowed down or dried up, affecting the livelihood of both newspapers and towns.

Rural Eldon, Missouri, is thirty miles southwest of the state capitol in Jefferson City. Eldon was once called "The Gateway to Lake of the Ozarks," but that was a generation ago. The first time I called the *Eldon Advertiser* office in 2020 to find publisher Trevor Vernon, a secretary told me he was out delivering the latest edition of the newspaper to his ninety-three-year-old grandfather, Wallace Vernon.

Wallace became a partner in the *Advertiser* in 1948, and in 1953 he took over the business with his wife, Marjorie. They formed Vernon Publishing, Inc.

The writing was on the wall. Literally.

The *Eldon Advertiser* was first published on June 11, 1894. At one time in its early years, the paper was cut into sheets and printed on wallpaper due to a shortage of newsprint. Later, one issue had to be cranked out by hand because of the failure of the printing press's gasoline engine.

Yet, it has been printed every week, without missing an issue, since 1894.

Eldon (pop. 4,700) is an old railroad town. The Missouri Pacific Railroad and the better-known Rock Island Line once ran through Eldon. The Rock Island connected Kansas City to St. Louis. Wallace Vernon's father was an engineer on the Rock Island Line, which eventually left in the 1980s because it was no longer profitable.

There are no trains in Eldon today.

"My first reporter job at the paper was to meet the trains and the buses and get items to print in the paper," Wallace Vernon said. "I'd find out who was traveling. Three passenger trains came through Eldon every day. I found out where people were going. That was news back then."

Wallace was proud to talk about his town. He said, "I want to tell you why Eldon is where it is. The trains would change crews in Eldon, but the trains would never stay where they were. They would roll down to the lowest place in town. That's where Eldon was born. The place where the trains stopped."

The hit 1960s television comedy *Petticoat Junction* was modeled after the since-razed Burris Hotel that sat next to the railroad tracks in Eldon. The show's creator, Paul Henning, was from Missouri, and he also used the Ozarks as a template for his *Beverly Hillbillies* show. Henning was married to the granddaughter of the owner of the Burris Hotel and became a regular visitor to Eldon.

"Eldon is where it is now because of the Bagnell Branch of the Missouri Pacific Railroad from Jefferson City to the Osage River and the tie yards that were there," Trevor said. "The T. J. Moss Tie Company was one of, if not the biggest, suppliers of railroad ties in Missouri and one of the largest in the nation."

The Lake of the Ozarks is ten miles southwest of Eldon. Like Eldon itself, the tourist destination is trying to reinvent itself. The Tan-Tar-A resort opened in 1960 on Osage Beach as a getaway for residents of St. Louis and Springfield, Missouri. In 2017, the five-hundred-room resort became a Margaritaville Lake Resort, named after the popular Jimmy Buffett song. "When I was a kid, there was a bowling alley there," said Trevor, who turned forty years old in June 2020. "It was a great place for a family to have birthday parties, that kind of place.

"Eldon is trying to figure out where we fit in. We started off as a great railroad town. The railroad went away, and we became 'The Gateway to Lake of the Ozarks.' That was the town motto. We had a good run with that; it lasted thirty or forty years where we were the retail base for the Lake of the Ozarks. That dried up with big-box stores going down to the lake. For a long time we were the only newspaper in the lake area. Three or four years ago there were four newspapers, multiple radio stations, and a television station around the lake. That area has just exploded. It's no longer a mom-and-pop deal. So we're struggling to figure out our identity."

Also located in the middle of America, near the middle of Iowa, is a town named Carroll. It is not an easy town to get to. The historic two-lane Lincoln Highway (Route 30) gently winds through town. Visitors from the east cross over Storm Creek. The smallest of creeks can get stormy in central Iowa.

Carroll (pop. 10,100) was settled in 1867 along the Middle Raccoon River. It began as a Chicago & North Western Railway town. One year after the railroad platted the town, the first local newspaper was published in Carroll. The *Western Herald* was started by O. H. Manning, who later become lieutenant governor of Iowa.

The Lincoln Highway was dedicated in 1913 and goes 331 miles through the middle of Iowa. The Lincoln Highway was America's first coast-to-coast road for automobiles. "If you do a triangle with Sioux City [Iowa] on one end . . . Omaha [Nebraska], and Des Moines, we're in the middle of that," said *Carroll Times Herald* co-owner Doug Burns. "We're a retail trade center for an area about fifty miles. We're just far enough away from Omaha, Des Moines, and Sioux City that we're able to function with a great degree of autonomy. The biggest economic development issue here is getting Highway 30 to four lanes. It is spotty across the state."

Burns said that at one time, fifty to ninety Union Pacific trains rolled through Carroll on a daily basis.

Were they a connection to another world of journalism and ideas?

"In the 1920s and '30s there were two train depots here," Burns said. "At one time, you could take the train from Carroll to Lidderdale, which is eight miles away. It's remarkable to think how that kind of world used to exist. I've heard that when the train stopped in Carroll, they would throw off the *Cedar Rapids Gazette*, the *Chicago Tribune*, and the *New York Daily News*. By the 1940s and '50s we had wire services, so that would have had to happen in the first quarter of the twentieth century, the last quarter of the nineteenth century. There may have been some papers getting dropped off in the 1920s, '30s."

Small towns pay attention to their larger past. The *Cheyenne Post* in Wyoming didn't publish its first edition until July 2019. But the front-page masthead of the new weekly featured a roaring steam engine with the words "The Journal of the Magic City of the Plains." This was the name given to Cheyenne as the city magically sprung up and grew when the Union Pacific Railroad came to town. The idea was to make the newspaper look like it had been around since the 1850s.

It's easy to get nostalgic about newspapers. I still cannot break the habit of looking for a news box when I arrive at O'Hare or Midway on a late flight and all airport newsstands have closed. During my years of deadline writing at the *Chicago Sun-Times*, it was a thrill to land in Chicago, buy the *Sun-Times*, and see the words I had written several hours earlier.

News boxes are now a distant memory in most airports and along city streets. So are the trucks and truck drivers who delivered the newspapers to the airports and street boxes. People are reading news or listening to podcasts on their devices. There's still something vintage-warm about seeing holdouts reading a newspaper on the subway or on a train. They look like time travelers.

—

In 1904, a three-story interlocking tower was built where the Illinois Central and New York Central trains crisscrossed in Pana, Illinois, about forty-five miles southeast of Springfield.

Former *Pana News-Palladium* owner and reporter Tom Phillips Jr. bought the thirty-five-foot-tall Pana Tower from the Illinois Central for $1,000 in order to preserve it. In early 2019, Tom Latonis bought it from Phillips, his father-in-law. Latonis was a Springfield, Illinois, native who had just been let go as managing editor of the *News-Palladium*. He landed on his feet as a staff reporter for the neighboring *Breeze-Courier* in Taylorville.

The railroads began pulling up tracks in southern Illinois in the 1960s and '70s. By May 2020, downtown Pana was a dusty checkerboard of dark storefronts. The Union Pacific freight still rolls through town, as the UP bought the old CEI (Chicago and Eastern Illinois) route. The once stately

Fleck Hotel stood across the street from the tower. It was boarded up and forgotten. Even the Walmart next to the train tracks up and left in October 2019. The building was empty.

Sometimes you rebuild, even if it is in your mind.

"Look out the window down in the gulley," Latonis said during a conversation in the tower. "You can see the foundation of the old railroad depot [razed in 1967]. They used to unload the newsprint right here from Chicago and maybe St. Louis. And the Illinois Central ran on this side going north and south. This was a big railroading community."

Latonis looked at another empty building across a field. He said, "Freight would be unloaded there and delivered around town. Walmart also owned that building. It's pretty much gone to shit. Walmart won't sell it to anybody. Or give it to the city. A lot went on here. There were greenhouses all over."

In 1928, the Amling brothers built thirty-two greenhouses west of Pana. The greenhouses totaled 780,000 square feet of glass. They became a source of community pride. Refrigerated boxcars would pull alongside the train station and they'd be filled up with roses. "Especially on Mother's Day and around New Year's," Latonis said. "Most of the roses you saw in the Rose Parade [in Pasadena, California] were grown in Pana. Outside of town there was one greenhouse with forty acres under glass."

A local holiday tradition was the huge miniature train display that the Phillips family installed in 1989 in front of the downtown Pana newspaper office. The display was dismantled in 2017 and stored in the tower.

In the fall of 2019, Latonis decided to bring the model railroad back to life. He had left the Pana newspaper in January 2018. Latonis pointed out the miniature *News-Palladium* office on his layout. People were on the streets again. He said, "You have the guy taking the picture with the family in front of the newspaper office. Art's Barber Shop is the place where Tom [Phillips Jr.] got a shoeshine job. That was his first job. I also found a newsstand, which has a guy getting his shoes shined by a youngster. There used to be a place called George's Candy Shop where you would get your newspapers and magazines. So we have George's here. We're looking for a coal mine. The Penwell Mine [1889–1941] was right near here." In March 1949, "The Old Mine" in Pana was sealed by the Peabody Coal Mine. It was believed to be the oldest producing mine in America. Peabody ceased operations in Pana in 1957.

By February 2022, Latonis had extended his dream by acquiring a 1952 caboose for his tribute to the region's train history. He had to have the fifty-nine-thousand-pound caboose shipped from a small town north of Indianapolis to Pana. "I've inquired with Union Pacific," Latonis said. "Their tracks run through Pana. I'll eventually open it up to the public so they can see history. As my ten-year-old great-nephew asked me, 'What's a caboose, Uncle Tom?' I'm sure there are many others just like him."

Have you heard the news? The Union Pacific train blew its whistle as it rumbled by the tower on a gloomy afternoon in October 2019. Latonis raised his voice and looked at the model train version of the Baltimore & Ohio "Puddle Jumper." It made daily (130-mile, one-way) runs between Springfield and Olney, Illinois. Latonis said, "You can see it's partly passenger and partly freight. They stopped in Pana; if you wanted to go to Taylorville, you'd get on and ride to Taylorville or Springfield. If a farmer had a couple of cans of milk he wanted to take to the dairy, he loaded them on here. It stopped at almost every town." News, gossip, and community moved on those trains.

—

Budding journalists also moved on trains. Hillsboro's John Galer remembers the story of his grandfather Del Galer selling his car in 1945 and taking southbound trains from Wisconsin to look for work at the *Hillsboro Journal*. "He took the New York Central out of Chicago," Galer said. "There was a train station in Hillsboro. It was active until the mid-1950s. I remember as a kid how the Wabash and the Illinois Central ran out of Litchfield."

Between 1938 and 1971, the Blue Bird train (Norfolk and Western Railway) ran from St. Louis to Chicago with stops in Litchfield, Taylorville, and Decatur. Galer recalled, "We'd go to Chicago. I had grandparents in Lake Forest. It was a big connection. Back in the pioneer days the rivers and the streams were everything. That's how big commerce ran. Then in the 1800s, railroads tied together the whole continent. But after World War II the interstate becomes the driver of our economy. Litchfield [along Route 66] does great with that. If there's extra jobs, Litchfield is going to be the place. They have the factory jobs we had, and we're probably not going to have those again. We're looking at smaller things."

The proximity of Indiana's historic *Madison Courier* to the Ohio River suggests that news once moved along the waterways. Longtime *Courier* publisher Curt Jacobs said, "A lot of riverboats would stop here. And some had entertainment on them. They had newspapers. In my time here, the paper has been distributed by carriers on foot or rural carriers. Before cars, horse and buggy. When I was a kid, newsprint came in on railcars. In the '60s and early '70s, I remember there would be cars of newsprint at the west end of downtown. Employees of the paper had to load them in a truck and bring them over to the warehouse because the rail line didn't come to where the paper was. In my lifetime it's always come in by semi-truck, and that's been an adventure in itself, unloading semi-trucks in a small historic downtown area."

Eureka Springs Independent editor Mary Pat Boian has witnessed the evolution of media transportation and distribution routes firsthand. Her recollections are vivid. "My dad got up at four every morning to pick up the *Rocky Mountain News* in downtown Denver and take a carload of newspapers to a neighborhood garage where the paperboys would fold and deliver. At nine a.m. he was in a suit and tie selling ads for the *Denver Post* all day. I remember him hoping neither paper would find out he worked for the other because of loyalty, but he did have six people to feed.

"I helped my brother Woody with his *Denver Post* paper route after school. It was the daily afternoon paper. We had to fold the *Post* [a broadsheet] into thirds and lock in the ends. There were no rubber bands. Then we would stuff newspaper bags on his handlebars. My helping meant carrying four or five papers in my bike basket and following him in case he threw one on a roof."

Hillsboro *Journal-News* owner John Galer said, "The newspaper is like the family farm. You're helping the family out in every way. That's how I got here. The news moved. I started as carry boy when I was eleven. I delivered to every house in this town. The tips were great at Christmastime, and in Hillsboro you wanted the Main Street route because the businesses were real generous. In the summer, old ladies would serve you lemonade. You got to know everybody on the route, and that's what small towns are about.

"We walked. We couldn't ride a bike because we didn't want the papers on the front yard. They had to be on the porch or at the house. We didn't rubber-band them. We didn't fold them. Some people had bricks and we'd put them under the bricks so they wouldn't blow away. I remember dogs chasing me. I got bit one time. It was a substitute route. I came home and was upset." Galer's father was editor, publisher, and co-owner of that newspaper he was delivering. "All my dad wanted to know was if I got the paper to the lady's house," Galer laughed.

That's old-fashioned Americana.

Chapter 6

Old-School Family Business

Historian Nancy F. Cott said, "Family has long been the cornerstone of American values; one of the few things most people can agree on." When it comes to multigenerational family-owned newspapers, sometimes family is a source of pride and cohesion. Other times family itself gets in the way as members navigate personal, political, and ethical issues, drama and scandal, perceived slights, and heightened emotions within their family, business, and community.

During a summer 2006 road trip through South Dakota, I stopped at Wall Drug, the historic roadside attraction and restaurant that opened in 1931. I enjoyed a cup of coffee with owner Teddy Hustead, the grandson of founders Ted and Dorothy Hustead.

We began discussing the challenges of third-generation entrepreneurs. Ted told me about a family business class he took at Harvard. His professor said that every culture in the world has an issue with third-generation businesses. "In America, they call it 'Short sleeves to long sleeves to short sleeves,'" Ted said. "A Brazilian classmate who was sitting next to me said in Portuguese, 'It's the wasted generation.' It's a countercultural thing. One professor said the third generation holds on to the steering wheel too tight and loses the entrepreneurial spirit. But it's important to understand what kind of business you are in."

Third-generation Missouri publisher Trevor Vernon knows his generation is the pivot point. Trevor's stocky build and red beard give him the look of a self-assured riverboat captain. "The first generation does the groundwork," he said. "The second one does all the work and builds it up. The third one gives up on it and does something else. For me, it's changed so much. It's not really the same business as to when my grandfather was there. We experiment with different things all the time."

The *Carroll Times Herald*'s Doug Burns leaned back in an old chair in the office of his mother, publisher Ann E. Wilson. Ann has had the same office in the same building at 508 North Court Street since 1984. The newspaper building was a grocery store in its previous life. It was just before Valentine's Day 2020 when I spoke with the family, and Doug knew there was minimal love for old-fashioned newspapers. His hair was frazzled and he spoke in a colorful staccato cadence. Doug is a quintessential newspaperperson. Fifty years old and never married, with no children—the newspaper is his baby.

Doug was later joined by his brother, Tom, who is in charge of advertising and circulation. Tom is two years younger than Doug and holds a master's degree in sports management from Western Illinois University. He is married with two children and is continuing his quest to see every Major League Baseball stadium with his kids.

Their sister, Jane Burns Lawson, is a teacher in Des Moines, ninety-five miles southeast of Carroll. She writes a weekly food column for the *Times Herald* and is on call for feature writing. She is also married with two kids. Doug said, "We are majority female owned." Rebecca McKinsey was editor at the time, Marcia Jensen is advertising manager, Sasha Backhaus is production manager, and Brianne Goins is circulation manager. "I'm adopted, my brother is adopted, my sister is adopted from Vietnam. Even though she's Vietnamese, you read her food columns and you think she comes from Iowa farm life. She cooks these Crockpot-type things. Her tastes are very rural Midwest in terms of food."

The Wilsons are a fourth-generation newspaper family.

Ann Wilson came aboard in 1984, becoming an equal partner with her brother, James B. Wilson, who was publisher. Ann was born in Carroll in 1941. Her mother moved to Carroll to become principal of a grade school, a job she kept until she got married. "At that time married women could not be employed by the schools in Iowa," Ann said. "Plus other strange requirements. She was one of six daughters and one son, who was a farmer. One of the girls died in childhood. The rest were all teachers. Female teachers were made to resign when they were married. They had to be seen in church three Sundays out of four.

"Very different from now."

On the wall over Ann's right shoulder there was a large framed portrait of Mark Twain with the caption "Out of public schools grows the greatness of a nation." On Ann's front desk there were pieces of Linotype from the *Times Herald* press that was dismantled and carted off into darkness in 2018. That was a sad event for the family.

The entire family was talkative and quick with answers.

Until they were asked, "Why are you all still here?"

Silence filled the room.

Finally Doug Burns answered, "We're kind of like the last Comanches that haven't been dragged onto the reservation. The book I can relate to the most that I've read in the past three years is *Empire of the Summer Moon* [a Pulitzer Prize finalist by S. C. Gwynne]. It's about the last tribe of Comanches and I feel like that. Books that help me figure out how to run a newspaper are books like [that] or books about Confederate generals." He laughed and continued, "Not that I sympathize with Confederate generals. Why are we here? Look, in 2013 we were Iowa [Newspaper Association's] Newspaper of the Year. You look around this community and you see my mom's influence, you see my grandfather's influence. Veteran's Memorial Park—I served on the committee that helped get that done. The middle school and the high school, Mom was a key player in making sure that those referendums got through."

The Wilson family fiercely advocated for the 2020 remodeling of the Carroll Public Library. Doug was vice president of the library foundation that raised more than $2.5 million in private funds. He said, "We're really involved in the community, and it is very rewarding to see your work make a difference. For better or for worse we always felt like this newspaper was almost a public utility.

"The work was so enjoyable. Obviously because of the catastrophic effects of social media and the predatory nature of Facebook, we're watching what we love be greatly diminished. We think it is still one hell of a product. And we think rural America is worth fighting for. Nobody is essential. But if we're not here and the newspaper goes to a chain, the community and a big part of rural Iowa will realize they lost their voice."

In August 2021, there were 253 newspapers in Iowa, and well over half were family owned. Locals say the state has the most family-owned newspapers of any state in America. Susan Patterson Plank, executive director of the Iowa Newspaper Association, could not confirm that, but she said, "We believe we have more newspapers per capita [not including online newspapers] than any state in the country."

Doug pointed out, "The largest part in the state are the really small weeklies. Those are mostly family-owned organizations. Those papers are too small for the chains. A great example of that would be the *Coon Rapids Enterprise*, [in] a town of about two thousand, southeast of us. It's run by a guy named Charlie Nixon. His dad ran it before him. If he died or decided he was done, I would have no interest in that paper because the entire brand is him. Without him, the paper has little or no value. There's a lot of papers in the state in that situation."

Doug leaned forward and had to repeat the question again in tones of disbelief.

"Why are we still here? It's painful to still be here. William Allen White was my hero, who ran the *Emporia Gazette* [Kansas]. I wanted this paper to be as good as that. And I think we got there."

William Allen White (1868–1944) was a newspaper editor, politician, and leader of the Progressive movement. He won a 1923 Pulitzer Prize for his editorial "To an Anxious Friend," after being arrested in a dispute over free speech following objections to the way the state of Kansas handled those who participated in the Great Railroad Strike of 1922.

"William Allen White was able to run a newspaper that informed the community and advocated fiercely for economic development," Burns said. "And change, not only in Emporia, Kansas, but the whole state. He stayed in Emporia and was always first and foremost the voice for rural Kansas and Emporia. He was somebody who national and political leaders looked to for advice on what was happening in rural America. I'm not going to compare myself to William Allen White, but as a family paper we were able to achieve some measure of something I think he would recognize."

Ironically, Doug's late father, Robert L. Burns (1931–2018), was from Emporia. He was married to Ann Wilson from 1965 until their divorce in 1984, and was a general manager of the *Carroll Daily Times*. He is buried in Emporia. His son said, "It's kind of weird. You are raised in a newspaper family that is four generations deep in Carroll, Iowa, and then when you travel to Kansas for the holidays you go to the town that, more than any small community in the United States, recognizes the importance of their hometown newspaper.

"I know the streets of Emporia. I remember as a kid being excited when the *Emporia Gazette* would arrive in the afternoon. I remember going to the *Gazette* offices. And going by William Allen White's house, which is now a state historical site. I've read many of his columns. I've read biographies on him. To me, I would have been a blend of Molly Ivins, William Allen White, and H. L. Mencken."

—

Tiny Eldon, Missouri, is just 235 miles straight east of Emporia, Kansas. And there are shades of William Allen White in young Trevor Vernon in Eldon. In January 2020, Vernon became president of the Missouri Press Association (MPA) after being elected at MPA's 153rd annual convention in Kansas City, Missouri.

In June 2020, nine days before his fortieth birthday, Vernon, the publisher of the *Eldon Advertiser*, was elected mayor of Eldon. He captured 367 votes, more than 53 percent of the vote in a three-way race.

That's real *Citizen Kane* stuff.

Or at least Joseph Medill. Medill was managing editor of the *Chicago Tribune* until 1864, when he entered politics. Medill became the mayor of Chicago in 1871, after the Great Chicago Fire. (He ran as a candidate of the "Fireproof" party.) In 1874, after resigning from the job, Medill returned to the *Tribune* to become editor-in-chief.

"It is really interesting," Vernon said during a June 5, 2020, interview. "I tell people all the time my editorial staff has free reign to be critical of the city. They look at me funny. We're a small, close-knit community and there are no secrets anyway. I hope they're critical of me because it makes everybody better."

After getting his feet wet as mayor, Vernon said his biggest surprise was witnessing the slow process of government. "In private business we make a decision and go," he said in January 2022. "Public business takes forever to get anything done." Vernon believes that hitting deadlines is a discipline that is baked into his DNA as a newspaper owner. "The beauty of a small business is that you can change directions quickly if something isn't working."

Vernon's great-grandfather Harry Tompkins was also elected Eldon mayor, on April 6, 1950. He owned a Chevrolet dealership, and the April 6, 1950, *Advertiser* masthead featured the motto: "A WEAK TOWN DIES." Vernon said, "Interesting tidbit in that he was a Democrat. Democrats don't win anything around here anymore."

Republican Joseph Medill removed himself from the newspaper when he became Chicago's mayor. "I am going to do both," Vernon said, in reference to being both mayor and publisher. "There's no ethical issues." The Eldon mayor does not run daily operations of the city. Instead, Eldon employs a city manager for those tasks.

"Early on I was asked if I was going to quit my job. There's no way I could quit for $400 a month," Vernon said, alluding to the mayoral salary. His main opponent ran an insurance agency in Eldon and received 33 percent of the vote. "His business is very flexible," Vernon said. "I've overcautiously tried to back myself out of the paper. This week there was an ad that thanked voters on page two at the top of the page. I said, 'No, put that at the bottom.' One of my employees put it there, but I had them move it down.

"I know people are going to shake their heads and say, 'Sure, whatever.' I probably won't read any of the articles before they're published in the paper. I'll let the city manager facilitate the work with the newspaper and stay away from it. I will reserve the right to write a column whenever I want. We give that right to every mayor. We don't get many who take us up on it. At least two mayors have." The *Advertiser* prints occasional editorials, but it does not do political endorsements. "We're too small for that," Vernon said. "It would be a nightmare."

Like political ethics, family ethics can be easier to scrutinize under the microscope of a small town. Susie Galer, wife of Hillsboro *Journal-News* owner John Galer, said, "Our son got a speeding ticket one time. Some of his friends were teasing him, 'Your dad will leave that out of the paper.' He said, 'No, I'll be at the top of the list.' And he was."

In a separate conversation, John Galer said, "I was asked to run for mayor. It would have been the most expensive decision I ever made. I would have been divorced. It's just one more road. And to tell the truth, if you own a business, and you take a public position, that can be detrimental to your business. Sometimes you are called to serve. 'If not me, then who?' Ethically, in small community newspapers we probably do cross lines. It's impossible in a small town. If you're in Chicago there's anonymity. You can write what you want. When you live here, work here, and still have trust and report accurately, it's a hard job. It really is. We all have biases. But any way you cut it, that's part of being in a small town."

In Madison, Indiana, sixth-generation *Madison Courier* publisher Curt Jacobs (who sold the paper in February 2020) is married to Nancy Jacobs, magistrate for Jefferson County. "We covered many cases that she was involved in, particularly when she was the elected prosecutor here," Jacobs said. "We often had discussions about the coverage after the fact, never before the story ran. We treated her cases no differently than any other news. If she pointed out an inaccuracy, we corrected it. If she did not agree with our coverage, she let me know, and if I disagreed with her take on it, I let her know in the same way I would with any other public official. Small-town newspapering is done in close quarters. She often said, 'That story should be above the fold.' I usually replied, 'I suggest you talk to the editor.'"

A 2014 report by Portland State University researcher Lee Shaker stated that civic engagement, such as contacting public officials or participating in school or other neighborhood groups, dropped significantly in Denver and Seattle after those cities lost one of their two daily papers, a decline not found in other major American cities that did not lose a newspaper.

The seeds for Trevor Vernon's campaign were planted in 2017 when he began examining the city budget. Vernon holds a bachelor's degree in finance from Southwest Missouri State University. He was told that Eldon was in fine shape. But when Vernon put numbers to paper, he saw the city was a quarter of a million dollars in the red. "I called the city administrator and asked what's going on," he recalled. "She argued with me and that got me going. I wrote a couple editorials about it. If we get in that position again, the town may cease to exist as we know it. Services are getting cut. We had one of the best small-town fire departments in the nation. Lots of equipment, six full-time firefighters for a town of less than five thousand. That's been decimated because of overspending."

In the summer of 2020, Vernon guessed he would continue to spend most of his daylight hours at the newspaper office. He mentioned his other office—the mayor's office at city hall. "I don't know I will be there much," he said. "I'll meet people there if I need to meet people there." There are city editors beneath his role as publisher and president of Vernon Publishing. "But nobody else does what I do at the paper," he said. "I still run all the operations [including the press]. There's no way I could teach someone to do all of that. And honestly, since I'm a finance major, I'm a real nitpicker."

Trevor Vernon is a prime example of how community meshes with a community newspaper. In the summer of 2020, he was mayor of his town, publisher of his town's newspaper, president of the Missouri Press Association, a husband, and father to two children. His wife, Molly Vernon, encouraged him to run for mayor. She is the circulation director for all Vernon Publishing holdings. Trevor was first approached by the superintendent of schools to apply for the city administrator position. He declined. Then it was suggested he run for a city office. He declined again. "My wife said, 'Quit bitching about the city if you don't do something.' I assume I was bringing it home at night."

Trevor told Molly that his four-year mayoral term would likely suffice. "My family has been really good throughout my life," he said. "At five o'clock my job ends. As a reporter, that doesn't happen. My job ends unless there's an emergency. I go home and I get to be a dad and a husband. Being mayor will change that a little. There will be more meetings at night. That bothers me the most. I may miss some things with my kids here and there. But it's a time where I'll have more energy than I'll ever have in my life. And my business hinges on this.

"If Eldon isn't as good as it possibly can be, then our newspaper can't bring in more revenue and continue to do the great things that we're doing."

The *Advertiser* (circulation 3,500) is the flagship newspaper of three publications under the Vernon Publishing, Inc. umbrella. The *Advertiser* has a three-person editorial staff (one dedicated mostly to sports), two graphic designers, a sales manager, a billing person, three pressmen, Trevor, and his wife. The entire company employs a little over twenty people.

The other two newspapers are the *Tipton Times* (circulation 1,500) in neighboring Moniteau County and the *Index* on Lake Pomme de Terre, a fishing lake about an hour southwest of Eldon.

Trevor said the Lake Pomme de Terre region "reminds me of Lake of the Ozarks thirty years ago. I think there's huge potential there. At some point it will become a destination for fishermen and big-box stores as well. Forrest Lucas of Lucas Oil bought a significant amount of land and built a state-of-the-art dirt track, off-road track, and racing lake there."

The *Index* is based in the town of Hermitage, the county seat of Hickory County. Hickory's population was just 460 in 2020, yet the *Index*'s circulation was 2,400. "It's crazy," Trevor said. "It's like going back in time. It is the only media in the county. There is no radio station or television station. It is very rural."

The *Advertiser* operates out of a century-old brick building in downtown Eldon. The building once housed a grocery store, and when the railroads were running through Eldon, a brothel operated upstairs. Trevor's office is now upstairs. His grandfather Wallace remodeled the building on and off when the money was good.

A piece of stained-glass artwork greets visitors as they enter the small lobby. The art depicts a young man reading a newspaper next to a ripe red apple. Wallace Vernon made the piece in the early 1990s. The newspaper was for Trevor's father. Trevor's mom was a teacher, so he made the apple for her.

The newspaper has been in the Vernon family since 1948. The *Advertiser* was founded by N. J. Shepherd, a freelance writer who had bylines in Chicago and St. Louis, and J. R. Helfrich. In its nascent years, the *Advertiser* was printed on a hand-cranked press, two pages at a time. Two of the pages were pre-printed in St. Louis with national news and advertising. Local news was printed in Eldon. All type was set one letter at a time.

In 2000, Trevor's father, Dane, and his mother, Sharene, bought out his grandfather.

Trevor attended the University of Missouri in Columbia for two years. He started in engineering and changed to business. In 2002, he graduated with a bachelor of science degree in finance from Southwest Missouri State (now Missouri State) in Springfield, Missouri. "I really thought I'd go somewhere else," Trevor said. "I had job offers in Miami and Denver. That was about the time the banking industry took a nosedive. My dad from day one knew he wanted to be in the newspaper. He went to J school right off the bat. I hated it when I was younger because the newspaper was always around the dinner table. We were always talking business. My dad would say, 'You're going to that volleyball game, here's a camera, take a picture.' I thought I'd never do it. But I'd been working at the office for three or four months of my last semester of college, driving back and forth to school. I told my dad, 'I really do love this.' The transition was pretty easy.

"I started in the print shop running the press. My dad said, 'There's one thing in this office I can't do and that's run the press. So if something breaks, I don't know how to fix it.'" Trevor stayed at the press for nearly a year before transitioning into the newspaper. He said, "I still run the press every other week at least to see how the guys are doing and help whenever I need to. I love that part. I had an old newspaper guy tell me, 'The one thing I'm upset about in my life is that I never physically made anything. I write all the time, but I never make a product that goes out. If you can run your press, you need to go do it.'"

Trevor has fallen in love with the family newspaper game. "I wouldn't do anything else," he said. "And now I'm doing the same thing to my kids that my dad did."

Would Trever Vernon lobby for a fourth generation in the newspaper? "My daughter shows interest right now," he said. "She's eleven. We'll see. Things are so different now than they were."

—

As with the extended Vernon, Galer, and Hussman families' effect on their communities, the community of Carroll, Iowa, would be much less than it is without the extended family of Ann Wilson. Ann's father, James W. Wilson, was named business manager of the then-titled *Carroll Herald* in 1929. James Rhodes of Newton, Iowa, purchased the paper and slotted in Wilson, his advertising manager at the *Newton Daily News*. On November 7, 1929, the *Herald* became a daily with the slogan "The Only Daily Newspaper in an Inland Empire of Eight Counties."

James W. Wilson purchased the Rhodes estate interest in 1944. He owned and operated the paper until his death in 1977. Ann's younger brother, James B. Wilson, joined the newspaper operation in 1967 and became publisher after the death of their father. Her brother died in 2013 and was not active for several years before his death. Ann took over as general manager in 1984.

Because of the Iowa caucuses, at least fifty presidential candidates have visited Carroll since 1984. "I remember talking to Jesse Jackson, so that goes back [Rev. Jackson ran for president in 1984 and 1988]," Ann's son Doug Burns said. "It's an endless number. We tell the hard stories when we have to, but I would say over the century our real calling card is that through my grandfather, my uncle, Mom, and myself, we're very active in economic development. The chamber of commerce just had its banquet and we're the only family in Carroll that's had four people win Citizen of the Year. That shows the value of the newspaper."

Ann recalled, "There were ample books and newspapers around the house I grew up in. Everybody read. Dad didn't buy a TV until I was almost through high school. And then he was the only one who watched it. He would rent one for the political conventions and then take it back."

Doug added, "Grandpa's idol was [Arizona Republican senator and 1964 presidential nominee] Barry Goldwater." James W. Wilson was an Iowa state chairman for Goldwater. Doug observed, "It was kind of neat, Mom was a regional leader for Barack Obama. And we were the first paper in Iowa to endorse President Obama. We endorsed him at the beginning of 2007." As a presidential candidate, Obama visited Carroll twice, although not at the downtown newspaper office.

Ann graduated from Carroll Community Schools and from Southern Methodist University in Dallas, Texas, where she received a degree in elementary education and religion. She was accepted by Grinnell and Carleton Colleges, but they were deemed too close to home. "I was also accepted at Columbia in New York City," she said. "Dad said he would not pay for anything east of the Mississippi because they were too liberal."

"I went to conservative SMU and became a liberal."

The rewards of teaching brought her back to Carroll. "I had taught in Des Moines," she said. "When the children arrived, I was running a daycare in our home so I could stay home. I knew I could not support myself with that. My ex-husband lost his job about that time, too." He was a professor who taught music at Simpson College in Indianola, Iowa. Robert L. Burns was minister of music for First United Church in downtown Des Moines when he met Ann Wilson. They were married at the same church where they met.

"I often wanted to escape from here," Ann said. "But it was the right thing for me. A newspaper editor, a superintendent of schools, maybe the pastors, they're just one of them in a town. It is hard to find somebody who understands your work and what you do. I did not have a business degree and I did not have a journalism degree. I had just lived it as a child."

The landscape for women in the media in 1984 was obviously different than it is now, especially in a small town in the middle of America. "There weren't as many women," Ann said. "Not at all. There were two men here. Every time my brother would leave, they would do something like hide an ad or something totally nasty so the paper would be late. They thought I would get blamed for it."

Ann pushed forward and got involved in a big way. In the late 1980s, she became the first woman and only non-golfer at the time to serve as president of the Carroll Country Club. (Doug and Tom golfed.) She served on the board of Friends of Iowa Public Television and eventually became president. She got on the board of the Iowa Newspaper Association (INA) during its early days.

During a 1985 INA convention, the late Grinnell, Iowa, newspaper publisher Al Pinder gave the new Carroll newspaper general manager advice that has stayed with her through her career. During an afternoon break he guided her to the bar, ordered a glass of Scotch, and declared he would give her some tips whether she wanted them or not. Her parents had known Pinder well.

With a warm smile Ann recalled, "First, he said, 'You have been given a wonderful family and talented kids. There is much potential there. Second, you have been given a good business. Pay attention to your family. Interesting things cross a publisher's desk that are worth doing. Do what you can of those, as long as you don't hurt those first two things we talked about.' That convention was in May. That summer, it came across my desk where they had a new wing on the art center in Des Moines. It was media day. I went; it was *Better Homes & Gardens*, the *Los Angeles Times*, the *New York Times*, and me. That started it. It was fun. Al Pinder was a wonderful human being."

Ann Wilson is soft-spoken but with the no-nonsense flair of a high school principal. She looks visitors in the eye, and her firm demeanor is a mash-up of the German Catholic and Irish Catholic stock of Carroll. The town was named for Charles Carroll, the only Roman Catholic to sign the Declaration of Independence.

"Some of the richest farmland in the world is here," Doug said. "And unlike a lot of other small communities, we're fortunate we're not a company town." The nearby Farner-Bocken Company distributes products to grocery and convenience stores. Pella manufactures windows and doors, and down the road there's American Home Shield. All three diverse businesses are headquartered on the Lincoln Highway.

Mulling over his family's role in the community, Doug observed, "My mom is a pioneer. She's been the first woman in a variety of roles in this community and statewide. She is in this matriarch role of newspapers in Iowa."

In a separate interview, Ann said, "Looking back, it was fun. But there was a lot of stress. All three children were very bright and involved in a lot of different things. I'd cook one weekend a month and put it all in the freezer. And now every one of them are good cooks. They had to do things like that. They were involved in lots of activities, and I couldn't go to all of them because of the paper. I think that bothered my daughter more than anything. She was involved in a lot of speech and music things. I couldn't make Tom's golf tournament."

Sacrifice.

Suddenly Doug Burns's cell phone rang loudly. It was a potential advertiser. He jumped up from his chair and excused himself from the publisher's office.

His mother said, "We don't pass those up."

—

During the early 1900s the Reverend Michael Galer, a Methodist minister in McGregor, Minnesota, owned a rural weekly newspaper. His son, Delford, left Minnesota for the warmer climate of Wisconsin. Delford worked in Lancaster and Delavan, Wisconsin, in advertising and typesetting. In 1945, Delford answered an Illinois Press Association advertisement offering a partnership in editorial and mechanical work at the *Hillsboro Journal* in Illinois.

Delford, his wife, Pauline, and their sons, Douglas, Gilbert, and Phillip, moved to Hillsboro in 1945. Phillip covered prep sports for the *Journal* during his senior year of high school. In 1952, he obtained a bachelor of science degree in newspaper management from the University of Illinois.

"He comes back here," said present-day owner John Galer. "I graduated Eastern [Illinois] in 1972 and I came back here. Now my daughter [Mary Herschelman] has come in with us. She wanted to get into photojournalism, so she went to Missouri and she comes back here. Five generations. We're lucky here."

Mary Herschelman talked about her path in the rear kitchen-office of the *Journal-News*. Her father was busy in the small newsroom and expressed no desire to lord over our conversation. He respected our privacy. Mary has a brother, John Phillips Galer, who is four years younger than her. (He is not a Jr.; their father is John Michael.) John Phillips Galer was a major in the United States Air Force who was working at the Pentagon in the autumn of 2019.

"Growing up, we were in and out of the office as Mom and Dad covered stuff," she said. She remembers the *Journal-News* being part of her life as early as elementary school and early middle school. "I used to tell people I was never going to be part of the newspaper business," she said. "I was going to be an elementary school teacher. I've since learned God didn't give me that much patience. In high school I started my first job here. The first thing I did was work in circulation. Then I started working in the darkroom. We developed film and that's when I caught the photography bug. I still wasn't going to come back to Hillsboro, mind you. I was going to be a nationally renowned photojournalist for *National Geographic*."

Mary looked at Eastern Illinois University in Charleston, where her father went. She also was interested in the University of Missouri in Columbia. As she recalled the Missouri visit, Mary laughed and said, "Of course my dad toured their press, he talked to everybody. He is the only person I know that not only can do every job that is here, but has. We get back in the car and he said, 'If you're serious and this is what you want to do, this is where you need to be.' It was the best decision ever."

Mary studied in London in 2001. She arrived only ten days before the 9/11 attacks in a program sponsored by the Missouri London program. She also worked for the daily *Columbia Missourian*. "Columbia is much bigger than little old Hillsboro," she said. "I found out that big-time journalism wasn't for me. I did some harder stories. I'm more of a close-knit, community kind of person."

After earning a bachelor's degree in photojournalism from Missouri in

2002, Mary became a photojournalist at the *Princeton Daily Clarion* in Indiana. The *Daily Clarion* was also a family newspaper at the time, owned by the Brehm family in California. In the fall of 2003, her father was having knee trouble. The Hillsboro Hilltoppers had made the state football playoffs. "He asked if I'd come home and shoot a football game," Mary recalled. "I said, 'Sure.' It was only a three-hour drive."

John Galer was in the process of buying the *Montgomery County News* in Hillsboro. As he reinvented the *Journal-News* with the merger, he said he could use his daughter's help. "I enjoyed what I did in Indiana," she said. "I worked a lot. I didn't have a lot of friends. I had a family in my church that was wonderful to me."

She came home to Hillsboro in May 2004.

"I went on the editorial staff and did everything," she said. "The other [newly merged] paper, that was a county-focused paper, where we were more of the Hillsboro-focused paper. I wanted to be outside of Hillsboro. I wanted to do something a little different. I worked a couple days a week in our Litchfield office and focused on bringing Litchfield in."

The *Journal-News* had a small bureau in Litchfield, on Union Avenue near Library Park. Mary worked there until her daughter Grace was born, then she moved back to Hillsboro.

In a separate interview, while working on newspaper postal reports, publisher Mike Plunkett said, "Family newspapers, like the family anything, are going away. Nokomis [*Free-Press Progress*] just sold to a chain [Paddock Publications] in Arlington Heights, the same chain that bought *Panhandle Press*. If you're small, you're vulnerable. John is retirement age, I'm still around, and Mary is going to be around. If Mary wasn't there, would John say, 'I'm going to have to sell this thing, too?' And the potential buyers would be a chain. We're a small community newspaper. We have a staff of six. A paper this size owned by a corporation would have, what, two? Because that money would be needed to pay for dividends. That's the difference.

"The Galer family invests in bodies to put on the streets, covering the community. We go to all the baseball games and basketball games. We still go to the courthouse and grab the news. All the events—we will be at every damn one. The county fair. When Farmersville Irish Days comes, we will be at the coronation. By and large those are weekend events, and it takes a lot of people from the staff, but we cover them."

In 2010, John Galer was president of the Illinois Press Association; he is a regional director for the National Newspaper Association and past president of the Litchfield Chamber of Commerce. His wife, Susie, worked subscription and the front counter at the now-defunct former competitor *Montgomery County News* before meeting John in 1978. "We lived next door to each other," she said. "He ran into my car one time on the ice. I had never met him. We had a lot of teasing. People would say, 'I guess you're the only one who has keys to both newspapers.' But we put the papers together."

John added, "We worked very hard at not talking about it. I didn't want to know anything, and she didn't want to know anything. But it worried everybody. Susie came from a big family and her dad was a Methodist minister. Everything ties together right here. This is what can happen in a small town. But it makes the world a pretty place."

—

Peter Shaw was sitting in his *Telegraph* office with Peoria Street behind him. A large oil portrait of great-grandmother Mabel Shaw leaned on a wall in front of his desk. Mabel sat on a chair, wearing a long peach-colored dress with a chiffon draped over her shoulder. The painting was done in Florida by Wallace Bassford (1900–1998), whose father, Homer, ironically, was a newspaperperson at the *St. Louis Times*. Mabel wintered in Florida. You would not call her pretty by this painting, unless it was pretty imposing. She had a stern smile. The painting had been hanging in the home of Mabel's granddaughter, and before that it was in an aunt's house in Palm Beach, Florida. Mabel's latest stop was in the Shaw Media corporate office in Sterling, Illinois, until it closed in 2019.

And that is why she was in Peter's office. She was awaiting her next move.

Mabel Driver Smith Shaw (1870–1955) is the heroine of the Shaw legacy. She was publisher of the *Telegraph* between 1909 and 1955 and led the newspaper through a couple of economic depressions with her sons as co-publishers. An aspiring opera singer, Mabel became known as the "First Lady of Midwestern Journalism." Her eyes in the portrait seemed to follow guests around the room.

"We say B. F. Shaw started the newspaper in 1851," Peter explained. "B. F. went to work for a newspaper in Dixon [The *Amboy Times*] and bought it from them. We go generationally from B. F., but everything is really about Mabel. She took over the company at a time women couldn't vote. She was B. F.'s daughter-in-law. B. F.'s son, Eustace, had taken over the company and died at a young age [forty-five years old in 1902]. She took over not long after. I hear my dad say that Mabel realized B. F. was gambling all the profits away playing poker with his buddies. When she started, there were three other daily newspapers in Dixon."

Mabel's shadow was indeed imposing. Peter Shaw resigned as the Shaw Media trustee in June 2021. He said, "I am proud and thankful for my twelve-plus years as trustee, including guiding the trust through an incredibly difficult period and helping chart the path forward."

Shaw Media made industry news in 2013 when family members went to court over control of the company. That was one of Peter's difficult periods.

Mabel had established the Shaw Media trust, which covered Mabel and her three sons. As each of her sons passed away by the early 1980s, Northern Trust Corp. became full trustee. "There was litigation going on from a small part of the family with Northern," Peter said in the summer of 2020. "So the beneficiaries got together and went through possible people. They asked me. I became trustee February 9, 2009. We did go through a lawsuit that ended in 2014."

According to a December 2013 *Family Business* report, the plaintiffs were William Shaw (former publisher of the *Telegraph and Herald*) and his brother Robert. They led a group of family members who collectively represented 35 percent of the trust that owned the publishing operation and real estate. The report said that William Shaw was "pushed out of the company" in 2004 and that Robert was fired as publisher of the *Northwest Herald* in 2002. The catalyst for the suit was the company's rejection in 1999 of a $120 million offer from Tribune Co. for Shaw's *Kane County Chronicle* and the *Northwest Herald*. The suit argued that Northern Trust and Peter Shaw should have started selling assets before the newspaper industry began tanking.

"That ended up with a bifurcation settlement [in January 2014], before we got to trial," Peter said in 2020. "What used to be 35 percent of the ben-eficiaries, four income beneficiaries were bifurcated out of the trust." Under terms of the family settlement, the family members that owned 35 percent of the company through the trust were cashed out of their ownership stakes for $5.25 million.

Retired Shaw Media CEO Tom Shaw is Peter's father. He is a cousin of William and Robert. In a separate interview Tom said, "There have been disputes. The issues weren't so much from the same generation, but there were distant cousins and multigenerational. When it got severe, it went to the board. There's an old proverb [27:17], 'Iron sharpens iron. And one man sharpens another.' That's part of the nature of the conflict. If you can keep the power from getting out of bounds, it can be beneficial. Because nobody's got all the answers. It's when it's taken personal and people are working behind the scenes with ulterior motives that it becomes destructive."

—

Peter Shaw made his exit as a sixth-generation family member, as did Curt Jacobs, the former publisher of the *Madison Courier* in Indiana. Just like with Mabel Shaw, the dreams of elders watch over younger generations. Jacobs recalled, "My grandfather [Don Wallis Sr.] was publisher when I was a child. I was close to him. So I'd come down to the newspaper on Saturday morning. He'd typically work half a day Saturday. I'd pick up scraps of newsprint around the press. He had a houseboat on the river. So we'd work here until noon and then go on his boat. I'd clean that up too. I had a paper route pretty young. I had that route from the time I was six. I carried thirty-five, forty papers. Pretty much everybody on my street got the paper."

Jacobs delivered the *Courier* by walking, riding a bicycle, and riding a skateboard. He had the newspaper route for eight years. "At one time I rode a mini-bike that you could fit in my parents' car," he said. "I later gave the route to a neighbor and then my younger brother took it over. When I got into high school I'd work in the mail room, the press room, and in the warehouse."

Jacobs went to Madison High School and then attended college at Indiana University in Bloomington, where he was a criminal justice major. He became a juvenile probation officer in Bloomington and Johnson County, Indiana. He is married to Nancy Jacobs, who was a two-term elected prosecutor in their home county of Jefferson from the 1990s to the early 2000s. In July 2019, she became a magistrate in the Jefferson County Superior and Circuit Courts.

"When I was twenty-nine years old, I decided to come back and give this a shot," he said. "And I've been here ever since. I came back in 1991 as circulation manager. I remember telling my wife in 1989—it sort of came out of the blue. My grandfather was still alive. I said, 'Hey, I'm switching jobs.' I was a juvenile officer. I was staying at my wife's family's house. I hadn't really thought about coming back. He passed away later that year.

"I don't know if that's what planted the thought in my mind. I never considered going to college for journalism. My grandfather was hands-off a bit. He had a somewhat contentious relationship with my uncle Don, who was a journalist. And Don never came back to the paper. Don grew up in the 1960s, but there was some tension. I don't know if that's why my grandfather never pushed me to come back."

The late Don Wallis Jr. was a reporter in nearby Vevay, Indiana (pop. 1,600) for a weekly newspaper that was owned by the *Madison Courier* during the 1960s. In the early 1980s he left to edit the *Yellow Springs News* in the alternative paradise of Yellow Springs, Ohio (pop. 3,500). Don Jr. also served as the member of the Yellow Springs Human Relations Council and was deeply interested in sustainable living and environmental care. "He was a hippie, very much so," Jacobs said. "My grandfather was very conservative, and that's one reason they didn't get along. When my grandfather passed away in 1989, my uncle Donnie inherited the Vevay paper." Don Jr. owned Vevay Newspapers until his death in January 2012. His daughters sold the paper to the newspaper's editor. While the *Madison Courier* no longer owns Vevay Newspapers, it still does Vevay's production work.

Don Jr. wrote the 1992 book *Madison and the Garber Family: A Community and Its Newspaper*. He had fond remembrances of his father, Don Wallis Sr., who was business manager of the *Courier*. Of his father, Don Jr. wrote, "Taking his family for Sunday afternoon rides in the country, he would stop at every *Courier* delivery box along the road that did not sit securely enough on its post to satisfy him; he would get out of the car and fix it. He would stop at country stores, so he could meet the people there, and talk to them."

On the day Don Wallis Sr. died, his daughter, Jane Garber Wallis Jacobs, became publisher. She remained publisher until her death in 2015, when her son Curt took over. Jane Jacobs steered the *Courier* into a new world of technology, yet her values remained close to the ground. She became a member of the Madison Presbyterian Church in 1952 and cofounded the church's preschool program. "She thought with the paper it was important to tell the story of everyday people," Curt said. "She saw everybody as equal. As the publisher, you're often perceived as somebody of some 'importance.' She didn't carry herself that way. I think that bled through to the paper. You didn't have to be somebody important to catch the attention of the paper. She was very strong in terms of ethics, and we continued to be that way. We had a pretty strong wall between advertising and our news."

—

Independent, multigenerational family newspapers maintain a commitment and desire to follow the truth, no matter where it may lead—including, sometimes, to one's own family members. In June 2019, the *Bakersfield Californian* concluded a 122-year run of family ownership. It marked the end of one of the oldest and more colorful family-operated newspapers in America.

Bakersfield (pop. 380,000) is a fertile landscape for American journalism. Located across the Tehachapi Mountains, about one hundred miles north of Los Angeles, Bakersfield is the county seat of Kern County, the most productive oil-producing county in America. With abundant almonds, citrus, and grapes, Kern County is also the most productive agricultural county in America, with $7.25 billion in gross value, according to a 2018 Farm Progress report. Around town they say, "If you want to know America, come to Kern County."

I rolled into Bakersfield in mid-July 2019, six weeks after the *Californian* was sold to a pop-up company called Sound California News Media.

Sound News Media, as it is called, was just three months old and named itself after the "Bakersfield sound" that birthed country music legends Merle Haggard, Buck Owens, Red Simpson, and many others. I learned Sound News Media was based out of downstate Marion, Illinois, which is the home of company CEO Melanie Walsh.

As evidence of how deep and intertwined newspaper roots can be, Walsh is the daughter of David Radler, who was publisher of the *Chicago Sun-Times* when I worked there. Radler was a confidant of then–*Sun-Times* owner and

Donald Trump biographer Conrad Black. Radler served twenty-nine months in prison for mail fraud that involved $32 million of non-compete payments made to Radler and Black in the sale of their Hollinger International newspaper chain. Black also served more than three years in prison before he was pardoned by President Trump in May 2019. Radler now runs the Alberta Newspaper Group in Canada.

The *Californian* began in 1866 as the *Weekly Courier* in Havilah, California. In 1872, it moved to Bakersfield when Bakersfield became the county seat. Then in 1897, the Kern County superintendent of schools, Alfred Harrell, purchased what was then called the *Daily Californian*.

I had a lengthy breakfast with longtime *Californian* columnist Robert Price. I knew Price from his extensive coverage of the "Bakersfield sound" and our mutual writing for the Country Music Hall of Fame and Museum publications in Nashville. In 2003, the *Californian* published Price's ten-page exposé, "The Lords of Bakersfield," which detailed the newspaper's crazy and lurid history of murder and pedophilia.

Price was still reeling from the sale of his beloved newspaper. He had been with the paper for forty-one years. It seemed like he needed someone to talk to. He spoke with candor and reflection. "The new ownership has been hands-off editorial so far," Price said. "They want to serve the community, blah blah blah, but they made it clear they're in it to make money. And that's understandable. Previous owners were doing it for the community, but after a while you can't lose a million dollars every year for ten years. They were going to lose their family fortune."

Alfred Harrell purchased the *Californian* for $1,000 at the age of thirty-four. He had no experience on the business end or production end of newspaper work. He ran the paper for fifty years until he died in 1946 at the age of eighty-three. He was still writing his own editorials at the time of his death. "But he had been 'The Man,'" Price said. "His wife took over for five years until she died. It became a matriarchy. Their daughter took it over, basically absentee. She lived in the Bay Area."

Walter Kane became the paper's general manager and ran the *Californian* until he retired in 1967. Kane began his career at the *Californian* in the 1920s as an advertising salesman.

"He had a controversial background," Price said—an understatement. "He was a pedophile. I worked with Joe Stevenson, a great, old, sweet man. A business editor. He told me that one day in the 1950s he got a call to come to the front desk." Until the 2019 sale, the *Californian* was housed in a resplendent 1926 Moroccan-influenced building that is on the National Register of Historic Places. The newsroom was on the third floor of the red brick downtown building. Visitors entered through a grandiose foyer. "The secretary directed Joe to this guy who was in tears, and he said, 'Walter hit on my son. What are you going to do about it?' What could Joe do about it? [Walter] was his boss."

Walter Kane was a suspected member of a 1950s organization called the White Orchid Society, a group of pedophile men. In his 2003 series, Price wrote that Kane "had an unusual arrangement regarding police reports," implying that illegal actions by Kane or associates would not appear in the newspaper. There is no record of Kane ever being arrested in Kern County. "They basically showed Walter the door," Price said. "They had a big retirement dinner, and it remained an absentee ownership."

But the Bakersfield controversy didn't stop there. Alfred Harrell's granddaughter Berenice Fritts Koerber had four children: William "Bill" Chipman Fritts, Donald Harrell Fritts, Virginia "Ginger" Fritts Moorhouse-Cowenhoven, and Theodore "Ted" Fritts. Ted was the youngest.

"Huntington's disease was part of the family DNA," Price said. "Speculation was that Bill Fritts had it. He ran the paper, moved to San Francisco, ran a men's clothing store, and then committed suicide. This was 1970. Then Don stepped up into a managing role, and Huntington's disease definitely killed him. . . . It jumped over Ginger and went to Ted—who was gay. One of his paramours, a seventeen-year-old boy, murdered the county's human resource director. There was a salacious trial, and they sent the kid off to prison—he recently got out. Ted stepped down and went to Los Angeles to work in theater." Ted Fritts died in July 1997 of AIDS complications in San Diego, California. He was fifty years old.

"I wrote each of their obituaries," Price said. "I'm the official family historian."

Meanwhile, Ginger Moorhouse was living in New Hampshire, acting as publisher from afar, and going through a divorce. She had three kids: Tracey,

Peter, and Ginny. Ginger moved to Bakersfield with her two daughters and took over ownership in 1994. Ginger had networked with then-chairman of the *Washington Post* Katharine Graham, who took over her family newspaper after her husband died by suicide. "Ginger embraced it," Price said. "She ran a pretty tight ship. She became part of the community. She loves horses. She has a little cowgirl in her walk. She leaned politically a little more to the left, more so than the average person in Bakersfield."

In 1998, Price wrote a feature story on the one hundredth anniversary of family ownership at the *Californian*. A newspaper broker told him the *Californian* was worth $100 million. "I put it in the story and of course they took it out," Price said. "After 1998, the fortunes of newspapers started going down. And Ginger starts thinking about the next generation. How are they going to survive the digital world and who is going to run it? She wanted very bad to keep it in her family. Tracey [her daughter] was involved with the editorial page at the same time I was. I was the editorial page editor. She was the letters editor, which was like a twenty-hour thing but a way to keep her in there. After a while she soured on it. She eventually took a nice buyout. She's out of the newspaper game, but she established the Bakersfield Californian Foundation [now the Virginia and Alfred Harrell Foundation]. She continues to manage that. The foundation continues to do good things. Tracey and her mother, Ginger, basically run the foundation."

Ginger's son, Peter, remained in New England, where he was involved in financial services. Price said that Peter had little to do with the newspaper outside of a stint on the board of directors. "So all the hope was invested in Ginny, the youngest," Price said. "She started in marketing. She was named associate publisher in 2015. Everybody gathers in the big foyer, and they make the big announcement. It didn't take. She had some serious issues." Richard Beene, then CEO and president of the *Californian*, had a falling-out with Ginny.

Ginny accused Price of embellishing his expense reports when he was asked to lead a panel discussion at the 2015 California News Publishers Association convention in San Francisco. After the Bay Area trip, the newspaper's board of directors voted to terminate Ginny. "I'm giving you good stuff, huh?" Price said. "I'd be more guarded about all this if they were still the owners. In the end, she's suspended. She's about forty, young. At this point things are disintegrating. I saw the writing on the wall. The paper had to get sold. Tracey is out, Peter's not interested, and Ginny had issues. Ginger is in her seventies; she is married to a nice gentleman who had some health problems. She donated one of her kidneys to him and it failed. He's on permanent dialysis so she needs to care for him. And that's what she's doing. We kept hearing rumors about being sold. We knew it was the beginning of the end when we were told we had to evacuate our historic building. We moved to the old press facility [six miles away] in Oildale. We finally got the word on June 1 [2019] that the sale had been consummated. We've been under new ownership for six weeks."

Just as amazing as the bizarre stories of the "Lords of Bakersfield" series is that Price had an editor and a publisher who gave him full autonomy to write about the darkest parts of the newspaper's, and the family's, history with transparent depth.

According to Price, the Kern County assistant district attorney, Stephen M. Tauzer, was murdered in September 2002 by Chris Hillis, the father of Lance Hillis, the young man Tauzer had been associated with. "[Lance] steals a car, gets in a crash, and kills himself," Price said. "The family was outraged because the DA [Edward Jagels] had used his influence to keep the kid out of jail. The family wanted him to go to prison and clean him up."

Jagels had a reputation as a tough-on-crime DA. In his January 2003 series, Price wrote that during Jagels's time as district attorney, Kern County had the highest per-capita prison commitment rate of any major California county. "I'm taken off my column and commissioned to do a deep dive into all these other murders in the 1970s and '80s and how some mirrored [Tauzer's] murder," Price said. "It became clear that Ted Fritts is a central figure in this."

By "this," Price meant the long history of men in positions of power in Bakersfield using their influence to protect each other.

Price wrote how Ted Fritts came into play after the 1981 murder of Kern County personnel director Edwin A. Buck. Within four days, Bakersfield police arrested a gay hustler named Robert Glen Mistriel and his friend. *Californian* reporter Steve E. Swenson learned of Fritts's ties to the murder case through police reports. Then–managing editor Owen Kearns Sr. told Swenson not to use Fritts's name unless it emerged in the trial. During the 1983 trial, Mistriel took the stand and implicated Fritts as an adult man he had had sex with as a minor. Price reported that Fritts finally made the pages of his family newspaper three times in 1983: twice on the "jump" (inside the paper, off the front page) and once on the last line of a small story.

Price wrote about this well-connected group of closeted gay men, some of whom were predators, adding, "Occasionally, however, the preyed-upon lashed out, leading to a string of murders involving young gay men and their promi-nent, older male suitors. Anybody who had been at the paper for any length of time was familiar with the Ted Fritts story, the little we knew."

Mike Jenner was managing editor and executive editor of the *Califor-nian* between 1993 and 2010.

"It was an interesting story," said Jenner, now a University of Missouri professor and faculty group chair of Journalism Professions. "Bob Price knows that story better than anybody, and he did a fabulous job writing about it. During the course of writing about it, we talked about the fact our former publisher and owner was also a prominent gay man and ran in these same circles. It was obvious to us that we had to acknowledge that fact. We never ac-cused him of any crimes, but he knew the people and was in the demographic we were writing about.

"So I talked to his sister [Ginger Moorhouse], who was the owner. I said, 'We're doing the story,' and she said, 'I know you are.' I said, 'We have to write about Ted.' And her response was, 'Of course you do and what do you need from me?' She was very honest and told us what she knew of her brother and his activities to some degree. When a lot of this was going on, she was on the other side of the country and Bakersfield was not on her radar."

Price said, "Ginger is confronted with, 'Do I allow my reporter to look into this dark aspect of our family? And this newspaper's role in this city?' And she allowed me to do it. I'd pass her in the hallway. She knew what I was doing. And she was cordial about it. So this comes out and the shit hits the fan. I'm interviewed on CNN. I'm still talking to people about a Netflix movie."

Jenner gave his reporter liberty, time, and space to tell the story right. "I thought and we thought—Lois Henry was an assistant managing editor who worked closely with me and Bob—that we had a unique obligation to tell the story," Jenner said. "Nobody else would ever do the story. The goal was to dig up the facts on these old stories and share them with the community. These stories had never been brought to light.

"First and foremost, Bob is a great storyteller. He had lots of sources. He'd come back with tidbits, and we were like, 'Keep going, keep going.' It made a big impact when it came out. We knew there were some people who would rather that we left the past alone. We weren't deterred by the likelihood that some would criticize us."

In January 2003, Ginger Moorhouse was named Publisher of the Year (2002) by *Editor & Publisher* (*E&P*) magazine. *E&P* cited "The Lords of Bakersfield" as a shadowy cabal of powerful local leaders with secret (and often evil, deadly) lives. *E&P* staff writer Mark Fitzgerald wrote, "Even more extraordinary was the story the family-owned paper told on itself. A long-ago general manager was revealed as a suspected child molester. The *Californian's* past practice of burying or killing embarrassing stories was documented. And former publisher Ted Fritts—brother of current publisher Ginger Moorhouse—was linked to an underage gay prostitute." And the *Californian* won the University of Oregon's Ancil Payne Award for Ethics in Journalism.

Ginger Moorhouse was named chairman and president of the *Californian* in 1989. Jenner arrived in Bakersfield in October 1993. "It's interesting in itself how she became in charge of the paper," Jenner said. "Her brothers either died or were incapable of running it. She was told when she was younger, 'The guys have this; you get married, have a family, and you'll get your share of whatever money is coming to you. But they'll run the paper.' They did, in their way. In the end, she ran the paper and she did a better job than any of them. She was a fabulous publisher."

As for the future, Price said, "It's murky and I'm not sure how people are connected. The CEO is Steve Malkowich, and he lives in British Columbia. The person he brought in for the transition is the editor of a small paper in Quebec. She was only here for a month. Everybody was terminated legally. Then they were offered jobs. They closed the entire printing facility so thirty-two jobs were lost there. There were three or four paginators who were near retirement. They walked out with nice severance packages per our contract. And one reporter was let go. The executive editor was let go. He was only here two years. I was the highest-paid person in the newsroom after him. And I took a bump down. The paper is now printed in Palmdale [California]. We're in a huge warehouse with presses—and it's a ghost building except for us."

Price had talked a long time in what was a candid and sometimes therapeutic conversation. He apologized for having to leave. The longtime reporter was running late for the wake of a dear friend.

In February 2020, Price also left the paper. He became digital managing editor for KGET-TV (Channel 17) in Bakersfield. He continues to freelance a Sunday column for the *Californian*.

—

Imagine the unenviable task of having family meetings with your in-laws on a daily basis.

That's one way Mike Plunkett could have looked at his role as the managing editor and then-publisher of the *Journal-News* in Hillsboro, Illinois. He took a higher road. Plunkett is the only non–family member in the *Journal-News* management. Even sports editor Kyle Herschelman is married to John and Susie Galer's daughter, Mary.

"It was challenging," Plunkett said in a conversation at the Black Rabbit coffee shop on Hillsboro's Main Street. "I grew up in a family business. I grew up with someone who got customer service. The Galer family is like that. At the beginning, the editorial team was John, his mom and dad. Susie was doing bookkeeping from home. The editorial meetings would be the four of us. At first I was apprehensive. But they always made me feel like a member of the family."

Plunkett has been with the *Journal-News* since October 1, 1990. In 2015, he was named Master Editor at the Southern Illinois Editorial Association annual meeting, and he has won several IPA (Illinois Press Association) awards for editorials and nutty headlines such as "Bitter Buzzer Beater Beats Big Red" and "Lance and Vance Enhance Lancers, Chance to Advance."

He graduated from Hillsboro High School in 1983 and found a seasonal job at the Dairy Queen in Hillsboro. He worked at the ice cream stand while attending Lincoln Land Community College in Springfield. Plunkett's warm personality and facial resemblance to talk show host David Letterman made him a popular ice cream server. "Like every kid, it was 'When can I get out of here?'" he said. "I had that until I watched *American Graffiti* and there were kids growing up in Southern California—where I wanted to be—going, 'When can I get out of here?' It must be youth and not the place."

Throughout much of my newspaper career, I enjoyed the company of drinkers, rounders, and roustabouts. A couple of them were even my bosses. Mike Plunkett, by contrast, teaches Sunday school at St. Paul's Lutheran Church in Hillsboro and is president of the Hillsboro Table Tennis Association. "My lifelong guilty hobby is table tennis," he confessed. "That's about the only times I've been to Chicago. When I was younger and had more time, I'd go up there for tournaments. When we go to the 'city,' it's St. Louis."

His father, Cleveland Plunkett, ran an insurance agency in Hillsboro. Mike, who was born in Springfield and adopted through DCFS (Department of Children and Family Services) into the Plunkett family with his sister, was born in 1965. "Growing up in our family, we never had the discussion of where babies come from," he said with a smile. "We knew. You went to Springfield and picked them up."

Mike and his wife, Heather, have a son, August, who is named after Cleveland's father. August was seventeen in the summer of 2019. "My dad will drop what he's doing to spend time with August," Mike said. "I think he's making up for not having time when I was growing up." Mike met Heather when they attended Millikin University in nearby Decatur. He was an English minor. She was an English major. Heather is from Illiopolis (pop. 891), between Springfield and Decatur. Of course, after they were married in 1998, Heather worked at the *Journal-News*.

She moved to Hillsboro as a teacher's aide but quickly became a copy editor and proofreader. Mike said, "I always told people if you want to know the definition of humility, work at a job where your wife's job is to find your mistakes. When we worked together we sat at desks and faced each other, so we were never far apart. When we had our son we decided it was important for someone to be home. We came to John with the idea that Heather would do proofreading part time from home. We did that for six years until he was school age. We probably would have not had a kid if they said we couldn't do that.

"It's always been family first with the Galer family."

Galer's daughter, editor Mary Herschelman, has a desk directly next to

Mike's. She remembers the spot as the pivot point for meeting her future husband, Kyle. "It was a Sunday paper night," she said. "I don't remember what I had on. I wore my glasses. Even on a Wednesday paper night, I might have jeans and a nice shirt. But on a Sunday paper night, I don't come in until four. Kyle worked at a bank in Springfield, so he couldn't come in during the day. He agreed to come in on Sunday night to be interviewed. His brother at the time was a freshman playing baseball for Lincolnwood. [Kyle] volunteered to write baseball for us."

The volunteer gig evolved into a job offer.

"My first thought was, well, he works for a bank and we're not a high-paid place to work," Mary said. "But it is something he really enjoys. I was not part of the interview process. I was sitting at my desk. After Kyle left, Mike Plunkett walked by my desk and said, 'I like him so much I think you should marry him.' He really did. I didn't even know Kyle. We started covering football together. We started talking. It took a while. We have a very similar work ethic. Very similar family values." Kyle started at the *Journal-News* in 2007, and he married Mary in February 2009.

Mary understands the pros and cons of a family newspaper.

"My mom would tell you she never wanted her kids to do this," she said. "Because she knows it is a challenge at times, although the lessons they've instilled in us carry over to so many things. You get out of something what you put into it. Or you make the best of something. If there's a dinner to be covered, my folks will watch our kids and my husband and I will go on a date night. The things we can cover when we can take our girls, we do, and we make it a family thing. I'm lucky that my husband shares some of the same values and, as someone who hasn't grown up in a family business, kind of understands. When we hired him, I was shooting Litchfield football every Friday night. And one of his responsibilities was to write Litchfield football. So the paper wouldn't have to pay mileage twice, we rode together."

Litchfield, by the way, is nine miles from Hillsboro.

"This is all such an interesting question," she said. "I never thought this is what I was going to do. It is what my folks did. I'm not sure I ever stopped to think about what my parents did and the kind of impact they made. The biggest pros to me now are making a difference in our community. The things that scare me are when places buy out longtime family newspapers. Because unless you have somebody from your family move home that has an interest in doing it, what are you going to do? As family-owned newspapers go by the wayside, who is covering those communities? It is so important. Someone has to be at government meetings and hold people accountable."

In many cases, it's not just the family-owned newspaper that is central to the community—it's the family itself. Such is the case in Hillsboro. Plunkett said, "My wife came here from Illiopolis, another small town, and she said it was different here. The health issue in John's family with his granddaughter [Grace]—they raised a quarter of a million dollars. How do you raise $250,000 in a county of thirty thousand people and a town of four thousand? And that's just one family. There's others."

The January 9, 2016, issue of the *State Journal-Register* in Springfield, Illinois, featured a story with the headline "Grace is among good people of Montgomery County." The story was about Mary and Kyle's daughter Grace Herschelman, who was four at the time and had been diagnosed with INAD (infantile neuroaxonal dystrophy). The paper reported she was one of thirty to forty children worldwide to be diagnosed with the genetic disorder. There is no cure for INAD.

"Our community has a great sense of community," Mary said. "It is heartbreaking for me to see so many community newspapers not being able to sustain themselves. I'm very grateful my folks put a lot of stock into what we do. On the flip side, I move home with my dog. I get married. I have two daughters [Charlotte and Grace]. I find out Grace has a terminal illness. And suddenly I'm on the other side. I'm on the other side of this great community and it's unbelievable."

Mary explained Grace's condition in slow, empathetic tones. "In layman's terms, everyone has two copies of genes. One from our mom and one from our dad. Somewhere along the way, Kyle and I each got one good copy and one bad copy. As genetics sometimes happens, we both passed a bad copy to Grace. So there's a gene in Grace that doesn't work. That gene is responsible for breaking down toxins and things. Because it doesn't, they build up on her nerves. It causes iron to accumulate in her brain. It affects her sight. She loses her functions. Respiratory issues are a big thing. Most kids with INAD live to be about ten. I know families where kids have lived longer than that. I know families who have lost them when they are three or four.

"The support we have been given is . . . the outpouring . . ." Mary stopped for a moment. She and Kyle took Grace to Springfield every Friday for physical therapy. Kyle wrote a *Journal-News* column about his daughter, and Mary created a *Grace Filled Journey* blog. She said, "Much like we went with our parents, Grace went everywhere with us. She went to sporting events with her dad. She still does when she's able. They held her up to dunk a basketball. I knew the community support was there. I had written those stories. I had just never been on the other side."

It is easy for journalists to identify themselves with their job. I did it when I was younger. It is not a healthy thing to do. Grace's challenges taught Mary a balance between real life and family business. "Balance is really tricky," she said. "I'm lucky I'm married to the sports editor, so I'm married to someone who understands that when I have a meeting to cover, he will be home with the girls. If the meeting is in the same town as one of the basketball games, I may shoot some of the game on my way home. Grace being diagnosed with INAD taught us a lot. We both did kind of identify with our jobs, especially since we did the same thing. Shortly after Grace was diagnosed, I stepped back to part time, although I probably still work forty hours a week."

Mary said her family now has a deeper appreciation for the finite boundaries of life. She reflected, "I'm not sure which is more challenging: to lose a child in a car crash—to see that child in the morning, send them off, and not see them again—or to be in the position we are. We understand that our days with Grace may be numbered. Anything can happen to any of us tomorrow. It helps us focus on what matters. I'm not sure she can see very well anymore or hear very well anymore. She loved going to basketball and volleyball games. She's always been in the gym somewhere with Kyle covering games."

Grace Louise Herschelman died on May 19, 2021. She was nine years old.

"Losing a child that young who is the daughter of our editor and sports editor, as well as the granddaughter of our owners, is something that we continue to deal with," Plunkett said in August 2021. "Of course our newspaper is family. Her journey with INAD was also a public one, and the community has been very supportive. The day of her passing, a small shrine with flowers, stuffed animals, and other memorabilia began appearing on the sidewalk in front of our office. It's amazing how one little girl—who spoke just a handful of words her entire life—touched her community."

Her parents were surprised at the outpouring of sympathy. Mary said, "Someone put a huge picture of her up on the front window of our office. I was surprised at the memorial outside of the newspaper. People here take care of one another and look out for one another. Grace was very well loved by her community in her lifetime."

—

Plunkett has always used community as a point of identification in hiring journalists. He used to find reporter candidates through the Illinois Press Association. "We'd get people who wanted a lot of money and a line on their résumé," he said. "We finally decided, 'Let's look for people who love the community and who we can teach to write.'"

A writer named Tori O'Dell was one of those people.

O'Dell was involved in the community group Imagine Hillsboro. "Tori had two children. One is autistic," Plunkett said. "She started blogging about that. It was very good writing. She fit the mold. She loves the community; she had writing talent. That's been our model for hiring people."

O'Dell grew up in Coffeen, about eight miles from Hillsboro. She lived in Coffeen until she was fourteen, then moved to be with her grandparents in Sarasota, Florida, because of an abusive home life in Illinois. She graduated high school in Sarasota in 2005 and moved back to the Hillsboro area in 2008. She lives with her husband, Corey, and their two sons in Panama (pop. 343), an old coal mining town about two miles from Hillsboro.

"Mary [Herschelman] and I had known each other through our kids," O'Dell said. Her son and Herschelman's daughter both went to Teamwork Rehab, the pediatric therapy department at Hillsboro Area Hospital. "They were looking for a reporter. I had stopped working to stay at home with our oldest son when we found out he had autism. They offered me a job with a lot of flexibility, and I was able to work with someone else who understood what it is like to be a special-needs mom. I was motivated by that. I didn't think of myself as a journalist. To be honest, I took the job because I wanted to be better friends with Mary." O'Dell laughed. "It has really honed my skills as a writer, to learn some of those style things. Mike [Plunkett] is a great teacher."

In the June 15, 2020, issue of the *Journal-News*, O'Dell wrote an outstanding piece called "A Column Written to Myself." She composed it a few days after her thirty-third birthday and after George Floyd's death in Minneapolis. O'Dell is biracial, and the catalyst for the column was her decision to revert to her natural hairstyle. She recalled being teased on the playground for her curly, frizzy hair and hand-me-down clothes. She eloquently wrote that she was tired of straightening her curls and "erasing the biggest tell of lineage—my otherness."

O'Dell wrote, "Patient does not mean quiet, and God became louder still. I started noticing the ways that hiding myself kept me from showing up, and how the deeply rooted belief of my own inferiority caused me to self-sabotage—how because I unconsciously didn't believe that I deserved a seat at the table, that I was there under the ruse of being something that I am not, I wasn't really showing up."

That's honest, big-city journalism in a small town.

"It wasn't easy to publish," said O'Dell, who was hired by Plunkett in 2018. "I didn't hand it in until three p.m. [on] our press day, which is very late. It was hard for me to let that go because most people around you might not want to hear it. But you realize the things that hold you back aren't very real. The response was very positive. I try not to read anything [after] I write it. I gotta put it out there and move to the next page."

Her husband, Corey, is an area electrician. Their kids were four and five years old in the summer of 2020. Corey and Tori made the decision to stay in the Hillsboro area because of the desire to have strong family and community support systems. *Journal-News* owner John Galer said, "Unless one of our reporters came from a small town, they're not going to be happy here. We've tried to build our own. Partly out of economic necessity and partly for stability and operation. People are going to be residents here and you will keep them for a while. It takes a while to train people to do what we want to do here. We try to hang on to them if we can."

Even Plunkett left his beloved newspaper for two weeks in 1998. He was on the verge of getting married, and he thought that the demands of the newspaper business might not be the most prudent path to follow when starting a family. He went to work for the Illinois State Senate Democrats. "I was told journalists have their advantages, but sometimes they're a bit too idealistic," he said. "They were right. I wasn't enjoying it. John [Galer] was killing himself at the paper. He welcomed me back. But the big question in front of the General Assembly in 1998 was, 'What are we going to do with the budget surplus?' There was a Chicago senator having trouble getting funding for radon [testing]. His chief of staff asked me to write a column presenting his case. I wrote it and he said, 'You got to come over and meet this senator, he's exceptional.' I took it over, he read it and said, 'It's about time we had a writer on this staff.'

"It was State Senator Barack Obama."

Galer likes to talk about local children taking newspaper tours that include the dark and gritty press room. The newspaper staff takes pictures of the kids at the press. "We make a mock-up of the front page," he said. "And put their story on the front page about visiting the *Journal*. Then they get it as a souvenir."

Hillsboro High School used to have a student newspaper called the *Hilltop Preface*. It ceased publication in the 1990s. "They didn't have as many kids interested in the newspaper as they used to have," Galer said. "The staff came here, and we let them have the run of the place. I'd just run the press for them. None of their things were very heavily edited. This was in the mid- to late 1970s. They didn't always go through the superintendent. The one I always remember was that two kids did a story on teenage marriage. They were Catholic and went to the priest to go through all the premarital stuff. They got wedding gowns and everything. But they weren't going to get married. They wrote this big story, and when it came out the priest was upset, but there really wasn't anything bad in the story."

A small-town, multigenerational newspaper is a performance in patience. Editors and publishers have seen it all, and they know many of the characters. The community's joys, heartbreaks, and even high school newspaper hijinks are handled with care. Empathy plays a role in their news-gathering process. When there is no corporate pressure from above, the heart on the street beats stronger.

Chapter 7

Seeds of Change

The ability to stay the course with a community newspaper can change the world. Some of these newspapers value inclusion and progressive thinking because they had no other options. There simply weren't papers in their communities that represented these views. Their bold voices led them to create more than legacy publications. They became leaders for the communities they serve.

The *Miami Times* is a polished weekly broadsheet that was launched in 1923. Its founder was Henry Ethelbert Sigismund Reeves (1882–1970), an immigrant from Nassau, the Bahamas. Henry first printed the *Times* on a small hand press in his home. In 1970, he was succeeded by his son, Garth C. (Coleridge) Reeves, who was also born in Nassau.

During his time at the paper, Garth C. Reeves wrote editorials that helped desegregate Miami's public golf courses and beaches. The *Times* grew into one of the city's oldest Black-owned businesses. Reeves also purchased the historic Evergreen Park Cemetery, a resting place for many of Miami's Black pioneers.

In 1980, Reeves bequeathed the paper to his son, Garth Reeves Jr.. But two years later, Garth Jr. died of colon cancer at age thirty. Garth Sr. returned to the newspaper until turning the *Times* over to his daughter, Rachel J. Reeves III. She died at age sixty-nine in September 2019. Garth C. Reeves died in November 2019 at the age of one hundred.

Garth Basil Reeves III is the only survivor in the family. He is Rachel's son and current publisher of the *Times*. Reeves became the fourth generation of the family to guide the paper.

He was just thirty years old in late 2019 when he lost his mother and grandfather in the span of three months. He found the family legacy daunting, but also realized the meaning of his product in today's world.

"Big shoes to follow," Reeves said in a January 2020 interview. "Very big shoes. But I'm coming up in a different age. We have a lot of the same problems, but we have a new set of challenges. We have no shortage of content. Our community is always bringing up new opportunities for coverage, new issues that are brought to life. We continue to play an important role like we did twenty, fifty, and seventy years ago. And without the support of our community, there's no way we would still be selling newspapers and have ads on the pages. Especially at the rate that newspapers are closing up these days."

Reeves likes to tell the story about how his grandfather told him he was destined to play a role in his community. He was never presented with career options as a child. Reeves recalled, "My mother never bothered saying, 'You can be a fireman.' 'You can be the president.' It was, 'You're going to be a newspaper publisher.' It helped growing up in the business. I learned to like it. Don't get me wrong, there are things about the business I find frustrating. But for the large part I like what we do at the *Miami Times*. I'm happy with it. And I do plan to keep it going. We operate a profitable business. I'd be foolish to walk away from that. And I'd be very concerned if we went away, what might happen." Such devotion to community is what connects Miami, Florida, with Hillsboro and Dixon, Illinois.

Garth C. Reeves studied printing at Florida A&M University. After college he wanted to stay on that path because the struggling *Times* was being subsidized by its printing operation. Garth C. Reeves was outgoing and "could be loud," according to his grandson. "He liked to put himself out there in the community," he said. "Which is what made him such a great leader and allowed him to accomplish so much for civil rights in Miami. At the same time, we're talking about a different generation and a different political climate." His grandfather served in the army during World War II. When his ship returned from the war, Garth C. Reeves was not permitted to disembark with white soldiers. He had to use a separate gangplank.

"My mother took over and as she started stepping away, I started taking over the day-to-day," Reeves said. He paused to collect his thoughts, which tumbled from the losses of recent months. He continued, "Okay, my mother and I are more the quiet, stay in the office, use the power of the paper, write editorials to get our point across. It was a different approach from my grandfather. We've been very successful in bringing change and improvements to our community, we just had different methods of going about it. I still believe our editorial page can be a real game changer for policy and perspective that people have on issues that are facing our community."

There are a multitude of challenges to keep any American newspaper alive. The *Miami Times* is a component of an eclectic melting pot of a new America. According to the 2015 American Community Survey, the makeup of Broward County in Miami was 62 percent white, 17 percent Hispanic of any race, 12 percent Black or African American, and 5 percent Asian.

Mohamed Hamaludin was managing editor of the *Miami Times* between 1985 and 1999. The elder Reeves hired him as a reporter in May 1984. Hamaludin had been working for *Caribbean Life & Times*, a monthly news magazine based in Miami. Before that he had been a correspondent for the Caribbean News Agency (based in Barbados) and deputy news editor for Guyana National Newspapers in his native Guyana. As a reporter for the Caribbean News Agency, Hamaludin was one of the first reporters to enter the commune after the deaths at the 1978 Jonestown Massacre in northwest Guyana.

"I had read the story of Garth and his son in what was then the *Miami News*," Hamaludin said. "And how it was going into the third generation. Then I learned his son died at age thirty. I applied at the *Miami Herald*, the *Miami News*, television, and everything. Garth responded. He hired me on the spot. He read my résumé, which even though I was from a small country, it was the kind of operation that paralleled what a community newspaper does. It is a minority country made up of Guyanese of African descent and Indian descent. Maybe most importantly, he didn't have an editor. His then-son-in-law, Miles Johnson, was running the operation. I went to the morgue and collected a year's supply of the *Miami Times* and made notes about some of the people who were making the news and the issues in the community. When

Miles left [in 1986] I was promoted to managing editor."

Reeves said that operating a Black newspaper in South Florida is incredibly difficult. "We have a largely Hispanic population, which as a result, a lot of governments in city and county have Hispanic leadership," he explained. "Many advertising agencies in town are Hispanic. From the advertising standpoint, people don't think 'Black' in South Florida. That makes it challenging for us, when advertising dollars are coming in and the vast majority is going to Hispanic and mainstream. There's nothing left for the Black community. That's something that people don't quite realize.

"The Black community is spread out throughout South Florida, which is actually quite nice. It's not necessarily tied together in one location. We're not all on top of each other. That's always made distribution a challenge. We go almost down to the Keys and well into Fort Lauderdale. And, if you are reading the *Miami Times*, you will never see, unless it is in a quote, the words 'African American.' We always use 'Black' because we have Haitians, we have Jamaicans, we have Afro-Cubans, we have Bahamians. But what we all share is our Blackness, our skin color. It's very important to unify us as a group, as opposed to breaking us down into smaller sections. That just makes it more difficult for us to accomplish important tasks that are beneficial to the community as a whole. The *Miami Times* is busier than ever. I wish we could have more reporters and writers on staff."

In January 2020, Reeves said the *Times* had thirteen full-time employees that included four in editorial. He said circulation fluctuates. "It depends on the time of year," Reeves said. "If we have our Newspaper in Education program going, circulation is anywhere from seventeen thousand to twenty-three thousand.

"One thing that separates us from a lot of the Black newspapers is that we have a building that we own," he continued. "Our headquarters. Other newspapers may be operating out of garages or storefronts. We provide our community with a place where they can come and bring their news. We're doing a $1.3 million renovation to our office right now. Our headquarters are a point of pride in our community. It gives us a sense of place."

The *Miami Times* is based in a historic Alfred Browning Parker mid-century building in the Liberty City neighborhood of Miami. There were once more than one thousand Parker-designed buildings in South Florida. According to a September 2016 article in the *Miami New Times*, there are less than one hundred left. (Parker designed the Miami Arena, the former home of the NBA's Miami Heat that was razed in 2008.) Liberty City is also home to one of the largest concentrations of Black residents in South Florida. Muhammad Ali had a home in Liberty City in 1964 when he defeated heavyweight world champion Sonny Liston in Miami Beach, and when Dr. Martin Luther King Jr. couldn't venture into places like Miami Beach, he stayed at the Hampton House Motel and Villas in Brownsville, adjacent to Liberty City.

The year 1980 changed the course of Miami's landscape. More than one hundred thousand Cubans immigrated to Miami during the Mariel boatlift. Refugee camps were established at decommissioned missile defense sites and the since-razed Orange Bowl, less than four miles from Liberty City. That same year, Liberty City burned in some of the most intense race riots in Florida's history following the acquittal of four Dade County Public Safety Department officers in the death of Arthur McDuffie, a Black former Marine. The four white officers had attempted to arrest McDuffie after a high-speed chase with him on his motorcycle. Property destruction after the acquittal was in the excess of $100 million. More than 600 people were arrested throughout Miami, 350 people were injured, and 18 people lost their lives.

Liberty City was Reeves's neighborhood. It was also his window to the world. "If I ever wanted to see my mother, from a young age I would need to be at the *Miami Times*," he said. "Because she was always there. When I'd get home from school, she might not get home until one, two, or three in the morning. I wanted to spend time with my mother, so I started going to the *Miami Times* after school. That's when my education began in the newspaper business, watching my mother work. It was exciting. They were still cutting and pasting the newspaper together with glue. The X-Acto knives and the grease pencils. Thinking back now on how technology has changed and the size of computers back then—it's shocking. For a Black newspaper, we had a pretty technology-savvy operation. But we've come a long way. And at a young age there were areas I was able to help in. It was a wonderful experience."

Reeves was coming of age during the mid- to late 1990s in the *Times* newspaper office. He kept his eyes as open as his mind. "Sometimes when you have an established newspaper, we get accustomed to doing things a certain way," he said. "Innovation is not necessarily the first thing that comes to mind. I was always around in the afternoons, and I would observe issues they were having. It might be technical things. I would ask staff members, 'Have you heard of X, Y, Z?' I was there when the newspaper transitioned to digital, which was exciting."

The *Miami Times* was an early adopter of Adobe InDesign (typesetting software) because Reeves had learned about the program while working on the yearbook staff at Miami Country Day School, a private high school just north of Miami. "There were many things I was able to chime in on that the older generation might not have been up to date on."

It was unusual for his high school peer group to be hanging with a budding newspaper publisher. Reeves has maintained the same group of friends for a very long time, many back to the second grade. "As long as they've known me or my family, they've known we're in the newspaper business," he said. "When I got to Miami Country Day, I'd take the newspaper with me every morning to homeroom. I read the business section of the [*Miami*] *Herald* every morning. That was startling to a lot of my classmates. Not because they were reading newspapers digitally but because I was reading news in general. I went to private schools in Miami. The number of Black friends I had were limited, unfortunately. Which actually is another reason why I valued my time going to the *Miami Times*. It was able to give me the balance I needed from the white, privileged, private school thing, then going to Liberty City and the *Miami Times*, where it was very Black, largely middle- to lower-income families. It helped give me a better understanding of the world.

"I would not have turned out the way I did."

A love of newspapers was in the family's DNA. Reeves said his grandfather read four newspapers a day. "He was one of the most informed individuals that I knew," Reeves said. "It made him quite savvy. At least when I was around him, he never made dark comparisons about fifty, sixty years ago. We were always talking about the latest happenings and the latest news. We always felt up to date [on] how the community was evolving, be it for better or worse. He loved Miami. He was proud to call it home. He was pleased to see how it had progressed. Certainly we would have liked to have seen more Black businesses, more opportunities for Blacks to advance themselves. But we're headed in the right direction as a community, and I think he recognized that."

Garth C. Reeves was able to attend his daughter's funeral. "He was one hundred years old," Mohamed Hamaludin said. "She was ailing for some time, so her death was not unexpected. He was very frail. He entered the church on his own and walked all the way up to the front by himself. He didn't want anybody to help him. He stayed at the service. He came out of the church by himself and stood in the parking lot. I gave him a hug and he said, 'Thank you for coming.'"

Garth C. Reeves lived long enough to receive accolades for all the chances he took in his remarkable life. In 2017, at the age of ninety-eight, Reeves was inducted into the National Association of Black Journalists Hall of Fame at their annual convention in New Orleans. Carolyn Guniss, a former executive editor of the *Miami Times*, was president of the South Florida Black Journalists Association. She told the *Miami Herald* that Reeves was sometimes criticized when his Black-owned paper depended on advertising from companies without minority ownership. "By doing that, he could've made economic disaster for himself," she said. "It's that sort of fearlessness that I don't know if we talk about enough with people of color."

Garth Basil Reeves III attended the conventions of the National Newspaper Publishers Association (NNPA) with his mother and his grandfather. He was always surprised at the absence of young people at the event that connected nearly two hundred Black newspapers across the United States. "I knew the other publishers had children," he said. "But I didn't know why they weren't pushing them more to be involved in the business. I thought it was a misstep not to encourage their participation. There needs to be generational planning. People start to die, retire. The question becomes, 'Where do we go from here?' For me, it was pretty seamless."

Reeves's mother told him that it was important to pay attention to other Black newspapers in America. Reeves said roughly forty different Black newspapers are delivered to the *Miami Times* office every week. "Sometimes you don't need to reinvent the wheel," he said. "And Black newspapers have lifted their fair share of good ideas from the *Miami Times*. But if we see something that we like and we believe we could adapt to our market, we will use that—

while also keeping in mind that our market is very different than a lot of other markets that Black newspapers are in. We produce an excellent newspaper, and if we had a market like Atlanta, we would be killing it. But we've done pretty well carving out our little space in South Florida."

—

The family tree of the *Chicago Defender* also cast seeds of progress across America.

In 1905, Robert S. Abbott founded the newspaper for Black American readers. After Abbott's death, his nephew John Sengstacke took over the *Defender* in 1940. That same year, Sengstacke also established the National Newspaper Publishers Association, then called the National Negro Publishers Association. The *Chicago Defender* became a compass for the Great Migration, writing about community and the promise of job opportunities in the North. Abbott biographer Roi Ottley wrote that only the Bible was more essential to Black Americans during the first half of the twentieth century.

Sengstacke founded the *Tri-State Defender* in Memphis, Tennessee, in 1951. The Sengstacke family saw the Memphis area as a wide-open market for Black American readers. The only competitor was the *Memphis World* (1931–1973). The *World* pledged that its content would provide "news of interest to the race" and "clean and interest-demanding features."

The *Tri-State Defender* (Tennessee, Mississippi, Arkansas) reported on the civil rights movement from the front lines. It included coverage of the 1955 murder of Emmett Till, the Chicagoan who was killed near Drew, Mississippi, after being accused of flirting with a white woman.

Tri-State Defender reporter L. Alex Wilson was part of the search party through Mississippi plantations looking for witnesses. He joined former *Tri-State Defender* reporter Moses Newson, who wrote about covering the Till case in a January 2003 edition of the *Afro-American Red Star* in Washington, DC. Newson broke into journalism in 1952 at the *Tri-State Defender*. In 2014 he was inducted into the National Association of Black Journalists Hall of Fame.

According to Ethan Michaeli's comprehensive 2016 book, *The Defender: How the Legendary Black Newspaper Changed America*, the flagship *Chicago Defender* dispatched a photographer and reporter to the Illinois Central Railroad Station when Till's body was shipped back to Chicago for his open-casket funeral. Several pages of impactful pictures and reporting on the Till death and funeral followed in the *Defender* about a week after the September 3, 1955, funeral.

From 1951 to 2001, the *Tri-State Defender* was part of Sengstacke Enterprises, Inc., a chain of Black American publications that included the *Chicago Defender*, the *Michigan Chronicle*, and the *New Pittsburgh Courier*. The *Defender* replayed stories in all their papers. The *Tri-State Defender*'s first office was in an older house next to the Black-owned Universal Life Insurance building on what is now the corner of Dr. Martin Luther King Boulevard and Danny Thomas Boulevard. In the 1970s the newspaper moved downtown.

Ethel Sengstacke, niece of John Sengstacke, still lives in Memphis. Ethel was a photographer at the *Tri-State Defender* before embarking on a long television career in Memphis. She was the first Black American woman to be a newspaper photographer in the state of Tennessee. Ethel maintains a no-nonsense demeanor and looks visitors in the eye. She was happily retired at age sixty-seven in November 2019. Ethel shared warm memories of growing up during the late 1950s and early 1960s around the *Defender* on the South Side of Chicago.

"There were two uncles: Uncle John and Uncle Fred," she said in a conversation at the Cafe Eclectic coffee shop in Midtown Memphis. "My father was head of classified ads. Uncle John was head of the paper. I didn't know titles. Uncle Fred had an office there also. It was happy times. My cousins and I ran around the office. It was a daily newspaper. Typewriters everywhere. Deadlines. I guess that's why I made it so well in television because I was used to deadlines. I was little, but it was kind of cool. The *Chicago Defender* was the biggest building on the block. It was an industrial neighborhood, not residential."

Was journalism her destiny?

"The thing about me was that my uncle transferred my father to Memphis," she said. Her father, Whittier Alexander Sengstacke (1916–1996), moved his family from Chicago to Memphis in 1959 when he became general manager of the *Tri-State Defender*. Ethel said, "I started there as a filing clerk. Then I said, 'I want to be a photographer.' My ex-husband knew photography. I knew other photographers. And I became a photographer for the *Tri-State*

Defender right out of high school in 1971." Ethel attended the since-closed Father Bertrand High School in Memphis. "I was young, but I knew the *Defender* did community things. In the Black community, it was social news, what was going on in the NAACP, the Urban League, and all of that."

Some of Ethel's family peer group is gone. All three of her uncle John's sons have passed away. Her brother, former *Tri-State Defender* editor Whittier Sengstacke Jr., died in February 2021 at the age of seventy-six. After the Emmet Till lynching, the newspaper continued to report on other lynchings in the Mid-South. The local printer would refuse to print the *Tri-State Defender* because of its consistent coverage of the lynchings, so Whittier Jr. flew to Chicago to have the newspaper printed at the *Defender*. Ethel's other brother and sister were still alive in 2021.

Wiley Henry is an award-winning Black journalist and lifelong Memphian. He sat across the coffee table from Ethel as the former deputy editor of what is now called the *New Tri-State Defender*. He wore a dapper blue and gray argyle sweater and a polka-dot print shirt. Henry said, "The *Tri-State* covered stories that mainstream newspapers wouldn't cover. We knew what was going on in the community. It wasn't all shootings. We focused on events that were positive in the Black community. There were socialites. Sports figures and college students who were doing great things in the community. They wouldn't get coverage in a mainstream newspaper.

"Our newspaper was in touch with all the neighborhoods. We knew the heads of the organizations, and that's why we were able to do as well as we did. By having all those people in place, that represents the totality of community. I've always been interested in community because I came out of a poor community. North Memphis. It's now run down. Dilapidated homes. Lots of crime."

After John Sengstacke died in 1997, the four-paper Sengstacke chain was held in a family trust until 2003, when it was sold for nearly $12 million to Real Times Media, a group of investors with business ties to Sengstacke. The *New Tri-State Defender* was purchased in 2013 from Real Times by Best Media Properties, Inc., in Memphis. In 2019, Real Times ceased printing the *Chicago Defender*, making it an online-only newspaper.

The *New Tri-State Defender* is a weekly print publication with the creed

"Information. Inspiration. Elevation" under its front-page nameplate. It's headquartered on the tiny second floor of a building across the street from Handy Park on Beale Street near downtown Memphis. "People can't find it," Henry said. "People used to walk in because they were friends of the newspaper. They would walk in and chat with us because it was home."

For the first time in more than fifty years, there's no Sengstacke name involved with the *Tri-State Defender*.

"My best friend, Linda Sengstacke, who married my brother, became the editor," Ethel said. "We worked together. My cousin [Thomas Maurice Sengstacke Picou] came down from Chicago and became general manager. Linda and I also worked for him." Picou later led the effort to assemble the Real Times investors.

Linda Sengstacke died in September 2019 at the age of sixty-seven. She had been editor-in-chief of the *Tri-State Defender* during the late 1970s and '80s. She was the first female editor of the newspaper. "She was fearless," Ethel said. "She sought the truth."

Ethel didn't feel any emotional sting when the *Tri-State Defender* was sold in 2013. "I wasn't involved in it," she said. "And my uncle [John] had died. Tommy was the inspiration to all of us. When he got Real Times, his goal was to sell it so we could all make money. I didn't want to be known as 'Ethel Sengstacke of the Sengstacke family.' I wanted to make my own way. My family tried to control me and tell me what I should and shouldn't do. My mother was, 'You need to do the family tradition.' But I didn't want to do that. Everywhere I went, it was 'Can you do this, can you do that?' I got burned out." Her brother Fred suggested she move into television.

In 1975, Ethel left the *Tri-State Defender* to become a projectionist at WREG-TV, the CBS affiliate in Memphis. She worked her way up to senior production manager and assignment editor. "I also had to fight there," she said. "They weren't used to a woman. I worked just as hard as the guys did. Eventually I moved up the ranks and made my own reputation. Fred also broke away from the family and went into news photography."

Ethel said she does not read the *New Tri-State Defender* or the Gannett-owned Memphis *Commercial Appeal* on a regular basis. "I read newspapers online," she said. "Things change. You have to go with it. The good thing was that the way I was brought up, because of the newspaper, whenever I saw injustice, I had to say something. And I had to get involved. I was class president in high school."

Ethel covered many civil rights events in Memphis.

"I can't remember the event, but I got to one early," she said. "I was standing on stage, and here comes CBS and ABC and it's 'Get her off stage.' I'd say, 'You move, I was here first.' I had to fight with a lot of people because I was a female. I always tried to get the photograph that nobody else had. I thrived as assignment editor. I covered everything. News is not all bad." In 2007, Ethel joined Fox13 in Memphis as operations manager and became assignment editor. She returned to WREG for a short stint and retired for good in 2018.

Wiley Henry remained close to the roots of the tree. He started with the *Tri-State Defender* in 1984 as a part-time layout artist and worked in various capacities with the newspaper over the next thirty years. "The *Tri-State Defender* advocated for the Black community," he explained. "Our editorials were about racism. How Black people were being treated. We shed light on atrocities in the Black community. And we wanted to bring it out. But we wanted to elevate the Black community. We told our own story because we knew the mainstream media wouldn't tell the story right."

The *Tri-State Defender* newspaper circulation was often inflated. "In the Black community the newspaper circulates four or five times," Henry said. Ethel pointed out, "That's how they gathered their numbers. In the 1970s and '80s I would guess the circulation was between thirty thousand and forty thousand."

Henry added, "Another thing about the Black press is that anybody could write if you knew how to write. You didn't have to have a degree. The *Defender* was a training ground for young journalists. A lot of young people didn't have the opportunity to go to college, so they started with the *Defender* and worked their way up. We learned so much more than just writing. My degree is in advertising design, but it was Thommy Picou who recognized my writing skills." Henry's first byline was a 1993 front-page *Tri-State Defender* story on a Napoleon Bonaparte exhibition in Memphis.

The *Tri-State Defender*'s commitment to community was tested during the April 1968 Memphis Sanitation Workers' Strike that brought Dr. King to town, where he ultimately met his death. "They didn't miss a beat as far as covering those stories," Ethel said. "And the mainstream newspapers didn't have minorities in the newsroom. After the [1968] riots and after Martin Luther King's death, then they had to hire minorities. They couldn't send white reporters and white photographers into Black communities."

Henry said, "It got to the point some of the mainstream newspapers saw what we were doing, and they started covering some of our community. But we knew what was going on."

At the *Miami Times*, Reeves said, "We've had three different perspectives. My grandfather was pretty adamant about hiring Black people. Almost exclusively. And while he was in charge, that's largely what took place. When my mother took over and as I became more involved and we were looking at our staffing needs, sometimes the Black candidates weren't always the best candidates for the positions we had open. It didn't make sense for us to weaken our product by hiring employees that weren't going to be as qualified just because they were Black. As a result, our office has changed in diversity. The community is very Hispanic, so it wasn't uncommon for us to have one or two Hispanics on staff. A white person has come in and out. The majority of our staff was Black, but we couldn't deny a talented, qualified individual. If we could find a role for them, we wanted them on our team."

—

Eureka Springs, Arkansas, is diverse in every way except the color of skin, according to *Eureka Springs Independent* publisher Mary Pat Boian. "It feels Southern to me, but people from Louisiana will call us a 'Yankee,'" she said. "People know how to skin a deer. You don't find a lot of that outside of rural America. It is country-wise and arrogant PhDs. They know who you are and what you're doing—and are interested in it. They're smart, interesting, and funny. The smaller the town, the more intimate it is. And that's where you run into problems big newspapers don't have. They can separate editorial and advertising. And they should. And we should. But we can't. There's three of us and if the phone rings, one of us has to get it. And it is probably going to be about an ad or an editorial problem."

In one of her weekly columns, Boian wrote, "We don't have to be unkind to anyone unless we want to be." I asked her to elaborate. "Well, it's kind of like racism," she said. "We're not born racist. We learn it. And we learn it from racists. You can be kind."

Graphic artist Perlinda Pettigrew-Owens was born in Eureka Springs. She assembles the *Independent* with a warm and colorful eye. Her father was a machinist who grew up along the Kings River in northwest Arkansas. Her mother grew up across the state line in the mountains of Missouri. She was a homemaker who raised four children and also a bookkeeper for the family machine shop. She also taught in a one-room schoolhouse before Pettigrew-Owens was born.

Boian and Pettigrew-Owens guessed that outsiders looked at the idea of women starting a newspaper as unusual. "We didn't feel it," Boian said. "It might have been talked about."

Pettigrew-Owens added, "We didn't go into it thinking how we're going to be 'powerful women' and own a business. We just don't think about it. Then something happens where it's . . . they treated us that way because . . ." and her voice trailed off. Then she added, "They do. They wouldn't have done that to a man."

Boian continued, "It's a subliminal thing, a learned thing. I mean, how could you not like us? The community is like that. The school of the arts is run by a woman. The CAPC [City Advertising & Promotion Commission] is run by a woman. The community center is run by a woman. And the newspaper is run by women. A lot of professional women have brought their brainpower to town and they're making a living. It was more male when we started. Women could be editors.

"They weren't publishers."

Another journalist breaking the publishing mold is Tracy Baim. Her strong vision was formed while growing up in a three-story brick apartment building on the North Side of Chicago. Her parents were Chicago journalists. In her adult life, Baim became the founding managing editor of the *Windy City Times*, a Chicago weekly LGBTQ newspaper, and publisher of the *Chicago Reader*, one of the oldest alternative newspapers in America. The *Reader* started in 1971.

Baim had to make sense of the fast-paced news of the late 1960s and 1970s. "I put up a huge cardboard wall in the crawl space of where we lived," Baim said in a lengthy January 2020 interview in the *Reader* offices on the Near South Side of Chicago. She sized up an office wall, then guessed the wall in her childhood basement was at least eight feet tall and ten feet wide. "Anytime anybody brought a magazine or a newspaper in the house, I would cut the front-page banner," Baim said. "I had a wall of every font you could imagine. I just loved the physicalness of print. Every term paper I did, even in grammar school, was almost designed like a newspaper.

"I started a newsletter for my family at age ten that was designed like a newspaper. It had many different names, but one was *Tribune News Today*, 'TNT.' 'All the News I Could Fit, We'll Print,' or something. I absorbed from everything I was reading and reinterpreted it into my ten- or twelve-year-old lens. In college, when I wasn't sure I would be able to fulfill my path, that heart where you think you're going to be something, and everybody tells you because [of] who you are, you can't be it—and many generations of people of color and others have experienced this worse than me—it was devastating. Luckily, for me, my mom had created this weird, independent path for herself that I admired."

Baim's parents are deceased. Their imprint lives on in her work. Her mother was Joy Darrow, a white journalist who made a name at the Black-owned *Chicago Defender*. She was the *Defender*'s managing editor between 1973 and 1983 and had a section named "Joy" in her honor. Darrow was grandniece of iconic defense attorney Clarence Darrow. She interviewed Baseball Hall of Famer Hank Aaron early in his career and interviewed Fidel Castro in the mountains of Cuba before the revolution. Darrow died in 1996 at age sixty-three.

"She stumbled around," Baim said. "She worked with [architect-inventor] Buckminster Fuller. She worked with Dempsey Travis at the United Mortgage Brokers of America, redlining." Joy Darrow assisted Travis on his comprehensive 1981 book, *An Autobiography of Black Chicago*. Travis introduced her to John Sengstacke, and that's how Darrow started at the *Defender*. Baim said, "I know she was managing editor in 1973 because I had a kid's consumer column for her."

When Baim was ten years old she began writing "The Child Consumer" for the *Defender*. Here's a bit of her twelve-year-old critique of kids' toys that appeared in the February 27, 1975, issue of the *Defender*: "Many of the things advertised in magazine and comic books that try to get children to send away for are both plastic and breakable. They are often too small to be usable and they don't always do the things they're promised to do. One '7-foot monster' that is made to look like a really big and thick and plastic scary thing in the ads turns out to be a thin sheet of plastic that wouldn't scare my goldfish." Tracy Baim—a budding Ralph Nader, uncovering truth.

Baim said her mother left the *Defender* full time in the early 1980s but continued to freelance for the newspaper. She traveled with church groups monitoring elections. Darrow traveled to Cuba and South Africa multiple times, often writing political travel stories. "She was not a happy person," Baim said. "She was frustrated in her career. I've been lucky because I've stayed in one place for a long period of time—she never stayed in one place, mostly because she couldn't. Or they wouldn't allow her. The *Defender* was probably her longest stint. I felt she was pretty happy there. She was always reaching for something that maybe was unattainable for her and something few of her generation of women journalists could achieve."

Baim's stepfather was journalist Steven Pratt. After cutting his chops at Chicago's legendary City News Bureau, in 1968 Pratt joined the *Chicago Tribune*, where he met Darrow. Darrow eventually left the *Tribune*, Baim said, because "she wanted to cover hard news and they didn't want women to do that." Pratt worked on the newspaper's "Action Express" column in 1969 and 1970, and in 1985 was named editor of the *City Trib* insert. "When my mom died in 1996, he quit," Baim said. "At that point he was food editor." In 1996, Pratt won a James Beard Award for his three-part series, "America's Plate," on eating habits across the United States. After leaving the *Tribune*, Pratt moved to Key West, Florida, where he suffered a fatal heart attack. He was sixty years old.

Darrow was from Milwaukee and attended Marquette University there. She was gang-raped at a young age when she moved to Chicago. Baim did not know this until after a horrific 1978 invasion at the same home where she once pasted newspaper headlines in the crawl space. In a January 13, 2009, tribute to her mom, Baim wrote, "The men who attacked her were Black, as was the man who tried to attack me in our home, stabbing me, Steve, and Joy. So my mom finally opened up to me, only briefly and very cryptically, about her own experience. She wanted to make sure I did not allow that incident to drive my life, to turn me into a racist, or to cripple my dreams. . . .

"She pushed so hard for civil rights, cared so much about the rights of others, especially Asians, Cubans, South Africans, and African Americans, that I often feel it was a way to avoid the crushing defeats of her own life."

Baim, who was fifteen, was stabbed in the left thigh in the 1978 invasion. The perpetrator jammed the knife into Pratt twenty-seven times. Darrow suffered broken ribs. The man was apprehended and imprisoned. Baim was against the death penalty in 1978 and remains against the death penalty. These are the seeds of empathy and truth that were planted in Baim's young spirit.

Socially fueled journalism seemed to be her destiny.

Baim's mother wanted her to go to Northwestern University and stay close to home. "She wanted me to be a journalist, but Northwestern was the last place I wanted to go," Baim said. "Not only because it was close, but I would have never made it through Northwestern. The type of people, the type of school. I never would have fit in. And I would have hated it."

She chose Drake University, a private university in Des Moines, Iowa. Baim liked the midsized vibe of the school and the fact it was 340 miles from Chicago. Drake graduates include author Bill Bryson and former Iowa governor Robert D. Ray. "At the time it had a good reputation for a newspaper program," Baim said. "It was more Iowa-friendly. What Northwestern would have done to me could have been damaging. I was openly gay in college. I was working on a feminist newspaper in college. My professor and dean didn't know where I fit, and they admitted it. And the words 'alternative journalism' didn't mean anything back then."

Baim started the women's soccer team at Drake. She wrote about feminist issues for a Des Moines–based wire service. She wrote in depth about comparative worth, the feminine nature of poverty, and gender mutilation. "Some other papers picked it up," she said. "In a newsletter I did for the school, I wrote tons of stuff about race issues and gender and pay inequality on the faculty. I never felt ostracized. I felt Iowa was relatively progressive. I had a good experience at Drake. I wouldn't say it was perfect."

Baim attempted suicide during her sophomore year at Drake.

"I don't say that lightly, but it was a pivotal point in my life," she said. "I think it would have happened at whatever school I went to. I got through it. I had a professor who came out to me and didn't have to say or do much. He just wrote something in my journal, 'It gets better. No kidding.' Dan Savage did it later but my professor actually said it in my thing." In 2011, Savage published the popular nonfiction anthology *It Gets Better: Coming Out, Overcoming Bullying, and Creating a Life Worth Living.*

Of her professor, Baim explained, "I knew he was closeted, he was gay, and he was miserable. But it got better for him later. He had optimism. And if he can have optimism, married to a woman in the English department at Drake University in Des Moines, Iowa, and he thinks it's going to get better for me, then that was it. I said, 'Okay, nobody is going to tell me what to do or how to do it. I'll be a typesetter the rest of my life.' Which thank God I didn't have to be. But that's how I paid my way through college. I said, 'I'll just typeset insurance forms the rest of my life and be a feminist activist on the side and not be a journalist. And that's fine because I'm not going to compromise to be something that fits into the *Chicago Tribune* or *New York Times*.' The job I wanted was to work at *Ms.* magazine."

Baim returned to Chicago after graduation. Her mother told her about the fledgling *Gay Life* newspaper in Chicago. "It was like, 'I'm there!'" Baim said with a smile. "I didn't even know there was a gay press. And I certainly didn't know there was a career in a gay press. I walked in and they had the typesetter I used in college. I said, 'I can typeset. I can take photos. I can write. I can edit. And hours don't mean anything to me.' I was managing editor in a year [at age twenty-two]. I luckily don't have to do four days in a row without sleep anymore. But that's what it took."

This kind of work ethic sounds great for the mainstream press as well. Baim's keen and diverse observations would have been invaluable at any Chicago daily newspaper. "I'm so grateful the mainstream press didn't want me," she said. "I was openly gay in 1984. My stepfather let me freelance a couple pieces at the *Tribune*, but he said, 'Tracy, you'll never be happy here.' Because he knew gay people there who were very unhappy, and they couldn't be out. There were like five openly gay journalists in mainstream media in 1984. I don't even know who they all were. I knew Randy Shilts [1951–1994, *San Francisco Chronicle*] was one of them." She said everyone told her that she wouldn't be happy in the straight press, "sometimes paternalistically, sometimes realistically. But it was the truth. I would have loved to work for the *New York Times*. First of all, all my peers who graduated from journalism school in 1984—none of them were in newspapers after ten years. It was economically not viable, career not viable. I thrive in an environment of challenge and being told I can't do something."

In 1985, Baim became founding managing editor of the *Windy City Times* (*WCT*), still the go-to source for Chicago's LGBTQ community. In 1987, Baim left *WCT* to become founder of *Outlines*, which competed with *WCT* for thirteen years. In the summer of 2000, *WCT* was on the verge of closing when Baim gambled to buy the publication and merge it with *Outlines*. In September 2020, she dropped its print edition after thirty-five years.

"I couldn't get a loan for *Windy City Times* for twenty years," said Baim, who remained as majority owner in 2020. "I finally got one when I bought the name back from my cofounders. But with *Outlines*, banks laughed at me. So really, the 'no' helped me be a better businessperson to do the journalism I love. I have zero training in business. But what's fun is that some of my side projects, like working on the Gay Games in 2006, people on the board of directors became friends. One of them in particular works at the Chicago Mercantile Exchange. Super nice guy. My volunteering, doing work for youth homelessness, have not only taught me skills, but brought me connections to the work.

"So now I'm not intimidated when I go to a funder. I never would have learned that being a journalist. Once I got the *Reader* job, I said this to my partner, who is a saint, twenty-five and a half years: everything I learned in the prior thirty-four years, every nonprofit thing I did led to that confidence that I could do the *Reader*. It wasn't just being the publisher of a weekly paper. It was everything else. Making a couple of movies, doing the Gay Games with a bunch of other great people. Doing a book [*Out and Proud in Chicago: An Overview of the City's Gay Community*, 2008]. Doing the Chicago Gay History website. It led to that point in time."

The point in time was Baim's decision to approach the owners of the *Chicago Reader*.

In 2018, the *Reader* was owned by Sun-Times Media, a group of private investors, and the Chicago Federation of Labor, led by former Chicago alderman Edwin Eisendrath. Baim called Eisendrath.

"It would have been a mistake to take it then," she reflected. "He said we could have it for a dollar. I said, 'No, I want to come work for three months and see if I want it for a dollar.' And it would have been gone in a week. But having waited, and then said, 'Yes,' that was perfect timing for me, timing for the owners. Just even calling Ed Eisendrath and saying, 'I can come run the *Reader* for you.' That wouldn't have happened having just been a journalist for thirty-four years."

The *Chicago Reader* was cofounded in 1971 by Robert A. Roth, who grew up in the Chicago suburb of Arlington Heights. He was a student at Carleton College in Northfield, Minnesota, and talked classmates Robert E. McCamant, Thomas Rehwaldt, and Thomas Yoder into going in on the alternative weekly.

Roth liked the *Phoenix* weekly in Boston, which was sold on newsstands but also given away. The *Reader*'s founding fathers thought outside the box with an unprecedented magazine-style design on newsprint. They wanted their publication to be free, which the *Reader* still is today. In its first anniversary issue, the *Reader* reported it had lost nearly $20,000 in its first ten months of existence.

"What I did at *Windy City* was very transferable to the *Reader*," Baim said. "I wasn't intimidated by a weekly paper deadline. I never missed one in thirty-six years. I can do every aspect of the job, from typesetting to taking a photo to delivering the paper. It was also, 'Why the hell do you need this many people?' That was shocking. What do you all do? This is a weekly paper that is forty pages. *Windy City* is thirty-two, thirty-six [pages]. *Windy City* was five people, peaked at eight." In January 2020, the *Reader* employed twenty-six people full time and more than one hundred freelancers and vendors.

For a generation of boomers, the *Reader* was the most important, iconoclastic publication of the 1970s and '80s. It would hit the streets on Thursday evening and was gobbled up by midnight at North Side music clubs and long-gone music outlets like Tower Records. The *Reader* was a fat three sections, filled with music and movie listings, personal ads, and classifieds for cheap apartment rentals. The journalism was long form and featured the popular question-and-answer column "The Straight Dope" (which stopped appearing in the *Reader* in 2018) and a now-defunct media column called "Hot Type." By 1996, *Crain's Chicago Business* projected the newspaper's revenue at $14.6 million.

A decade later the *Reader* was operating at a loss. The alternative newspaper shared one pivot point in common with mainstream newspapers: the power of the internet. The classified ads that bulked up the paper moved to Craigslist and other online outlets. All those sexy personal ads that the *Reader* was known for? Fugget about it. Entertainment listings were available on numerous websites. Long-form journalism went out of style in favor of more biting, opinionated writing. The original owners left. After the decline in profits, Rehwaldt filed a lawsuit against the company. The lawsuit led to the 2007 sale of the *Reader* to the Atlanta-based alternative newspaper *Creative Loafing*.

A downward spiral began that continued through Baim's regime.

What was the *Reader*?

And what is it today?

"The term 'counterculture' would have been the appropriate word in 1971 when it was founded by a few white college guys," Baim answered. "They did a good job of presenting different news than the mainstream covered. They weren't perfect—nobody is in covering the whole city. But of all the media in the 1970s and '80s, they tried the hardest among the general-circulation publications to actually cover marginalized communities, people of color, queer people. They were always weekly, feature, news investigative. They never tried to be breaking news. What we're trying to change is not just diversifying the types of stories, but you can't do that without diversifying the people who tell those stories—and also the distribution."

Expanding diversity was a parallel operation. The *Reader* began buying new newspaper boxes and placing them in previously underserviced West and South Side neighborhoods of Chicago. They hosted a couple of freelance open houses on the predominately Black South Side to encourage new writers, illustrators, and photographers.

"We've tracked our diversification on our bylines and it's terrific—on women, on people of color, and other groups," Baim said. "We inherited a nineteen-person staff, eighteen of them white. There were a few females but mostly men. Since then, we have layered on our business side and other parts of the editorial side. The two editors-in-chief are people of color. We now have eight people of color on staff. We have queer and straight. We obviously hire white people too, but we make sure that when we're interviewing and hiring, we're doing it in a diverse way. We're recruiting from multiple skill sets, experiences, and experiences in writing about different communities. We had an issue at the end of the year [2019] that showed all the covers of the last fifty-one weeks. It was every kind of person: disabled, Asian, Latin, African American, young, old. It was wonderful to see."

It was another community newspaper planting seeds of change.

Chapter 8

Selling a Family Newspaper

Selling a family business can cause hurt within the family and confusion within the community. Choices are often driven by harsh economic realities. Apprehension becomes part of the deal, especially when the business is sold to an outside interest.

Unlike so many of today's newspapers, Bill's Toasty has never sold out. The family-owned, workingperson's diner is just off the town square in Taylorville, a former coal mining town of ten thousand people about thirty miles southeast of Springfield, Illinois. Since 1932, Bill's Toasty has been open twenty-four hours a day, serving breakfast, burgers, and deep-fried pickles to loyal locals and passers-through like the late country singer Charley Pride. The tiny restaurant contains generations of low-flying secrets and stories.

Tom Latonis walked into the diner on a gloomy and rainy afternoon in January 2020. He was a loyal local. Latonis was a popular staff reporter for the Taylorville *Breeze-Courier* (est. 1894), Christian County's only daily newspaper. He carried the final newspaper he produced for his previous employer, the *Pana News-Palladium*. Pana is about fifteen miles west of Taylorville. The newspaper was carefully folded at the crease.

Latonis had been the *News-Palladium*'s managing editor from 1989 until 2018. The front page of his final issue of January 3, 2018, featured two main stories: the *News-Palladium* sale to the Daily Herald Media Group (DHMG)

in Arlington Heights, outside of Chicago, and the obituary for Cindy Latonis, Tom's wife of twenty-seven years. She died on January 1, 2018. Cindy was
the daughter of *News-Palladium* publisher and owner Thomas J. Phillips Jr.

"This was the last paper we produced as a family," Latonis said.

Thomas J. Phillips Jr. stepped down on January 5, 2018, ending a fifty-
six-year run of family involvement. A Pana native, Phillips had been sole owner of the twice-weekly since 1975. His father worked in the Peabody coal mine
in Pana. Thomas Joseph Phillips Sr. had a fatal appendicitis attack when Tom
Jr. was eight years old. Tom Jr. worked as a shoeshine boy in high school and
delivered groceries. He gave his money to his mother for family expenses. His
father also built a neighborhood grocery store and other small properties in
Pana. Tom Jr. began his journalism career by delivering the *Pana News* on his
bicycle, slipping and sliding on the small town's oiled roads.

The *News* and the *Palladium* merged in 1948. Both were daily newspapers early in their histories. In 1956, Tom Jr. came on as a reporter-
photographer for the *News-Palladium* and became a co-owner six years later.
He would eventually serve as president of the Illinois Press Association.

"As my father-in-law got older, he started leaving me with more decisions
to make in the day-to-day operation," Latonis said. "The reason I got the [edi-
tor] job is because he bought a newspaper in Nokomis in 1984, and in 1998 he
bought the paper in Morrisonville. The [Morrisonville] publisher, John Len-
non, passed away during the holidays. He was from Chicago and bought the
thing sight unseen." In 2005, Phillips acquired the newspaper in Assumption
(pop. 1,093). The company ran all four newspapers out of its Pana office. The
small chain operated under the umbrella of Pana News, Inc.

"Resources kept dwindling and dwindling until finally he had to sell,"
Latonis said. "Myself, my wife, and her sister Trish [were] involved with the
newspaper. We had no input. He just decided to sell it. Paddock offered him
what he thought was the right amount and he sold it. It was the first offer."

DHMG/Paddock acquired the *News-Palladium*, the *Golden Prairie
News* in Assumption, and the *Free Press-Progress* in Nokomis, which incorporated the *Morrisonville Times*. Paddock already owned weekly newspapers in
neighboring Farmersville, Girard, Palmyra, and Virden.

Latonis called John Galer, the fatherly owner of the *Journal-News* in neighboring Hillsboro, to gauge his interest in Pana News, Inc. "He looked things over, and he wasn't interested," Latonis said. In a separate interview, Galer said, "Truthfully we didn't have enough staff here to go there. If I had been ten years younger, I would have gone for it."

Latonis said, "I knew the bottom line was bad. Tom was subsidizing the paper and it got to the point where he couldn't do it anymore. He thought, 'The first offer that comes along, well, I'm going to do it.'"

In mid-January 2020 I found Tom Phillips Jr. at Heritage Health Nursing Home in Pana. He was eighty-seven years old. "I'll be eighty-eight if I make it to March 20," he said, and he did. He was hard of hearing and had lost most of his eyesight. "I didn't have the money to do what I needed to do to keep going," Phillips said. "I went through three presses. Raised a family. I don't think I was frivolous. Never gambled except for shooting Kelly pool. Unless you're an Irishman you probably never heard of that. But it was sad to sell."

Latonis said most locals were unaware of the impending sale. "When they started talking about it, they assumed I was going to stay and that my sister-in-law [Trish] was going to stay," he said. "That didn't happen. That's when people started getting up in arms." Cindy's oldest sister, Beth Bennett, was a lobbyist for the Illinois Press Association (IPA). In 2010, she became executive director of the Wisconsin Newspaper Association in Madison.

"I'll be honest with you," Latonis said. "They never let me go. Nobody came to me and said, 'You're done.' There was no buyout. My father-in-law provided nothing for me. The new owners provided nothing for me or my sister-in-law." Trish, who passed away in February 2019, worked in the graphics department. Latonis sipped from a Sierra Mist at the diner counter and continued in a hushed cadence: "No severance. No paperwork. Just check 'unemployment status.' If Cindy hadn't passed away, I probably would have showed up and sat at my desk. My father-in-law and Mr. Paddock were great friends," he said, referencing Robert Paddock Sr. of Paddock Publications. "They knew each other from the IPA. But this whole thing just reeked. The first day they took over, about five or six corporate people came in. They were going through the computers. They knew who I was. One person out of the whole bunch offered their sympathy." Cindy's death was front-page news.

"No one else said a word to me."

Doug Ray, publisher and CEO of Paddock Publications, which includes DHMG, said making personal connections takes time. "We're not aware of everything going on in these towns," Ray said. "I knew Tom Phillips in Pana. He's in a nursing home. I think a lot of him. He liked the idea since he knew me personally. It was not 'Let's make a deal with the numbers,' but more about what we were going to do with the paper. We have to make some money on it, too. We're not doing it for practice.

"You don't break in overnight in these small towns. Everyone knows everyone else. But basically the staff, the editor in Pana—they've lived there forever. Maybe there was the outsider impression at the beginning but now I don't think they'd say that. I don't think they care where the paper is printed. It's about who is on the street and the personalities in the paper. Not the people from out of town. We did not import staff, except for the overall manager who basically runs all the [regional] papers. And she lives there and works there."

In the summer of 2020, Stefanie Anderson was the general manager of the company's papers in central and southern Illinois. She had been DHMG's production director in suburban Arlington Heights. She moved downstate when the acquisition process began. Ray said, "One newspaper after another would contact us. Most of them were concerned about maintaining a legacy for what their dad had done or grandfather had done. We tried to do that too. We've been buying one after another."

In early July 2020, DHMG launched the *Shelbyville Eagle*, a free weekly tabloid. "We did that because CNHI [Community Newspaper Holdings, Inc.] eliminated its print edition," Ray explained. "Here's a town of 4,700 people and one of the biggest recreational lakes in the Midwest. A robust retail environment for a small town. So we're going to start a newspaper there. We're finding that we can create a modest profit and at the same time provide these communities with a voice."

Shelbyville is the county seat of Shelby County, south of Decatur and west of Pana, which is headquarters of DHMG's Pana News group of weekly papers. In the summer of 2020, Ray said they owned twenty papers in central and southern Illinois. "I don't think Pana would have necessarily gone away," Ray said. "But some others would have gone away or been a shell of themselves. They were headed that way when we came in."

The most compelling family history of DHMG's southern Illinois news group is the weekly *Benton News*. Benton (pop. 7,000) is about thirty miles north of Carbondale, Illinois. Between the 1940s and 1987, what was then called the *Benton Evening News* was owned by the family of acclaimed actor John Malkovich. DHMG's Paddock Publications acquired the Benton newspaper from GateHouse Media in 2016.

I learned about the Malkovich newspaper family in 2001 when I wrote a *Chicago Reader* story about Beatle George Harrison's 1963 visit to Benton. A Beatles-inspired bed and breakfast had opened in the former bungalow of George's sister, Louise. Becky Malkovich, the effervescent younger sister of John, was an *Evening News* staff reporter. She told me she had "The Beatles Beat" in proud small-town tones. Becky's brother Danny Malkovich was the *Evening News* managing editor and he wrote an editorial in support of saving the house.

Becky laughed and said, "It's such a tenuous connection to George Harrison. My brother comes back to visit, but he's never stayed there. We joke about starting the *In the Line of Fire* Bed and Breakfast. We'd have a *Places in the Heart* Room and the *Con Air* Room." Becky was not a cynical newspaperperson.

The Malkovich family encountered hard times after my visit to Benton.

Their sister Amanda Joe "Mandy" Malkovich was a staff writer and photographer at the *Evening News*. She died in July 2010 of cancer in a St. Louis hospital. She was fifty.

Danny Malkovich was publisher in February 2011 when he died of an apparent heart attack. He was fifty-nine. John Croessman, publisher of the *Du Quoin Evening Call*, told the *Evening News*, "We both go back to that time when newspapers were family owned. Danny and his family were just amazing; he was so proud of the family history and connectivity with that paper."

Then, in September 2014, Becky died in a St. Louis hospital. Becky was fifty-three. She had moved on from the Benton newspaper to become a reporter for the *Southern Illinoisan*. Her father, Dan Malkovich (1926–1980), was publisher of *Outdoor Illinois* magazine and her mother, Joe Anne (Choisser) Malkovich (1928–2009), came from the Choisser family that owned and operated the *Evening News*. John Malkovich's only surviving sibling is

Melissa, a former CBS-TV associate producer who lives in Florida.

And the historic *Evening News* building was demolished in 2020 to become a parking lot. The Benton newspaper is now located in Carbondale.

"Yes, there's still a paper in those towns," Galer said in reference to DHMG's holdings. "But your commitment to the community is much different. It's not where you have somebody hands-on in every town that sees what is going on. I admire what they pull off. I could have never done something like what they did, pick up all the little papers and find a way to make it work. It's a huge investment of time, but still, it is different."

DHMG has been on the other side of the sales fence. Ray said the company has been approached many times over the years to sell. "When Stu Paddock was around, he wouldn't even entertain them," Ray said. "Remember David Radler?" Radler was the publisher of the *Chicago Sun-Times* between 1994 and 2003. In 2000, Radler brokered the sale of the *Sun-Times* building to Donald Trump, who built a glitzy Trump Tower in its space on the north bank of the Chicago River. Ray said, "Radler had a guy named Todd [Vogt]. It was a long time ago. He says, 'I want to come out and see you.' I was the general manager at the time. I said, 'What's on your mind?' He says, 'David Radler wants to buy your paper.' I said, 'Well, it's not for sale. Don't waste your time.' And then he said, 'You don't understand. David Radler wants to buy your paper.' So we ended up having a meeting. He would have bought it. And he would have paid a lot of money for it. He bought the Copley newspapers for $120 million, something like that. But again, we weren't for sale. And we hadn't been for sale."

Selling any heritage family newspaper is gut-wrenching. For many owners, their employees are part of the family. In February 2020, publisher Curt Jacobs ended his family's amazing six-generation run at the *Madison Courier* in Indiana. "The day we sold, one of my ad reps came in to give me two weeks' notice," Jacobs said. "He didn't even know we were selling. We had a going-away party for him and we reminisced. He was working for us when we adopted our two children. He had seen my children grow up. I saw his kids grow up, going through college and having a family. That's a lot harder to let some of those employees go than some guy sitting in a distant place that doesn't know them. They don't have the baggage I had. I had two people who worked at the paper longer than me. They'd come to the paper when I was in college to see my grandfather." Jacobs said there was no question he would have had to make staff cuts, just as new ownership did.

Tom Latonis bounced back and was hired by the *Breeze-Courier* in March 2018. He covered felony cases at the Christian County Courthouse and his old beats in Pana, including city council and occasional Pana prep sports. "I thought I was ready for the *Breeze-Courier*, but I probably wasn't," he said. "Your wife dies on January 1." He looked at his newspaper on the diner counter. It was filled with fresh memories. It was difficult to turn the page. He continued, "We put this newspaper out on the third. And you're out of a job on January 4. It's tough.

"I kind of wonder to this day. I had family, a son, a niece who doesn't live too far from me. I was thinking about them and how I have to press on. Because they're going to need me. I had to look to the future."

Cindy was a diabetic who had a fatal heart attack while in St. Mary's Hospital in Decatur, Illinois. The couple had one son, Jacob, who was studying at the University of Wisconsin–Madison in the winter of 2020. "Our son graduated high school June of 2017," Latonis said. "She got sick right after Christmas 2017. On New Year's Eve, they did a procedure for blood flow in her legs. When she came back, she looked at me and said, 'Help me die.' My wife was a large person. They needed some extra help to get her from the gurney into her bed." Latonis heard a code yellow from her hospital room. He was fearful that she might have fallen off the gurney. But she suffered a heart attack. Cindy died on a Sunday. Her weekly dialysis appointment was on Monday. "That Monday I got up at five thirty like always and drove to dialysis," Latonis said. "I didn't know what else to do. I talked to the nurses. Several of them had already heard. We commiserated. Last Christmas I had them over for lasagna and garlic bread."

Such is the common fabric of small communities in the center of America.

"When one of us is hurting, the town hurts," Latonis said. "And then when they found out I wasn't staying [at the newspaper] they started letting loose. People would see me and say, 'What the hell is going on with that newspaper?' I said, 'You're not talking to the right person. I don't work there anymore.' I don't know if subscriptions went down or whatever, but I know people are dissatisfied."

Family newspaper people are resilient. On April 1, 2021 (no joke), Latonis was named editor of the *Breeze-Courier*. The paper had been sold to Better Newspapers, Inc., in Mascoutah, Illinois, about ninety miles south, near St. Louis. The *Breeze-Courier* had celebrated its 125th anniversary in 2018. Its former publisher, Marylee Rasar, was a third-generation newspaperperson.

Like his father-in-law, Latonis grew into the fabric of the community. He knew what a community newspaper meant to Pana residents. Latonis was a Pana City Council alderman for twelve years and past president of the Pana Chamber of Commerce and the Pana Jaycees.

But it hadn't always been his plan to stick around.

In 1978, Latonis obtained a bachelor of arts degree in radio-television from Southern Illinois University–Carbondale. He planned to go to Chicago and take the late WLS-AM rock jock Larry Lujack's spot. "Didn't quite work out that way," he said. "I started at a little radio station [WSIU] just north of Carbondale." He later moved to a small radio station in Pana. At the same time the Pana station was sold, an opening came up at the Pana newspaper. "I said, 'Why not?' I always liked Pana and I wanted to stay." Latonis began his journalism career in 1984 in the advertising department of the *News-Palladium*.

When DHMG took over, Latonis was replaced by group editor John Broux. Broux was a local journalist whom Latonis actually hired for the Nokomis paper. "They still have the local coverage like I insisted on," Latonis said. "The way their deadlines are, city council meets on Monday night and generally it's not in the next paper, which comes out on Wednesday. It's a week later. We used to print right there. We'd put the paper together. We had our own press."

The *News-Palladium* is now printed in Virden, about sixty miles away. Stories and ads are sent to Arlington Heights in northwest suburban Chicago, where it is assembled and then transmitted to Virden and printed. "It's not as timely as it used to be," he said. "Especially with obituaries."

During the winter of 2020, music from satellite radio was piped out twenty-four hours a day through the Christian County Courthouse near Bill's Toasty. As Latonis talked, you could hear a soft rock instrumental version of "Do You Know the Way to San Jose" outside the diner. After leaving Bill's Toasty, he'd be off to mass at St. Patrick Catholic Church in Pana.

Pana and Taylorville are similar, according to Latonis. Immigrant coal miners settled each community. The *News-Palladium* offices were in a Montgomery Ward department store that left town in the mid-1960s. Before that, the building was the site of Pana's first opera house at the end of the nineteenth century. "Tom [Sr.] and his partners bought the Ward's building shortly after they closed," Latonis said. "They moved the press and all the linotypes over a weekend, and they put out the paper on a Monday."

But Pana was defined by the rose business.

The romance of roses is what separated Pana from any other community in Illinois. At one time there were more than one hundred greenhouses in Pana. "One place in Pana had forty acres of roses under glass," Latonis said. "We used to ship roses all around the world from Pana." From the end of World War I to the mid-1980s, most of the roses used in the Rose Parade in Pasadena, California, were grown in Pana. Roses were shipped out via refrigerated boxcars. The greenhouses had boilers for heat in the winter and air-conditioning in the summer. It was local Pana journalists the Jordan brothers who came up with the Pana motto "City of Roses."

The motto under the *News-Palladium*'s front-page masthead seems to celebrate a different time: "Containing More News About the Pana Trade Area Than All Other Newspapers in the World."

Latonis looked around the small-town diner, reflecting on the transition away from the *Palladium* in 2018. "Now, two years away from it, it's probably the best thing that ever happened to me," he said. "There's no pressure. I come to Taylorville, cover my beats, do my stories, and go home. When I went home with the Pana paper, I'd go home and think, 'Do we have enough money to do payroll on Friday?' 'Did the light bill get paid?' 'Who is not going to be at work tomorrow, whose job plus mine am I going to have to do?' That's all gone." Outside of Bill's Toasty, the courthouse music continued to play into the winter night.

—

What is it like for a family to sell a legacy newspaper?

"It's definitely emotional," answered newspaper broker Phil Murray. "Having done this for twenty-five years, you see lots of different dynamics. In the last one, two to three years, the decisions are driven principally by economic issues. It's becoming increasingly difficult for owners of single properties or properties in one geographic location to remain profitable. It's not impossible, but it certainly is harder to do. You see emotion because it's a choice driven by economic realities.

"Ten years ago or more, a lot of independent newspaper sales were driven by family dynamics. You've got a third or fourth generation, and by that point the family tree has gotten very large, and you've got pressure from some shareholders to sell and others who don't want to sell. Succession issues would sometimes play into it. Those were more the driving factor than economic issues. But now, when you're losing 8 to 10 to 15 percent a year in advertising revenue, and you have to take on that expense, it is really hard. And it's hard on a family because in many cases you've got longtime employees. There are very difficult decisions you have to make."

A June 2020 report released by Penny Abernathy, professor at the University of North Carolina Hussman School of Journalism and Media, said that the number of newspapers in the United States declined from 8,891 in 2004 to 6,736 at the beginning of 2020. Most of the losses were in small communities.

Hillsboro's John Galer conceded, "There's a very small number of us left. Partly it is economics. Your bigger towns—Springfield, Bloomington, Champaign—those were all family papers. They've all sold out to bigger companies. And then it is a hard job. When you're a newspaper publisher you're not just dealing with one little thing. You're covering the whole community. But if you're going to be successful, you have to put lots of hours in this job."

Robert Halpern owned and published the award-winning *Big Bend Sentinel* in Marfa, Texas with his wife, Rosario. They sold in 2019 after a twenty-five-year run. "To sell was wistful, emotional, happy," Robert said in the summer of 2020. "We did what we needed to do. We did our readers right. We raised a family with the income. It was kind of bittersweet, but we were ready to go. Then there was the political climate and the divisiveness that started a decade ago. It became more difficult to balance the minutiae of all this stuff." The Halperns were featured in a full-page ad with a thank-you from Marfa Public Radio, Johnson Feed and Western Wear, Marfa National Bank, and others in the July 4, 2019, edition of the *Sentinel*, the first one published by new, young owners Max Kabat and Maisie Crow.

Phil Murray has been in the newspaper brokerage business since 1994. During a couple of our conversations, Murray dreamed of ski trips and other outdoor vacations. He put that into play when he retired from the Dirks, Van Essen, Murray & April brokerage firm in 2020. He was replaced by Sara April, who had joined the firm in 2006 after working in magazine publishing.

Murray began his career in the 1980s as a journalist covering public schools at the *Daily Press*, his hometown newspaper in Newport News, Virginia. He moved on to become a business reporter at the *Virginian-Pilot* in Norfolk before leaving to obtain an MBA from the University of Virginia. "My thought was to get out of the newsroom and onto the business side of publishing," he said. "But this happened instead."

Murray is sensitive to issues around newsrooms because he worked inside them for a decade. He said, "As much as GateHouse, Gannett, or any of the big companies get criticized for cutting newsroom jobs, they're actually in a better position to support newsrooms because they've cut other aspects of the business. They've consolidated production. They've consolidated graphics, business offices, those kind of things to try to help support newsrooms.

"But I get hired to find a buyer for the Champaign, Illinois, *News-Gazette*. It's my job to get them the best price. We do our best to bring them multiple options and generate multiple offers so they do have a choice. A lot of owners don't want to make a public announcement that they're for sale. And if you don't do that, then it is difficult to find that 'local' buyer in the community."

For Champaign, the firm found the family-owned Champaign Multimedia Group, LLC, an affiliate company of Community Media Group. The deal closed at the end of August 2019—one hundred years after the *News-Gazette* was founded. News-Gazette, Inc., filed for bankruptcy along with subsidiary DWS (David W. Stevick), Inc., the radio station. The bankruptcy filing was the condition of the sale, according to publisher John Reed. In early November 2019, the company laid off thirty-four people in Champaign, including nineteen people in editorial. The *News-Gazette*'s Monday print edition was also eliminated to cut costs.

Murray said he puts any noble thoughts aside.

"I have to," he said. "I'm hired to do a job. Which is to get them the best deal. I do think some of the big companies get an unjustified bad rap."

Reed was publisher of the *News-Gazette* when the paper was sold. He was previously the publisher of the Danville *Commercial-News*, about thirty-five miles east of Champaign-Urbana. Before newspapers, he had been in the software business. In early 2008, Reed befriended his *News-Gazette* predecessor, John Foreman. The *News-Gazette* was exiting its longtime deal with the *Chicago Tribune* to print its downstate edition. "John was going to lose a couple million dollars' worth of revenue a year," Reed said. "He needed someone to focus on the digital side of the operation." Reed arrived in 2008 and replaced Foreman when he retired in 2014 after thirty-seven years at the paper. "The board landed on me to sit at this desk," he said with a slight smile. "It took me five years to figure out we had to sell to somebody, right?"

The transaction process was very emotional for Reed.

"Going through a sale—there's a lot of different levels," he said. "There's the level of an executive where you're part of the decision that you're going to sell it. Then there's the middle managers that come into it as the process is nearing completion, at least from the deal being done, and you're preparing for the transition. Then there's the employees who find out about it on the day you announce it. They're left reeling or in shock and their lives are about to change dramatically. Sales happen all the time, but when it's a sale in an industry that is in decline, it's particularly gut-wrenching."

Reed was sitting in the *News-Gazette* executive office that he would soon be leaving. He stopped to gather his thoughts. He had already gathered most of his belongings. Although Reed was no longer publisher, he remained at the paper to find a buyer for the *News-Gazette* building. He continued, "There are those out there that would say this is just the natural order of things. Newspapers are about to be extinct, and this is what happens to people on the way down. Well, it may very well be, but it is still people, and it still happens to them. And it is very emotional."

Mary Schenk began work at the *News-Gazette* in 1983, and she remained at the paper as we talked in 2020. She is part of Champaign's stand-up DNA, not unlike Roger Ebert or Dick Butkus. She was also president of the now-defunct Local 14407 of the Printing, Publishing, and Media Workers Sector of the Communication Workers of America.

Schenk recalled, "The sale was torture."

She was sitting in the same office with Reed and longtime *News-Gazette* columnist Tom Kacich. Reed said, "We had a deal in place. I announced it to the staff at nine a.m. on August 30."

"We had to pick up our paychecks in person that day," Schenk said. "They brought us in on a ruse."

Reed replied, "It wasn't a ruse."

Schenk continued, "Of course, everybody shows up instead of getting our direct deposit. And we get an envelope that says there's a WARN [Worker Adjustment and Retraining Notification] notice in it." Under the WARN Act, the seller is responsible for providing a notice for a mass layoff that occurs before or on the effective date of the sale.

Reed leaned forward on his desk and explained, "Through the negotiating process, we knew someone was going to reduce head count—us, the buyer, whatever—by a magnitude of such that it would trigger the federal [WARN] Act. So part of the announcement was the distribution of those WARN notices. You have to use the phrase 'mass layoff.' That's what happened. We announced the sale. We weren't making the decision about layoffs. That would be up to the new owner. Our responsibility was to keep things essentially going the way they were going and not let things get worse between the time we announced it until the time the sale closed."

Schenk is of diminutive stature. But she did not let up. She sat at a conference table a healthy distance from Reed's desk. And she continued, "Which was eleven weeks later. So for eleven weeks we dangled. Are we going to have a job? Are we going to have health insurance? What's going to happen to our 401(k)? Am I going to get contractually all the things they are obligated to give me? The answer ended up being no. We're still owed money by the *News-Gazette* [as of March 2020]. It was painful. On the day the sale was completed, which was Sunday, November 17, the new company notified us by text. 'You have a job' or 'We don't want you.' They never introduced themselves to anybody in the newsroom."

How were the survivors chosen?

"Beats me," Schenk answered.

Reed said, "I was not one of the ones retained, so I wasn't privy to it."

According to guild figures, of twenty-three non-managerial employees in editorial, fifteen were gone. Two of them ran the Danville bureau. They were not replaced. Six copy editors lost their jobs, as did two news clerks and one full-time librarian. One photographer was laid off, which left just one staff photographer. "At one time there were fifteen photographers here," Schenk said. "Reporters take their own pictures. The sales staff was mostly spared. Circulation was mostly spared. Composing lost two and they were already way down from the cuts that happened before the bankruptcy-sale process."

Paul Barrett is executive vice president and publisher of Champaign Multimedia Group. He came out of semi-retirement in September 2019 as part of the Champaign acquisition team. During the 1980s and '90s he ran newspapers in the South for Thomson Newspapers. In 2018, he ended a ten-year run as the publisher of the *Finger Lakes Times* in Geneva, New York. "The Champaign purchase was an asset buy," he wrote in a June 25, 2020, email. "We purchased the assets of the operations, which didn't include personnel. We rehired the people needed based on weeks of interviews with employees and especially with department heads. We didn't 'fire' anyone. In fact we've added seven new employees to the staff and are continuing to grow. We consider the newsroom the heart of the operation. You do everything you can not to screw around with it. We have a great newsroom here, the foundation of the previous owners."

While the Champaign newsroom soldiered on, the Champaign group shut down the neighboring *Rantoul Press* in late September 2020. The Rantoul (pop. 13,200) newspaper had been in business for 145 years. Jobs lost? By the time it closed, the paper only had one full-time reporter, one part-time reporter, and a few carriers. With fewer than six hundred subscribers, Barrett cited financial losses as the reason for the paper's demise. (It brought to mind the old *Wall Street Journal* joke about how the number one reason the *WSJ* loses subscribers is when they die.) A form of the paper re-emerged in the spring of 2021 as a free weekly shopper with *News-Gazette* articles, but the newspaper's website and social media remained dormant.

Over in Champaign, at the time of the sale, the *News-Gazette* had 128 total employees. Of that number, twenty-eight were covered under union contracts. Because the editorial department had been hit so hard, the staff opted to shut down the local union at the end of 2019. The union had been voted in back in 1975, and the local had only *News-Gazette* employees. They never merged with anyone. They stood proud and strong. Schenk said, "I did not have the energy to try to resurrect the troops or carry on in a leadership position, and no one left was willing to do so either."

Schenk and her surviving colleagues tried to assess the damage. "We looked around the room to see who were the heavy lifters. In editorial. I can't speak to the business end of it. I know in the newsroom the negative personalities are gone and the people who didn't produce are gone. The ones that always worked for free are still working for free. We used to have a full copy desk and now we don't. It's been painful. I call us 'reactionary.' We've always been a proactive paper, out ahead of the stories. That's damn near impossible right now."

Kacich added, "And thank God there's no paper on Monday now. Otherwise, you're working ninety hours a week. The first day we didn't have a Monday paper the publisher wasn't even here. He has made himself scarce."

Reed declined to answer how Champaign-Urbana has reacted to the sale. "I don't think I'm a good source for trying to discern the community's reaction," he said.

Schenk said, "Well, may I, then? The way they announced there would be no Monday paper was to bury it at the end of the Sunday paper on the jump. So Monday morning the phones started ringing. 'Where's my paper?' It crashed the phone system. For the first week there's nothing but ringing phones. Finally, our superiors said to not answer them. It took weeks to dig out from that. People were so ticked off and we lost a lot of subscribers."

Reed, Schenk, and Kacich agreed that the Monday edition was axed because it was the thinnest paper of the week. "Saturday's now the thinnest day," Reed said. "People don't like change. I loved every single one of our readers, but boy, you talk about a group that is really resistant to change. As a brand-new publisher fifteen years ago, I got the idea that nobody reads the bridge column. So I made the decision to take the bridge column out. That lasted about three days because I did nothing but talk to people about the bridge column." Ironically, new publisher Paul Barrett's mother was a "Life Master" bridge player, traveling around America to play as a tournament partner.

Schenk was feisty during our two-hour conversation. Kacich, semi-retired, was semi-resigned. Reed kept his game face on. "You hire a broker with the hopes that with the money you're spending on the broker that they're going to bring you the best possible price for the assets you're selling," Reed said. "Phil [Murray] did that. You're looking to maximize the return for your shareholders. This particular buyer also was the only one we were able to locate who was interested in continuing the multimedia approach. This company has been in newspapers and radio since WDWS went on the air in 1937. We always had run them as separate businesses. In late 2017, we put everybody into this building. Certainly you get some efficiencies and there's some benefits on the cost side for doing that. But we also felt that between the print operation, the broadcast operation, and increasingly the digital operation that the synergy for operating as consolidated entities would ensure our longevity into the future. It didn't pan out like we hoped, but this buyer also shared that vision."

—

Every newspaper sale has a unique story. *Arkansas Democrat* publisher Walter Hussman Jr. recalled a twelve-year battle to buy the *Arkansas Gazette*, the competing locally owned newspaper in Little Rock. The *Gazette* was owned by the Hugh Patterson family, and its legacy included powerful editorials against Arkansas governor Orval Faubus when he tried to prevent the Little Rock Nine from integrating Little Rock High School in 1957.

Hussman was named publisher of the *Arkansas Democrat* in 1974 at the age of twenty-seven. In 1977, the upstart publisher floated the idea of a joint operating agreement (JOA) with the *Gazette* as the dominant morning paper and the *Democrat* as the afternoon paper. The Patterson family rejected that idea and filed a federal antitrust suit against the *Democrat* in 1984, accusing the Hussman group of trying to cripple the *Gazette*. "They lost the lawsuit and sold the paper to Gannett in 1986," Hussman recalled. "Al Neuharth [the late Gannett chairman and founder of *USA Today*] came to town and said, 'We will use our considerable resources to make sure we prevail in this market.' It was a daunting deal.

"Once Gannett bought it, it was a circulation war. It got crazy. We competed with them for five years and they lost more money every year. And by the fifth year they lost around $29 million. And that's not after depreciation. They lost $110 million in five years! They decided to throw in the towel and sell. We couldn't buy the paper because we didn't even know what all the liabilities were. We were only interested in an asset purchase. The justice department wouldn't let us look at their financial statement because they wanted somebody else to buy it. The only way we could buy it is if nobody else would buy it."

No one wanted the forlorn *Arkansas Gazette*, founded in 1819 and considered to be the oldest continuously published newspaper west of the Mississippi River. It was losing money and market share.

"They were gentlemen about the whole thing," Hussman continued. "When it was all done, Doug McCorkindale [then chief financial officer at Gannett] came in. He put his hand out and said, 'I want to congratulate you on a great victory.' I thought, 'Wow, that's pretty first-class.' This is one of the most interesting things about the whole deal: the day it closed I was in our attorney's office. They said, 'Okay, you're now the owner.' I said, 'Bring me the financial statements to the *Arkansas Gazette*.' I had never seen them. I looked at them and I was dumbfounded.

"We had $19 million of property, plant, and equipment on our balance sheet. That was before depreciation. And the *Gazette* had $49 million of property, plant, and equipment. I thought that was amazing. That's all the presses, the trucks, the computer system. They had twice as many assets as we had to compete. So then I said, 'Let me look at the income statement.' I looked at the total operating expenses. They were spending $10 million a year more than we were! They had double the assets, and they were spending $10 million each year more than us—and we were gaining market share on them. I thought, how could this be? And then it occurred to me, the most important thing in an organization is not the money, not the assets, not the printing press. It's the people. Plus, we had a lot more riding on it. If we won, we got to keep our jobs. If we lost, we all lost our jobs, including me. If people at Gannett lost, they just got transferred. Money does not make the difference. That's been true in so many businesses."

Hussman did not know the colorful Neuharth at the point of purchase.

Several years after the deal, Hussman received a phone call. "My assistant said, 'Al Neuharth is on the phone.' I said, 'Well, that's interesting. I wonder why he's calling me.' I picked up the phone and he said, 'Walter, I'm in Arkansas. I'm in an RV with my grandchildren. We got up this morning and we bought a copy of your paper. We're getting ready to drive through Little Rock, and it took me two hours to read your paper. Your paper is fantastic. It's got so much news in it.' A couple years later, he wrote a column in *USA Today*, and he listed the five best newspapers in America. The *New York Times*, the *Wall Street Journal*, the *Washington Post*, the *Miami Herald*, and the *Arkansas Democrat-Gazette*.

"He was pretty gracious."

—

Several years ago a large truck delivered a mysterious, long tube to the offices of the *Madison Courier* in rural Madison, Indiana (pop. 11,700). Inside the tube there was a poster that was produced in 2000 by the Dirks, Van Essen, & Murray (DV&M) newspaper brokerage group. It ranked the *Courier* back then as one of the top three oldest continuously running daily newspapers in America. Madison is a historic town founded in 1809 along the Ohio River, about forty-five miles north of Louisville, Kentucky.

The *Delaware Gazette* in Ohio was at the top of the 2000 list, having started in 1818. The *Gazette* was sold in 2004. The *Deseret News* in Salt Lake City, Utah, was also near the top of the list, although it is published by a large family known as The Church of Jesus Christ of Latter-day Saints. The *Deseret News* was founded in 1850. (The *Deseret* name comes from the word for "honeybee" in the Book of Mormon.)

Until February 29, 2020, the *Madison Courier* had been owned by the same family since 1849. The DV&M effort tracked corporate and family ownership between 1900 and 2000. "It obviously ended up being families that owned newspapers that long," brokerage partner Phil Murray said.

The *Madison Courier* had been the oldest continuously family-owned newspaper in America, published under the same name in the same city. "I have not encountered one older than us continuously run under the same family," said *Courier* publisher Curt Jacobs, the sixth generation to work at the newspaper, in a December 2019 conversation. "I do know the others have sold out."

And then, on February 28, 2020, Jacobs sold his beloved *Madison Courier*.

"It was a hard decision and definitely bittersweet," Jacobs said in a follow-up March 24, 2020, interview. "We sold because the industry headwinds make it so hard for a small independent paper. My son and my brother's son had carried papers, and my son also worked as a photographer for the paper in high school. We did not see the next generation as interested in the business. Due to the precarious nature of the industry, it is hard to pause them that way. We felt it was important to get the paper in the hands of an organization that has more resources to ensure the continuation of the paper."

Jacobs sold to the Paxton Media Group of Paducah, Kentucky.

Ironically, Jacobs and his siblings contacted the same brokerage group—now Dirks, Van Essen, Murray & April (DVM&A)—that had honored the *Courier* for its endurance. "They know the players," he said. "They asked me if I knew of anybody who would be interested. But I didn't know of anybody who had the wherewithal in terms of finances or the ability to run it. Maybe that's unfair, but I didn't see it. So they look around the industry."

They landed on Paxton, a privately held media company that dates back to 1896. In March 2020, the company owned thirty-two daily and weekly newspapers ranging from the *High Point Enterprise* in High Point, North Carolina, to the flagship *Paducah Sun*. Paducah is about 270 miles southwest of Madison.

The market is the key component in selling a newspaper these days, according to Murray. "Quality of market—good job base," he said. "Stable employers like universities or government facilities that don't tend to expand and shrink. People that live and work in the community, so they're invested in it. You look for that loyalty. You want a community that has a local identity and still has a good subscriber base, although everybody is losing circulation. If you're going to be an absentee owner, management makes a difference as well.

"These days, much more than ten or fifteen years ago, the buyer is going to come from a company that owns newspapers nearby. You can rationalize costs easier in a region. And you can appeal to a broader base of advertiser because you're offering bigger coverage than you could otherwise. It makes a difference digitally as well to have a bigger footprint. It's easier to try and get digital dollars out of a car dealer because you have a region as opposed to a single market. It's still a problem to sell ads digitally." The reason is easy to understand. Even at a local level all that digital oxygen gets sucked up by Facebook, Google, and now Amazon.

"And then brick-and-mortar retail is under siege as well," Murray said. "All the Kmarts are going to be gone. Sears stores will be gone eventually. You can list lots of retailers that have closed stores, that twenty-five years ago, when I started doing this, would have been in the top ten advertisers in any daily newspaper. Then car dealers—twenty years ago, I bet you three of his top five were local car dealers. The other two were grocery stores. All those are either gone or moved the bulk of their advertising dollars to digital."

Jacobs had veto power if he felt Paxton wasn't the right fit for the sale. "We had another bidder," he said. "They wouldn't have been better. This is as good an option as we got. To be honest, we considered selling in 2015 before my mother [Jane Jacobs, the previous publisher] passed away. And as the one running the business, I was in charge of doing that. It was easy to put that off. Shortly after we made that decision her condition worsened. And about six weeks before she passed away, I was diagnosed with a rare form of cancer. And I'm trying to run the paper."

Jacobs again explored selling the paper in 2017. "I just couldn't do it," he said. "This has been a difficult decision for me. People locally asked me if my cancer impacted this decision. I said, 'None,' basically, except for the fact it had changed my perspective in the ability to let go of some things. It was very hard to let go of the family legacy. And the bigger thing is your commitment to the community. That was very hard to let go of.

"My cancer is not technically curable. On the same token, I've done very well over the five years since I've been diagnosed. I haven't been sick from the treatment. It's immunotherapy and it's being held in bay. I'm upbeat about it, as upbeat as you can be about that. You'd never know I have cancer unless I told you. I just got done lifting weights for an hour. But after you get hit in the face with that diagnosis and you live with it for a while, you realize things aren't as absolute as you think. I realize I don't have to carry that burden [of the newspaper] on my own, and I can contribute to this community in other ways. The paper existing is not dependent on me, and maybe I'm not the best person to be running it. You realize all those things, and you come to terms with cancer. So it was easier for me to let go."

After selling the paper, Jacobs spent more time in the community working with Jane's Kids, a Jefferson County charity that helps low-income children have access to quality summer programming. Jane's Kids is named after Jacobs's mother.

The *Madison Courier* ownership was split between Curt Jacobs, his brother, William, and his sister, Sally, who is an attorney in Falmouth, Massachusetts. Each of the siblings has two children. No one in the family expressed interest in keeping the legacy alive. "Nobody rejected this newspaper," Jacobs said. "It wasn't like we tried to get anyone to do it and they were unwilling. But I never encouraged them to get in it because who knows where that business is going to be? And now, in four months?" he asked, referencing the uncertainty of the pandemic. "It doesn't make sense to push them to it or make them feel a duty. It was just time. My brother was doing the press. He wasn't enjoying that anymore either. We could have overcome that. We could have outsourced the printing. And then of course with this [COVID-19] happening. Wow. I don't know what to tell you. It's bizarre.

"One good thing is that people need newspapers in this time."

Up until February 2019, the *Courier* had been a Monday through Saturday paper. Before selling, Jacobs cut the print publication to three days a week. And then he changed the delivery procedure. "We used to have our own delivery force," he said. "Motor route drivers. Youth carriers. When we made the switch to three days a week, we also made the switch to delivery by the Postal Service. There were approximately twenty-five contractors, most of whom were adult, but several were youth carriers. That was the hardest part. Many of them had carried for years and were very good to our company." In 2019, the *Courier* staff consisted of eighteen full-time employees, five of them in editorial. Two years previously, the *Courier* had employed eight full-time editorial employees.

The *Courier*'s print circulation in 2019 was 4,500 on every Tuesday, Thursday, and Saturday. The paper's circulation reaches across the Ohio River into Kentucky's Carroll and Trimble Counties. "Madison was a daily until early 2019," Murray said. "What's a daily anymore? In a couple years from now, papers like the *Chicago Tribune* will be in print one or two days a week. Is that still a daily?"

Jacobs said, "Longtime residents knew about our legacy. Others didn't. My mother and myself in particular are low-key people. My grandfather was not so much. He would blow the horn a little more. I'm proud of it. The legacy is important, but I try not to overemphasize it.

"Because what's real important is what you are doing now."

In the summer of 2021, Jacobs was enjoying retirement while keeping an eye on his beloved newspaper. "The staff is still all longtime employees of mine," he reported. "In fact, they hired a former reporter of ours to replace a younger one that left. They are still in our building, and they tell me what is going on. Paxton has continued to buy at a good clip. They recently bought the Landmark papers [a chain of forty-six dailies and weeklies based in Shelbyville, Kentucky], which gives them two weeklies in our old circulation territory.

"Consolidation moves on."

Chapter 9

Outsourcing and Rural America

Outsourcing has become the siren song to the newspaper industry's dwindling bottom line. The advances of technology have made it easier for jobs to be dispatched to other places at less cost, especially when it comes to paying workers' benefits.

Local newspaper people are replaced by distant voices, severing the connection to community. This is especially true in advertising, design, and production departments, but in some cases a local city council meeting has been covered by people out of state. Newspaper beats are eliminated, and the surviving reporters are forced to cover a multitude of topics. Outsourcing is the clown car in the circus. Accountability is lost. The truth can be harder to see. Like the farm-to-table movement, healthy family newspapers honor their local roots.

Mary Pat Boian is the straight-talking editor of the *Eureka Springs Independent* in Arkansas. Her parents met at the *Dayton Daily News* in Ohio. Her father, Harold, was a sportswriter and her mother, Mary, wrote for the society page. In 1953, they decided to move to Southern California. They packed Boian and her brothers into a 1952 two-tone green Chevy. But they only made it to Denver, Colorado.

"So my dad got a job with the *Rocky Mountain News*, where he delivered to garages for paperboys to fold and deliver at four thirty in the morning," Boian recalled. "He also got a job selling ads for the *Denver Post* and was afraid they would find out he was also working for the *News*." Harold Boian became advertising director at the *Post* and retired after thirty years.

The colorful Boian has a bit of cowgirl in her DNA. She was living in Denver in 1979 when a friend was moving to Eureka Springs. Boian hitched a ride. "It was April and there was a snowstorm," Boian said during a July 2019 conversation in the *Independent* office. Her friend "came down in a 1972 orange Chevy Suburban, hauling a trailer. She said, 'I can't drive in this.' So I drove her and her daughter, who was four or five, and their dog. It was winter all the way down until we crossed the [Arkansas] state line. Then it was springtime. There were peepers, frogs, crickets. A lot of noise I never heard.

"Eureka Springs was a magnet."

By 2010, Boian was editor of the *Lovely County Citizen* in Eureka Springs and was happy as an Ozark meadowlark putting out her weekly newspaper and driving around northwest Arkansas listening to her favorite singer, Willie Nelson.

Then things got crazy.

The *Citizen*'s owner, MOAR, LLC, a subsidiary of Rust Communications, outsourced advertising graphics to contractors in India and the Philippines. Production jobs were lost. Boian was worried editorial would be next.

Boian and her graphic design director, Perlinda Pettigrew-Owens, quit the *Citizen*.

On the day after Independence Day 2012, they published their first edition of the weekly *Eureka Springs Independent*. Eureka Springs (pop. 2,075) is a freethinking gay- and biker-friendly community nestled in the Ozark Mountains. It is out of the way, but not too out of the way—Willie Nelson has appeared in concert seven times in Eureka Springs.

Boian took on all kinds of odd jobs after she arrived in Eureka Springs. She sold bait at Beaver Dam. She was a bartender at the historic Crescent Hotel (circa 1886). There were seasonal jobs in the tourism industry, which drives the economy in Eureka Springs. "I was tired of hourly wage jobs," she said. "In 1999, a friend and I decided to start the *Lovely County Citizen*." That friend was Bill King, who later became a co-owner of a Eureka Springs tavern. "Neither one of us knew how to start a newspaper. We bought a book at Barnes & Noble in Fayetteville on 'How to Produce a Newsletter.' That was the closest thing we could find. It's all a game anyway. Who in their right mind would think starting a newspaper in an electronic age was a good plan? I graduated fifty-third in a class of fifty-seven, so I wasn't exactly voted most likely to amount to much."

Boian and King started writing, taking pictures, and working sixty-hour weeks. They ran the *Citizen* for five years and sold it in 2005 to Rust Communications, based out of Cape Girardeau, Missouri. In the summer of 2020, Rust had thirty-four independent newspapers (nineteen dailies, twenty-five weeklies) across Arkansas, Missouri, Indiana, Iowa, and Kansas. "It's a good, strong, small company," Boian said. "Not as small as we are."

Rust brought Boian back as editor in 2010.

"Then they moved in with cost cutting," she said. "It was uncomfortable. They were sending jobs out of the U.S. It had more negatives to employees. Of course, to employers, it was 'Look at all the money we made.'" So Boian and Pettigrew-Owens both quit.

Boian's and Pettigrew-Owens's Ozarks wisdom proved prescient. In March 2022, Rust flipped the *Citizen* and eight other community newspapers in Arkansas and Missouri in a sale to CherryRoad Media, Inc., a subsidiary of CherryRoad Technologies, a Parsippany, New Jersey–based technology company. CherryRoad entered the newspaper industry in late 2020. By March 2022 it had acquired sixty titles.

Pettigrew-Owens was the *Citizen*'s graphic designer. She sat across the room from Boian and remembered how she was told advertising was going to Chicago. "But from Chicago it was going out to Philippines or whoever was available and cheap to do the ad design," Pettigrew-Owens said. "The micromanaging was intense. You had to fill out a sheet and account for every minute of your day. The ad design portion of my job was being outsourced. We had to leave."

To be the best, you have to take risks.

In July 2012, Ron Kemp, regional vice president at Rust, told the *Arkansas Times* the company had indeed contracted with a Chicago firm to help with graphic design at the *Lovely County Citizen*. "Many American newspaper companies are doing the same thing that Rust is doing," he said. "The purpose of any such changes is to allow local newspapers to allot maximum resources to news gathering, advertising services, and customer relations—the things we do best on the local level." He said no jobs were lost at the *Citizen*.

Boian said, "The software was there to go to a Eureka Springs city council meeting, upload it to India, and they would sit, watch, and write it. They didn't do that. But it was talked about."

One family newspaper publisher who wished to remain anonymous said, "Companies saved enough money to overlook someone messing with their ads. They didn't have to pay salaries, vacations, overtime, and so on for creative departments. They thought it was good business to pay pennies to the dollar to people who never provided customer service but knew a lot about software and their own culture."

Bakersfield's Robert Price had been a business reporter specializing in the oil industry during his long tenure at the *Californian*. "As we contracted, we got rid of that beat and it became a component of the overall business coverage," he said. "And now there is one guy who covers business and four other things." In May 2018, Bloomberg's CityLab reported that in the three years following a newspaper closure, the costs for municipal bonds and revenue bonds increased in those communities. There weren't as many small-town reporters to cover the big investigative stories.

Newspaper broker Phil Murray said the selling landscape in small towns has shifted. "The local Target manager is not making that advertising decision," Murray said. "That decision is being made in Minneapolis [Target headquarters]. You might have three or four really good salespeople at the newspaper, but there's a limit to what they can do. As good as a relationship they might have with their local Kia dealer, he's been told he has to have 80 percent of his budget digital. It's amazing. Ad salespeople do a great job with the playing field.

"I don't know how you cut into that market share if you're in Madison, Indiana; Eureka Springs, Arkansas."

Hillsboro *Journal-News* publisher Mike Plunkett said, "One of the things John Galer and his dad did for this community that I don't think people realize because everybody here has grown up with them, is that we have a large editorial staff. How many papers of this size have an editorial staff of five and a half people? That's what separates us from the corporates. They're making sure the stories get told. Every one of our readers has grown up with that."

In a separate interview, Galer referenced the Coffeen Power Station that shut down on August 21, 2019, after a fifty-four-year run on the outskirts of Hillsboro. Texas-based Vistra Energy closed four of its Illinois plants. "People don't like coal, but that built the economy here for a lot of years," he explained. "We didn't have anything to replace that. Same thing with newspapers. A hedge fund is like an investment banking firm. It's sad because when you see that, you're not seeing things run for the purpose of what they were built for. You see bankers running stuff and bankers are good people, but there's a difference to when you're running what you're doing because you love what you do and you're doing it for a specific purpose. When everything is done just for the money, it doesn't work anymore. It really doesn't. I say that and I'm a dinosaur.

"I'm not in the real world today at all."

Galer's real world consists of neighbors and community members seeing each other around town. The Texas-based energy plant and media hedge funds are not accountable to the communities they land in.

Printing is the most obvious function to outsource in the newspaper business. The new plant can print the paper at very little added cost. Labor is in place and printing supplies are purchased in bulk. Business operations and management are other areas ripe for outsourcing because they can be spread out over multiple publications: one publisher, one advertising manager, and an advertising representative. The same is true with production layout and design. The real game is about reducing head count. This is where real money is made.

—

On the afternoon of my Eureka Springs visit, graphic artist Perlinda Pettigrew-Owens was in the A-frame chalet house that serves as the *Independent*'s office, and her twenty-one-year-old son, Jeremiah Alvarado, was doing real, old-school newspaper billing at the desk near the front door.

I asked about the staff.

Boian looked around the room and replied, "You're looking at it." This small staff, working long hours together, has managed to avoid outsourcing.

Besides handling billing and operating the *Independent* website, Alvarado is the newspaper's photographer. His dream is to run the newspaper someday. Freelance contributors include a fishing columnist, a local astrologist, and a University of Arkansas sports columnist. Pettigrew-Owens's husband, Michael, sells advertising but is not on staff.

Tuesdays are the biggest day for the small staff. City council meets on Monday night. The staff arrives around eight the next morning. Pettigrew-Owens wraps up ad design and the classifieds. Alvarado gathers photos and writes cutlines. "We proofread when it comes in and print it out," Boian said. "Jeremiah and I go through it. We do it again when we print the pages in the evening. And we go through them all again. Then, after we proofread the pages, we proofread all the cutlines. And we still manage to call a hat shop a hate shop. It just happens. You can't beat yourself up. But everyone else can. We really try to make it better every week. We know excellence will find an audience. We're generally out of here by eight or eight thirty. Because all the restaurants close at nine."

On Wednesdays the staff can often be hard to reach.

All three staff members are out delivering the latest edition of the *Independent* from the back seat of a Nissan Juke. They make up to 120 stops, bringing their own flat rocks to keep the papers down in the wind. They also take time out to tidy up news boxes. "We do the whole highway and then we go to Oscar's [Cafe] and get lunch," Boian said. "Then all three of us are back here at the office. By then Jeremiah has all the subscriptions stamped and addressed. When we finish lunch, we pack up the car again, deliver downtown, and drop our subscriptions off at the post office."

Pettigrew-Owens added, "We have people wait for us. They take them out of our hands and bring them into the store. It's very satisfying. It makes late night Tuesday worth it."

The *Independent* has a website, but Boian said, "It seems everybody does social media except us. It's a time stealer." She looked at a copy of her newspaper and added, "This is a life enhancer. I see social media as competitive. Jeremiah takes care of our Facebook page and website."

"We can put out breaking news in a short amount of time," Alvarado said. "But people always know when the newspaper comes out." He began his newspaper career writing press releases for the *Independent* while attending Eureka Springs High School. "My goal is to run this someday. I was raised in a newspaper office, almost since diapers. I didn't get a journalism degree. I have a degree in creative writing. But I was raised on this and I think I know more than what some people go to school for. It makes me curious. Mary Pat taught me how to edit. It was absorbed through osmosis, I suppose.

"My friends know what I do. They read the newspaper to get the information they need. The ones who moved away will go to the website. High school kids read it online. They are interested with things going on like city council and school board because it affects them."

Boian said that young people around Eureka Springs view the *Independent* as a curiosity. "How relevant is it?" she asked. "They do pick it up for the music schedule." She stopped, looked across the room at Alvarado, and added, "He doesn't have to do this. And he is not well paid."

Boian herself had to figure out how to sustain in Eureka Springs.

She spent twenty years residing in a five-room stone house in Butler Hollow at the south end of the Ozark Mountains. The house was a work of art created by James Dobbie, who came from Ireland to assist stonemasons in stacking the historic Basin Park Hotel in downtown Eureka Springs. The house was built on the edge of the Mark Twain National Forest, 1.5 million acres that roll like a welcome mat through Missouri. The house had been abandoned for years and has since burned down. "Owls, whip-poor-wills, wild turkey, rattlesnakes, tree frogs, snapping turtles, and a million other creatures called it home," Boian said. "I had no idea how to cut and stack wood so it would dry, pop a clutch to start a pickup with a dead battery, know when a paw was ripe, or how to talk to a redneck without pissing him off."

Boian's father and her Eureka Springs banker told her not to try to start a newspaper in 1999—and in 2010. "My dad told me about [James] Scotty Reston, who retired from the *New York Times* and started a paper in Cape Cod or someplace like that," she recalled. "He said it was the hardest work he had ever done. It is grueling. It's late-night and it's all about details. But it's satisfying."

Like many big-city journalists, Reston had dreams of exiting metropolitan life for small-town charms. In 1968, Reston and his wife, Sally, purchased the *Vineyard Gazette* in Martha's Vineyard. Reston was still at the *New York Times* and his staff thought he was rolling in high finances. In 1975, Reston bequeathed the paper to his eldest son, Richard, and daughter-in-law Mary Jo Reston.

"I knew the importance of news, or in our heads, it was important," Boian explained. "Why does anybody have a hobby? This newspaper is a hobby. We do this because it is interesting and fun."

The *Eureka Springs Fun Guide* is the moneymaker for the company. The *Fun Guide* is a free monthly magazine-style publication geared for tourists. It comes out ten times a year and is filled with ads for the Basin Park Hotel "Ghost Adventure," the weirdly hokey *Great Passion Play* in Eureka Springs, and the Cosmic Cavern, as well as various restaurants, wineries, and art galleries.

Eureka Springs is a Democratic stronghold that goes against the grain of the rest of Arkansas. The *Independent* has taken a stand on the advancement of gay rights, abortion, and other controversial issues. "We pick our fights for sure," Boian said. Pettigrew-Owens added, "We like to have both sides. We had two preachers sending letters to the editor back and forth. One highly intelligent one supported gay rights and the other used Bible scripture quotes. They had strong points and presented them in a great manner." Boian continued, "Both sides bought a lot of advertising. And we print both sides—if you submit it, [if] it is not libelous or hurtful. Our criteria is not very high or low."

The terrain of Eureka Springs is characterized by its ups and downs. The *Independent* offices are in a former house on a sharp curve along Federal Highway 62, the main highway through town. Highway 62 goes from Niagara Falls, Ontario, to El Paso, Texas. Through Eureka Springs there are switchbacks, zig zags, and wild hills that attract motorcyclists from across America. "Driving here is dicey on a good day," Boian said. "If you're going uphill, it will take you the crookedest, quickest way you can get there."

The *Independent* offices are in a loft-like, cedar-tinged home. Ironically the house was once owned by Irene Trimble, a former *Chicago Tribune* secretary. Trimble attended high school in Chicago in the late 1930s and retired to Eureka Springs. Trimble's son and daughter-in-law owned the building. "Her ghost is here," Boian said matter-of-factly. "Sometimes the TV is on when we walk in. One night this winter we were working late and Irene—or someone—touched Perlinda's arm. That was eerie. We blame everything on Irene, but she seems happy to be here. We say, 'Goodnight, Irene' each night when we leave." The *Independent* has been in the space since 2012.

A couple of times during our conversation, Boian, Pettigrew-Owens, and Alvarado got up from their chairs at the same time. They all walked to a rear patio window and started waving outside. I was confused. Was this some kind of Ozarks ritual? Boian later explained it is their summer tradition. Newspaper staffers do the wave at eleven a.m., one p.m., and three p.m. daily during the summer to cheer up frustrated automobile and tram tourists who are stuck in traffic along the bend on Highway 62 in front of their office.

"Half the people are from here and half are from somewhere else," she said. "Tourism is big. It's hard for people to find help here because people can't find anywhere to live."

The *Independent* began life as a large tabloid. Pettigrew-Owens said, "Of course paper prices were skyrocketing so we jumped on the broadsheet, which was frightening. We wanted it to be fresh and visually easy to read." The *Independent* is printed about an hour away from Eureka Springs in Hollister, Missouri, near Branson.

The *Carroll Times Herald* in Iowa also moved its printing operation. In 2018, the newspaper shut down its printing press of more than fifty years. Printing was outsourced to Sheldon, Iowa, about two hours away from Carroll. "It was excruciating," said *Times Herald* co-owner Doug Burns. The press was removed bit by bit over a month's time. The pressmen did the removal as they were looking for new employment.

"I still miss hearing the presses roll," Burns said almost two years later. "My office was right by the press. Having to dismantle the press and outsource was extraordinarily painful. It was a fully functioning 1974 press. We had to scrap it because there was no market for it. It was weird to take something we cared so deeply about . . . we actually had a replacement press in the basement. So we had spare parts. That press could still be running right now. We had great pressmen. The flexibility we had to put an ad in or change a story out twenty minutes before was incredible."

The paper is sent to Sheldon electronically. "They bring it back on the truck," said Doug's brother, Tom. "It works pretty well. It was not fun to do that, but it was probably the right call."

"It saved us money," Doug said. "We used to be classified industrial and now we're just office space. We shut down the mailing and got rid of people involved in mailing, which broke our hearts. I thought that I would die in my office as I would hear the presses run."

The paper is now printed on a six-tower, twenty-four-unit Heidelberg Harris Mercury press. White Wolf Press, a regional printing center in Sheldon, imported the new press to Iowa from Philadelphia. The Pulitzer Prize–winning *Storm Lake Times* moved its printing operations to Sheldon in 2016. White Wolf prints about sixty newspapers from Iowa, South Dakota, and Nebraska, many of them far away from home.

Chapter 10

Insourcing Spirit

While small papers may be exploring or actively outsourcing functions to feed the bottom line, there are certain mainstays that are ingrained in their DNA. The enactment of values like empathy and the respectful treatment of employees are tactics that require no cost-benefit analysis, yet they help boost morale, increase productivity, and reduce employee turnover.

Walter Hussman Jr. was like a cool breeze along journalism's stormy waters when I met him in October 2019 at an Inland Press Association event in Chicago. He was of diminutive stature and spoke in humble and humorous rhythms. The chairman of WEHCO Media in Little Rock, Arkansas, was not the bodacious cigar-chomping titan you see in the movies about big-city newspapers.

Just a month before our encounter in Chicago, the Hussman family gave $25 million to the journalism school at the University of North Carolina at Chapel Hill. It was the largest donation in the journalism school's history. None of the money came from company funds. The school was renamed the UNC Hussman School of Journalism and Media.

"I just have a positive outlook on life," he said. "We get to live a certain period of time and try to make a difference if we can. That's what we're trying to do with our involvement with the journalism school. I think you start feeling a little more empathetic about that as you get older. I'm seventy-two. The time I've got left is certainly shorter than it used to be. So what can I do to make a difference? How can I try to save this newspaper that is going to celebrate its two hundredth anniversary of us and its predecessor? The *Gazette* was started in 1819. It is the oldest newspaper west of the Mississippi River that's been continuously published."

Empathy! Bravo!

—

Tom Shaw retired from Shaw Media in 2017 at the age of sixty-nine. He had spent twenty-four years as CEO of Shaw Media, headquartered in Crystal Lake, Illinois. Long before that, he'd joined his family's company in 1970 in the circulation department of the *Telegraph* in Dixon, Illinois. In all his years with the company, Tom Shaw was most proud of changing the culture at Shaw.

In 2003, he crafted the original four-paragraph "Shaw Culture" statement. Other officers and top leaders of the company collaborated on editing the final draft of the culture statement. In part it said, "The Shaw Culture is one that is characterized by friendliness, professionalism, high ethical standards, and mutual respect for all persons. It is a culture that strives to be the dominant media company in our communities, serves our customers well, maintains high expectations from all associates, operates efficiently and profitably, and uses its capital and human resources prudently."

Tom Shaw was certainly ahead of his time on issues of ethics and mutual respect in the newsroom. "It was a process," he said in a July 2020 interview from his Dixon home. "There were calendars with nudie girls in the press shop. There were managers' attitudes towards subordinates, attitudes towards females. Use of disrespectful language in the workplace. That type of thing. Incident by incident I tried to move away from that. That was the beginning."

The culture statement was distributed through bulletin board posters, placements in the company news magazine, and on the Shaw website along with other values statements. Shaw said, "The biggest thing is that people saw they were viewed on an individual basis. They had valuable contributions to be made to the organization. They didn't feel like they were going to have the rug pulled out from under them. Although that kind of behavior goes on, we really worked at it. We wouldn't call people out publicly. We'd mentor and get people to think about maybe what they had done wasn't in the best interest of the company or their future. I was proud how we started off [the culture statement] by saying Shaw Newspapers is owned by the Shaw family trust. And that's all we say about the company. We talk about the culture, and it is probably our most valuable asset. We thought it was a fair reflection of our culture. On the other end, in its purest form, it was a reflection of our highest goals and aspirations. I was passionate about it. Much of this is still here, it just plays out in different ways with the changing times. There's things you don't just tolerate."

Shaw is a deeply religious man. Daily prayer and scripture study or meditation are key components in his forward spirit. "I try to fashion my life, as hard as it is, around a Judeo-Christian precept," he said. "An important part of that is the concept that we're all created in the image of God. I see that as meaning that every individual is uniquely important. I try to understand what that unique value is. That's where you get into not tolerating leadership lording over individuals just because they have the position. That doesn't make them any more special. That's something we talked about within the company. Everybody's job was important. People appreciate that."

Porter, Indiana, resident Jamie Hogan worked in advertising and editorial at the *Telegraph* between 1977 and 1980, when the leadership reins were held by three generations of Shaw family members. "All three of them—Ben T., Doug, and Tom—were active," Hogan said in a 2021 interview. "They were a presence in the newsroom, but I never had a sense there was editorial influence on us beyond Ben's measured, conservative voice on the editorial page. They noticed the camaraderie among the staff and let us know in subtle ways they were entertained by it. They were easy with praise and genuinely appreciated our work. Ben sent handwritten notes of acknowledgment on something he particularly liked. I was closer to age to Tom and there was more of a connection. He made a point of joining some of our newsroom after-hours social time.

"Beyond covering assigned stories, there were no boundaries to our beats. Except 'serious' reporters avoided anything that might have been society-related, like oversized vegetables from a reader's garden and ladies' teas. The society editor of that time [Suzanne Hanney] is now an award-winning writer and editor for Chicago's *StreetWise*." Established in 1991, *StreetWise* is a magazine distributed by people without homes or by those at risk of homelessness.

Unique company culture can be based on unified motivations. In a free-falling business like newspapers, there is little time to pull rank. The best model is when everyone is pulling the same end of the rope. Trevor Vernon is the third-generation owner of the Vernon Publishing chain in Eldon, Missouri. Born in 1980, he is just embarking on what he hopes to be a legacy career. He tells prospective employees they will not be working for him. "Whenever I hire someone, I tell them as soon as you walk through this door, you're no longer my employee," Vernon said. "Especially advertising people. You now work for [the] businesses you go in to talk to and that we're trying to help. If it is a sign that they need, tell them they need a sign. If it is newspaper advertising, tell them they need newspaper advertising. Obviously we're biased towards newspapers, but there's some businesses that nobody knows about because there's no sign to tell people how to get there. We'll tell them about the person who makes the sign. For us it is about connecting people."

Iowa's *Carroll Times Herald* publisher Ann Wilson also sees the value of a two-way street. She said, "Our staff was always well-educated, committed people. We felt that if we treated them right, they would come back and treat us right. And for the most part they have."

In a February 2020 conversation, her son Doug Burns said, "Right now if you look at our newsroom, our executive editor [Larry Devine] has been here for forty years, but he worked for the *Salt Lake Tribune*. Our day-to-day editor is Rebecca McKinsey, who has worked for the *Arizona Republic* and the *Times of Israel*. I worked on Capitol Hill for the *Palm Beach Post* and went to Northwestern. We have firepower. Anybody from our newsroom in the last seven to ten years could have instantly gone to the *Des Moines Register* or the *Omaha World-Herald*."

Wilson added, "We also have good interns. Rebecca was an intern for us, and we got her to stay."

Burns continued, "One thing Mom and I have tried to do is bring in interns from urban areas. We've had a number of Latino, African American, gay interns . . . kids who have never seen rural. . . ."

Then Burns said, "Nik Heftman [associate producer on *CBS Morning*] just called me three minutes ago. He came from Los Angeles. African American kid. He interned here for three months. He and I became close. Elyssa Cherney [*Crain's Chicago Business* reporter] was here. We have somebody working for Marvel Studios. I think it's important we have people in key urban decision-making or opinion centers who understand rural America. I like to have readers in our community interact with somebody who is Jewish from Chicago, African American from Los Angeles, or Latino from Washington, DC. That helps our community, but more importantly, when these young people move on to bigger jobs, generally in urban areas, they won't carry some of the stereotypes about us. Those rural-urban connections get overlooked. When I am in national newspaper meetings or similar settings . . . everybody else in the room, regardless of their race, religion, gender, sexual orientation—they're all urban. So I'm the only rural guy in a lot of the rooms I go into. I celebrate that, and I look at that as being an important part of diversity."

Wilson explained, "Well, we're Trump country. There's no doubt about that. For the most part, after readers get to know the people we brought in, they're pretty well accepted. We haven't had any major problems that I know of."

In a heartbeat her son answered, "I've found that people tend to be racist towards groups and not individuals. So when they're able to interact with an individual, some of those barriers break down."

Rebecca McKinsey was editor of the *Carroll Times Herald* for three years. McKinsey interned for four months in Carroll in late 2013, then headed off to Jerusalem, where she was an intern at the *Times of Israel* through Ohio University's John R. Wilhelm Foreign Correspondence Program. The *Times Herald* offered McKinsey a full-time gig in February 2014, the first week she was in Jerusalem. She returned to Carroll as a reporter in May of that year and was promoted to editor in October 2018. Then in late 2021, she moved on to work as project manager and editor of the *INvisible Project*, a magazine produced by the U.S. Pain Foundation.

McKinsey grew up in Lakeland, Ohio, just outside of Cleveland. She drove her 1999 Ford Taurus station wagon from Cleveland to Carroll. It was the first car she owned, and she was still driving it in 2020. "I came here on my own," said McKinsey, who was twenty-nine years old in May 2020 when we spoke. "Everything I owned was in that car. I had no connections here. It definitely was a process. Sometimes I feel it is still an ongoing process." McKinsey had also been an intern at the *Arizona Republic* and a general assignment and public affairs intern at the *Columbus Dispatch* in Ohio.

She had never worked at a rural newspaper. "One of the first things that stood out is when you go through journalism school and intern at bigger papers, you learn journalism purism," McKinsey said. "It's big on no conflict of interest. If you cover an event, don't eat there, don't take gifts. That's what had been pounded into our heads. That's very much not the case at a paper like Carroll's. You're mixed into the community. I write stories about the animal shelter where I also volunteer. I'm a hospice volunteer in Carroll. Community journalism really involves being a part of the community. You can't do it well without doing that.

"The other big difference is that everyone wears different hats. That's different than what I experienced at bigger papers. Here, my title is 'editor,' but I write, I take photos, I edit photos, I copy edit, I do layout, I run our website, I do social media management. Working at a small, independent, family-owned newspaper, you are a jack-of-all-trades."

At a smaller paper like the *Times Herald*, McKinsey was given space and time to dig deep into issues. "We have the freedom to chase the things we want and are important to us," she said. "That's fun for me coming in here as an outsider. I had a column for quite a while. I was writing sort of a liberal, feminist stance on sexual assault and women's issues. Things like that maybe hadn't run in the paper much before. One of my most talked about but also needed pieces was about Trump right before the election."

In the October 11, 2016, edition of the *Times Herald*, McKinsey wrote that in her past, in the space of a week, two men had grabbed her in a sexual manner without her consent. The column was in response to Trump's "Grab them by the pussy" statement from *Access Hollywood*. In part, McKinsey wrote, "What Trump doesn't seem to understand is the fear, the shame, the negative effects that linger for years after a man puts his hands on a woman who isn't willing."

McKinsey told me, "When we publish those kind of pieces there's backlash, but we also see how they resonate with people. Where I volunteer at the animal shelter, another volunteer is a city attorney. He's fairly conservative. He came up to me at the shelter and thanked me for writing that. He thought it was important. It's a different aspect to community journalism where you get the immediate reaction of a person."

McKinsey and her fourteen-person staff often discussed the realities of working at a small-town family newspaper. "Our conversations are more about what it would be like being in a chain as opposed to stockholders," she said. "Sometimes in a rural area the attitudes towards journalism aren't what you would want. You could dwell on those things, but on the flip side is having this small group of us knowing each other really well, and this is where the decisions are going to be made instead of someone in another state. That's huge. We understand as a staff that it's something we're lucky to have."

Hillsboro *Journal-News* editor Mary Herschelman said the togetherness creates an omnipresent fun element. "I remember going to Six Flags and we had to meet one of Dad's suppliers on the way home," she said. "I was like, 'No!' If we had to do something for the paper, my parents always made it fun. Before automation we did odd jobs. We would help with labeling. My dad would create contests to see who could do the most, so we'd work very fast. Before color printers we had circulation maps. So he'd buy us a new package of highlighters so we'd sit in the back and color circulation maps."

Trevor Vernon does not shy away from injecting fun into the community-centric workplace. In 2019 and 2020, he enlisted neighbor Elijah Hart to become a real-life "Newsboy." Elijah is the son of Jeremy and Jennifer Hart, the owners of the beautifully restored Historic Randles Court motel down the road from the *Eldon Advertiser* headquarters. Elijah, then ten years old, stood in front of the *Advertiser* office and regularly sold between forty and eighty newspapers on every Wednesday's publication day. "On a great day, maybe a hundred sold," Vernon said. "People still line up to wait for their paper. There are also elderly readers that don't want to get out of their car. Old-fashioned service. But a lot of it is that he is a fun kid. He is polite but will cut up if you tease him. I always open my window when he is selling and listen from my 'second desk.' Sometimes I sing to him. I can't carry a tune, so I try to make him laugh."

During the early days of the COVID-19 pandemic, toilet paper was scarce across America. On March 19, 2020, Vernon rolled out his sense of humor and created a full-page ad that read, "Almost out of TP? We have you covered. The *Advertiser* is printing a special cutout below for those last-resort moments. The *Advertiser* . . . Helping the community since 1894!" In a June 2020 update interview, Vernon said, "We did that at a time we had to get some levity. People were scared to death. Nobody could find toilet paper. Nobody could find eggs. What are we going to do? We like to have fun. We're not really struggling right now. A lot of people are and we're not. Our salesperson [Benne Myers] is really good and thinks outside the box. We have a couple newer people that don't think traditionally, and they are breaking molds. I won't lie that it's been painful sometimes, but it's been fun."

Countless community diversions were sidelined by COVID-19. The Orpheum Theatre in downtown Hillsboro celebrated its one hundredth anniversary in 2020. Sadly, the theater was dark for most of the year. The Orpheum was opened by a bootlegger from nearby Panama, Illinois, who owned a speakeasy during the coal mining boom in southern Illinois. The theater is currently owned by Jeff Eisentraut of Hillsboro. The Orpheum opened on March 22, 1920, and a throwback celebration had to be canceled due to COVID-19. "I feel so bad for them," John Galer said. "It's a family operation. They have five or six theaters, in Iowa and in Pana, one in Gillespie. They're going to be hurting for money. The Eisentrauts originally came from Iowa. My mom was still alive. Hillsboro can be cliquish. If you weren't from Hillsboro back then, it was difficult to get close to people. You hadn't earned your way into the world."

The Eisentrauts arrived in Hillsboro in 2003. They were so unfamiliar with the area that they originally had to look up Hillsboro on a map. The *Journal-News* did a feature story on the new kids in town. Galer recalled, "My mom was a teacher, a real people person. They were here three days and Mom brought them an apple pie to welcome them to Hillsboro. They still talk about the apple pie."

Eureka Springs's Boian said, "What's the saying from Shakespeare? 'Strive mightily but eat and drink together as friends.' We are that way. People don't pull weapons on one another. It happens. Mostly not out of anger and more out of fear."

The *Eureka Springs Independent* has a regular front-page feature honoring "This Week's Independent Thinker." For the January 26, 2022, edition the *Independent* honored the Vietnamese Zen Buddhist monk Thich Nhat Hanh, who had died on January 19, 2022. His photo appeared next to a story about the Eureka Springs City Council passing its 2022 budget. The newspaper wrote that Nhat Hanh "taught that we should regard ourselves as part of all of life rather than the dominant life-form." That message goes beyond local.

That's hugely spiritual.

Many times, the larger the paper, the less fun there is to be had.

Toward the dusk of my career at the *Chicago Sun-Times*, a new editor arrived from the stodgy *Chicago Tribune*. The *Sun-Times* was generally the more freewheeling publication. In our first features staff meeting, the new editor promised that we would have "fun." That was a warning sign to a bunch of cynical journalists. Fun is organic. We had weekly staff meetings where we were instructed to bring in a minimum of three story ideas. Folk singer Jim Croce's wife, Ingrid, was on a book tour for *I Got a Name: The Jim Croce Story*. I interviewed her and wanted to do a "fun" sidebar.

One of Croce's biggest hits was "Bad, Bad Leroy Brown," about a menacing dude from the South Side of Chicago. After some research I found a real Leroy Brown on the South Side of Chicago. The fun-loving Mr. Brown met most of the requirements of the Croce song: treetop lover (he was tall), junkyard dog (he had one), and he liked to gamble.

After I handed in my short sidebar, the same editor who said we were going to have fun spent time walking around the newsroom polling younger staff members to see if the 1973 hit "Bad, Bad Leroy Brown" registered with them. Another editor intervened, and my Leroy Brown sidebar appeared, much to the delight of our irreverent music fans. But it was at this turn of events I knew my time at my beloved *Sun-Times* was nearing an end. I was getting too old to fight over things like this.

So now I wander around smaller family newspaper offices and ask staffers if they are having fun. It is important to keep an open mind. In 1979, Dixon *Telegraph* reporter Jamie Hogan was assigned to do a profile on the late banjo player Earl Scruggs, who was headlining the Dixon Petunia Festival. "I didn't want to do that story," she said. "I was covering hard news and I got to see my byline every day on stories I thought were important. . . . I was in for a surprise because that interview opened my eyes and changed my life. That put me on a lifelong love affair with bluegrass, steel strings, and twang. It was the only piece I wrote for the *Telegraph* to be picked up by the AP [Associated Press] and syndicated for distribution, which was quite a distinction back then."

After Dixon, Hogan moved on to the Galesburg *Register-Mail* in 1980. A personal drama pushed Hogan to leave Galesburg in 1981. "I needed to go," she said. "Before I had appropriate employment lined up and was nervous about the next step, Tom Shaw invited me back to Dixon and told me there was always a place for me at the *Telegraph*. I think about his kindness and how meaningful it was to have the option. But I knew it would be a mistake. I was definitely still in career-growth mode."

Longtime *Tri-State Defender* reporter Wiley Henry reflected, "I loved the newspaper because it was camaraderie. We had people we practically spent the night with on press night." Henry smiled and recalled deadline orders of huge trays of macaroni and cheese and Kentucky Fried Chicken. "We were all like family," he said. "I loved it even though I wasn't paid what I was worth. I started at $75 a week [in 1986]. I lived with my parents. By the time I left the paper in 2013, I was full time, making about $30,000 a year. That's on the lower end of the spectrum. People always told me to leave, but I stayed because I felt this was my calling. I was tied to the Black community. Where else would I go?

"I felt a close kinship with the Sengstackes because I had been there longer than any other person who worked at the newspaper. I called John Sengstacke 'Uncle John.' We remained friends over the years. I wasn't that concerned about the money because I loved what I was doing."

Trust and loyalty grow out of a community of kindness.

Larry Gavin, former senior editor of the *Evanston RoundTable* in Illinois, sighed and said, "We do look at the newspaper as a community service. Some of it is fun. When we get attacked by someone, it is not fun. There's a group of thirty or forty people here who attack everything. I don't know if Trump created a climate where people are more willing to do that." His wife, writer and former publisher Mary Gavin, added, "It has gotten very vitriolic and not for the good of the community."

Longtime *RoundTable* reporter Bob Seidenberg said, "It is becoming more complex. The more corporate-owned things aren't as concerned about that [criticism]. They're concerned about stories that create a lot of hits. When it is publicly held stock, you have a whole different group."

Positive change comes from a newspaper environment built on trust, respect, and the willingness to take chances. The *Arkansas Democrat-Gazette*'s Walter Hussman Jr. obtained a business degree from Columbia University in New York. He said one of the most interesting sections of business school was when they studied declining or failing businesses. "And someone would come in and try to turn it around, whether it was an entrepreneur or a big corporation," Hussman explained. "To me, that involved a lot of creativity, innovation, and collaboration. To me, it was an exciting challenge."

There is no question that if you don't evolve, you die.

"You have to take risks," Hussman remarked. "When we bought the number two newspaper in Little Rock, it had half the circulation of the dominant paper. That was a big risk. It doesn't work to be a complementary newspaper in a two-newspaper market. You have to be a substitute. So we said, 'Let's try being a substitute.' And it actually worked. It took seventeen years, but it worked. If we had known it was going to take seventeen years on the front end, I don't know if we would have done it. But you have to evolve."

Chapter 11

The Truth About Fake News

Whether they're reporting on their own family member, neighbor, or child's teacher, reporters and editors at hyper-local papers work as hard as those at larger newspapers to report without bias or self-censorship. Yet big media is facing unprecedented levels of animosity and distrust. The strong, trusting, community bonds formed between readers and their local-paper staff have largely enabled family papers to evade the "fake news" accusations that have become so prevalent today.

In January 2017, Walter Hussman Jr. joined seven couples on a bicycle trip in Cambodia and Vietnam. Hussman travels regularly, and every time the former publisher of the *Arkansas Democrat-Gazette* is outside of the United States, he tries to watch American news on television.

"The only way you could do that in 2017 was CNN International," Hussman said. "I'm watching, and [CNN chief international anchor] Christiane Amanpour comes up. She's done great reporting on the Middle East and such. But she wasn't doing any reporting. She was doing an ad for CNN. She said, 'I don't believe the false equivalency of giving both sides.' I stopped buttoning my shirt. I was getting ready to go down to dinner."

Hussman could not believe what he'd heard. In his soft homespun drawl, Hussman reflected, "She said her job was to determine what the truth is and share that with the viewers. Yeah, we like to share what the truth is, but a lot of times we think we know what the truth is, and as we find more evidence it turns out to be different than what we thought it was." Hussman said the role of a newspaper is not to define the truth but hopefully arrive at the truth. That is best accomplished by giving readers as much information as possible and letting them figure out over time what the truth is.

"A lot of our readers are smarter than we are," he explained. "We have doctors that know more about medicine. We have executives that know more about energy. That CNN ad really bothered me. So I came home and told our readers what we do believe. I drafted core journalistic values. It's six paragraphs. We publish it on page two every day and we've been doing that in all of our newspapers."

These are the *Arkansas Democrat-Gazette* core values. They were first published in the *Democrat-Gazette* on January 11, 2017:

> *"To give the news impartially, without fear or favor."* *(Adolph Ochs, 1858–1935) Impartiality means reporting, editing, and delivering the news honestly, fairly, objectively, and without personal opinion or bias.*

> *Credibility is the greatest asset of any news medium, and impartiality is the greatest source of credibility.*

> *To provide the most complete report, a news organization must not just cover the news, but uncover it. It must follow the story wherever it leads, regardless of any preconceived ideas on what might be the most newsworthy.*

> *The pursuit of truth is a noble goal of journalism. But the truth is not always apparent or known immediately. Journalists' role is therefore not to determine what they believe at that time to be the truth and reveal only that to their readers, but rather to report as completely and impartially as possible all verifiable facts so that readers can, based on*

their own knowledge and experience, determine what they believe to be the truth.

When a newspaper delivers both news and opinions, the impartiality and credibility of the news organization can be questioned. To minimize this as much as possible there needs to be a sharp and clear distinction between news and opinion, both to those providing and consuming the news.

"A newspaper has five constituencies, including first its readers, then advertisers, then employees, then creditors, then shareholders. As long as the newspaper keeps those constituencies in that order, especially its readers first, all constituencies will be well served." (Walter Hussman [Sr.], 1906–1988)

In 2016, the University of North Carolina at Chapel Hill approached the Hussman family about raising money for their journalism school. Hussman was a 1968 graduate of the UNC journalism school. On one of her trips to Little Rock, the dean, Susan King, brought up the idea of naming the school for the Hussman family, who had been in the newspaper business one hundred years. "I said we were honored but we didn't have the financial resources to make a donation large enough," Hussman said. Hussman later told King that the journalism school should adopt a statement of core values, which could assist in fundraising.

"Some people now are disenchanted with what they see in media today," he said. "They feel there's way too much bias. They must be saying, 'What are they teaching these kids in journalism school?'"

Hussman still considered the gift over time. "I said I'm not going to do this unless you adopt the statement of core values that I would agree with." And UNC did. The core values are chiseled into a stone wall in the lobby of Carroll Hall, where the journalism school is located. In September 2019 the school was renamed the UNC Hussman School of Journalism and Media. Notable alumni include CNN host Brooke Baldwin, *New York Times* Pulitzer

Prize winner Emily Steel, and the late beat poet/City Lights bookstore owner Lawrence Ferlinghetti (class of 1941).

In September 2019, Dean King told the *Democrat-Gazette*, "For journalism to have someone at this moment of such cataclysmic disruption and lack of trust to say journalism is so important that he wants to invest in the future for the pipeline of great journalists and media leaders—that is the most optimistic thing I have felt in a long time. At this moment, many people may run the other way, but Walter Hussman and his family are running straight toward the issues in supporting journalism."

Hussman said, "UNC is probably one of the top five journalism schools in the country. You got Columbia, Medill, Missouri. If we could get University of North Carolina to do this, why not get other journalism schools to do this? Other newspaper groups to do this? Then we can slowly try to re-establish trust with the media."

—

By the fall of 2021, Hussman was embroiled in a major controversy at UNC. Pulitzer Prize–winning journalist Nikole Hannah-Jones was offered the position of the Knight Chair in Race and Investigative Journalism at UNC's school of journalism, but without tenure that had previously been part of the package. Hannah-Jones obtained her master's degree from UNC at Chapel Hill.

UNC journalists discovered that Hussman had sent messages to the journalism school, the chancellor, and the vice chancellor expressing concerns about Hannah-Jones, who created the *New York Times*'s 1619 Project, a collection of essays and other materials that explore the legacy of slavery in America today. The North Carolina–based digital magazine *The Assembly* obtained copies of Hussman's emails and shared some with its readers. For example, in September 2021 Hussman questioned Hannah-Jones's essay on America's post–World War II struggle for civil rights in which she wrote, "For the most part Black Americans fought back alone."

In an email uncovered by *The Assembly*, Hussman wrote, "I think this claim denigrates the courageous effort of many white Americans to address the sin of slavery and the racial injustices that resulted after the Civil War." According to *The Assembly*, Hussman listed white Freedom Riders and other white people who had fought for equality, including journalists in the South. He continued, "Long before Nikole Hannah-Jones won her Pulitzer Prize, courageous white southerners risking their lives standing up for Blacks were winning Pulitzer Prizes too."

The UNC board of trustees eventually voted to offer Hannah-Jones the professorship with tenure. She turned down the offer, citing Hussman's meddling. Hannah-Jones landed at Howard University in Washington, DC. In an interview with NC Policy Watch's Joe Killian, Hannah-Jones said she had a good relationship with journalism school dean Susan King but added, "I just could not work at a school named after Walter Hussman. To be a person who has stood for what I stand for and have any integrity whatsoever, I just couldn't see how I could do that."

Hussman would not talk about his emails with *The Assembly*, and in January 2022, he told me, "I'd rather not comment on Nikole Hannah-Jones. I will comment on dealing with controversies. Any newspaper worthy of their readers' respect is going to find itself in controversial and unpopular positions from time to time. I learned long ago you can't live your life worried about what others say about you. If you do, you become a prisoner to what others say or think. You do what you believe is moral, ethical, and right and give others the chance to explain why you are wrong."

Hussman's dustup with Hannah-Jones has led some to suggest his core values at UNC should be removed. In the October 14, 2021, issue of the alternative weekly *Arkansas Times*, Austin Bailey (a UNC journalism school grad) called Hussman an "old white man" and wrote that his values are "an outdated code that perpetuates the 'both sides' journalism that help land us here in this hellscape that is 2021," adding that "it's not too late to peel [the values] off and change course."

In January 2022, Hussman said, "The very core of journalism is just human nature. Would we like other people to think like we do? And other people to agree with us? Sure, that's human nature. But that's why news reporting has to have guardrails. Your job is to keep your own bias out of reporting. You have to be impartial." This opens the door to a greater discussion about a new journalism that can be cynical about "both sides." Communities are changing and the playing field is more diverse than when Hussman was coming up in the family newspaper business. Each journalist—whether it is Hussman, Hannah-Jones, or myself—brings their own background and experiences into their work. Objectivity is impossible.

But we can be fair.

And what goes into being fair? The ability to listen. The gift of listening with measured compassion. Asking uncomfortable questions. Conducting thorough research while gathering facts and then following wherever the story may take you, without bias and blinders.

—

In the world of independent family newspapers, trust and community are united in purpose and spirit. Between July 2017 and May 2018, the family-owned *Carroll Times Herald* in Iowa published a series of stories about a local police officer's inappropriate relationships with teenage girls. Reporter Jacob Strong spent two months investigating Carroll police officer Jacob Smith's personnel records and public documents. Strong went on to interview the teenage girls. Smith resigned just before the paper published the first article. And then Smith sued the paper for libel.

Iowa district judge Thomas Bice ruled that the articles were accurate and the "underlying facts were undisputed." The libel lawsuit was dismissed in May 2018.

"Our family always felt our first responsibility was to the community," *Times Herald* co-owner Doug Burns said during an interview in his mother's office. "This is the way we were raised. That's why we stared down a libel suit and won."

But the expenses from defending the truth put the future of the legacy newspaper in jeopardy. Burns established a GoFundMe page seeking $140,000 to cover legal expenses and to keep the newspaper in the family. The paper raised $99,000. "It all worked out fine," said publisher Ann Wilson.

On the GoFundMe page, Burns wrote, "Standing up to the patriarchy, particularly in a rural reach of the nation, and especially now, is a financially perilous choice, one fraught with pressures from a host of sources and power centers, many of whom sought to kill the story and then retaliated against the newspaper."

In October 2019, Burns told the *Washington Post*, "'Fake news' rhetoric has trickled down to affect even local papers." The president of the United

States of America was consistently belittling American journalists for writing what he called "fake news," seemingly forgetting that the First Amendment to the U.S. Constitution guarantees freedom of speech, and of the press. The president's censorship efforts largely failed.

During a February 2020 interview in the publisher's office, Burns elaborated, "If you ran a story like our police story in 1998, there was still a level of respect for our institutions and a level of respect for truth. A majority of the community would have been outraged that there was an officer conducting himself in that fashion. The newspaper wouldn't have been targeted in the way we were. I'm glad I responded the way I did.

"When we were pressured to walk away from that story, and had I just done a 'good-old-boy, small-town-guy' thing and told our editor, 'He shouldn't have been sleeping with a seventeen-year-old girl, but he told me he was going to stop, and the police chief was going to find him a job in another town, she's going to be eighteen in a year, let's just drop the story. . . .' If I had taken that approach, do you know how much financial pain, personal pain, legal pain we wouldn't have had to go through? But that was a hill I was willing to die on. If you can't stand up for a teenage girl who had to deal with that sort of activity from a police officer, then you shouldn't be standing anywhere near a printing press."

As the owner of a private for-profit business, Burns was humiliated about turning to the GoFundMe model. The lawsuit forced the family to scramble for funds to recover from lost revenue and legal expenses. "The police chief was on a mission to see our paper sink," he said. "We know he was trying to sabotage our sources and prevent us to cover certain sensitive areas. Our attorney, who knows the case inside and out and was with us for a whole year, she was one of the contributors to the GoFundMe. She gave her own money."

Burns's effort generated national press and shed a light on the challenges of keeping a family newspaper alive in the tight quarters of rural America. "The vast majority of what we write lifts the community and celebrates success, whether it is a new business opening or kids doing well in school," he said. "A lot of rural America is a news desert. The papers that are left don't want to take the risk. We've gotten charges of 'fake news' on school board stories and city council stories. And the level of abuse that I take and some of the other journalists take would be shocking if you time-machined back to 1998. We're without peer in newspapers of this size and that's because we care about the community. We can't just celebrate it. We have to tell truth to power, too."

The *Eureka Springs Independent*'s Mary Pat Boian took a lighter attitude toward 'fake media.' "There's always been fake news, yellow journalism, and publishers who were printing money using newspapers as their bully pulpit," she said. "We're more interested in putting out a product that shows both sides. Making money is a concept we're not real familiar with. But it hasn't deterred us."

Tom Shaw, retired CEO of Shaw Media, said trust builds over time. "Just simple things like having the words in your story spelled correctly, delivering the news in a timely fashion—those types of things feed into the trust component," Shaw said in the summer of 2020. "The meat of the matter is to cover the stories accurately, and if you have opinion, label it as such. It seems to me 'fake news' hasn't been an issue in the smaller towns that it has been on a larger scale."

—

The late Lon Grahnke hired me in 1981 at the *Suburban Sun-Times*. I had written for the suburban *Aurora Beacon-News* and *Barrington Courier-Review*, and freelanced for *Chicago* magazine and the *Chicago Reader*. I prided myself on speed and hitting all deadlines. I was sloppy. Until Lon became my editor, I was hesitant to call back sources to double-check facts. Lon taught me to slow down, to reread and edit my copy over and over. Everyone makes mistakes, and I still melt down if an error of mine gets published.

Lon moved on to become features editor and television critic at the *Sun-Times*. He mentored a generation of Chicago journalists. He paid attention to detail. After all, he was the son of a carpenter. Lon was a proud union man. He looked like *NYPD Blue* actor Dennis Franz and acted like gruff but vulnerable television newspaper editor Lou Grant.

Lon was a compelling human being whose interests included acting, Van Morrison, pro wrestling, movies, and television. Pulitzer Prize–winning journalist Roger Ebert double-checked facts with Lon. He knew where the truth was. He was a relentless advocate for his writers, and he would never sell us out. Lon died of complications from Alzheimer's disease in 2006. He was just fifty-six years old. But he looks over my shoulder in everything I write. And that's the truth.

—

Paddock Publications in Arlington Heights, Illinois, deals with media trust using a variety of methods. "I don't know if there's any one way to deal with it," said Doug Ray, chairman, publisher, and CEO of Paddock. The *Daily Herald* features a Sunday "Facts Matter" column, a suburban Chicago version of the *New York Times*'s "Fact Checks" column. In 2019, the *Daily Herald* rolled out a semi-regular "Pulling Back the Curtain (A Behind-the-Scenes Look at the *Daily Herald* Newsroom)" section that features background stories on staff members and columns such as "How We Got the Story" and "Policy Corner," which explains how some editorial decisions are made. "We had an ongoing initiative to tell people how we produce the news and why we produce the news," Ray said. "We've been around a while, so a lot of our readers tell us. A lot of them know us. Our problem is less than what the metro papers would have."

The *Daily Herald* created its community advisory Sounding Board in 2018. In the summer of 2020, the Sounding Board leader was *Daily Herald* deputy managing editor Jim Slusher.

Former Naperville police chief David Dial was one of the community members the newspaper asked to volunteer on the board. Naperville (pop. 148,000) is the fourth-largest city in Illinois. Located twenty-eight miles west of Chicago, it is the hometown of actor Bob Odenkirk, *Jeopardy!* whiz James Holzhauer, and me. Dial was police chief from 1990 until he retired in 2012 at the age of sixty-seven. "They contacted a dozen people from a variety of backgrounds," Dial said. "They wanted people to give them opinions on editorials. And we are a diverse group. They've got a minister, people who have far-left and far-right political views. Our purpose is not to try and reach consensus but to give them opinions. We generally meet once a year in Arlington Heights."

Dial still lives in Naperville. He is an associate professor and chair of criminal justice at Aurora University. Naperville is constantly ranked among the nation's safest cities by *USA Today*. Dial has been on the other side of the media fence, where journalists are chasing him down for truthful answers. "Never ever lie to the media," said Dial, who has a deep background in homeland security. "If you're not going to respond to something, tell them why.

Because the matter is under investigation. Whatever it is. But don't give inappropriate information. I teach that."

Dial went back to the 1980s when he was assistant chief of police in Lakewood, Colorado. That's where the Vietnam vet first heard of a quote from Chicago mayor Richard J. Daley. "He said, 'Never start a war with people that buy ink by the barrel,'" Dial recalled. "When I worked in the field, I tried to have press reports available to the media. We had a press office. It's all digital now. Also to be responsive. It's a public interest. Quit trying to hide behind things. If we make a mistake, here's what we say about it. We're never going to be perfect. When you hold people accountable, there's a lot of forgiveness. If you try to cover things up, it doesn't work."

—

Sometimes a newspaper builds trust in its community one person at a time. Longtime Hillsboro pastor and newspaper fan Randy Sands is a cornerstone of that process. His church sits atop a slope on the southwest corner of the southern Illinois town. You drive by the Hillsboro Heights apartments, the Beckemeyer Elementary School, and the obligatory Casey's convenience store. "For a community of 6,400, we have three Casey's [stores] in town," Sands laughed.

Sands turned fifty-eight years old in February 2020. He had been pastoring at the Hillsboro Free Methodist Church for thirty-three years. He is the third-longest-tenured pastor in the Gateway Conference of the Free Methodist Church. When Sands arrived in Hillsboro in 1987, there were forty-five churches in the conference. During a March 2020 conversation, he said the number had dropped to twenty-seven.

The membership of the Hillsboro Free Methodist Church stood firm at two hundred in 2020. The average attendance number was three hundred. "When we got here, we had twelve members," Sands said. "On a good Sunday we had thirty people. In 1985, the conference almost closed the doors here because it was getting down to nothing. We had a church in Litchfield, but they closed in 1977, '78."

Small-town churches, like small-town newspapers, are going away.

The truth is still there; sometimes it takes more time and energy to find it. Sands reads the physical edition of the local *Journal-News* three times in one day. "I do the pictures first," he said. "Then I put it down and later on I'll read the story related to the picture. The third time, I read everything else. Thankfully it only comes out Monday and Thursday. I will go online to look at the obituaries, but that's the pastor in me. I'm married to a woman who goes paperless. She says, 'Why do you have to have those finance reports on paper?' I want to circle it. I want to highlight it.

"I still want to hold it."

Sands has held trust close to his heart throughout his career. He was sitting on a sofa in his spacious office on a late weekday afternoon in March 2020. Sands looked out through a window to an empty white-gravel parking lot. "Last fall a member of our church shot and killed his wife in our parking lot," Sands said. "Right at those rocks. They were going through a divorce. He shot her twice point-blank. They were exchanging their dog. They were both members of our church. He was retired from Graham Correctional Center [a medium-security prison outside of Hillsboro] and was president of the union for a number of years. She was a retired nurse."

Pastor Sands was not at the church at the time of the shooting. He was visiting his youngest son in eastern Missouri. "After the shooting, [the shooter] actually came back to see me," Sands said. "The cops were here and the yellow tape was up. He pulled up. He still had his sidearm and they told him to drop the gun. But I wasn't here yet."

The shooter, David Chesser, was taken into custody without incident in the church parking lot. The event had been captured on the church security camera. His wife, Mary Chesser, was able to drive away before crashing into a tree down the road from the church. She died eleven days later from injuries sustained in the shooting. Chesser was charged with murder and felony aggravated discharge of a firearm, having allegedly fired the shots within one thousand feet of Beckemeyer Elementary School while school was in session. Chesser spent his seventieth birthday in Montgomery County Jail.

These things just don't happen in Hillsboro.

"We couldn't figure out what the press was going to do with that," Sands said. "And the media that was going to swarm in here. So I called my superintendent and said I was on my way. My secretary was in here. My superintendent called his lawyer. He asked, 'How do we respond when the media shows up?' I thought Decatur, I thought Springfield, St. Louis newspapers would all come here. The lawyer told us what to say and what not to say."

Mike Plunkett, the publisher of the *Journal-News*, was the only local media to appear on the scene. He wrote a story and took pictures of the church parking lot and the spot where Mary Chesser hit the tree with her car. The shooting was front-page news. "They had to cover it," Sands said, and he started crying, ever so gently. "Dave was a good friend—we were fishing buddies—and not just a parishioner. The newspaper was very tactful. It was the hot topic for a while, and then people move on to something else."

Plunkett was on an advertising call in Litchfield and heard about the shooting on his police scanner. He drove the seven miles back to the scene in Hillsboro. In a separate interview, Plunkett said, "We have such a good relationship that the police chief called me over while he was on the scene and said, 'I gotta get a press release out. Can you write it for me?'"

Former Naperville police chief David Dial said, "That's a bit much. I've never heard of that one. I never worked in a town that small either."

Journal-News owner John Galer said, "Sometimes you think that's too close. But at the same time, they know we're fair. And we don't have to beat these guys to death for the information that we need. We're not going to go off the rails and do crazy, emotional stories. We just want to make sure people know the facts. It could be a real conflict in what you feel is right journalistically and what you're doing in the public interest. It's a hard line to walk. But in a small town you don't have the population density. You wear a lot of hats in a small town. Whether you're in public service or you're in the newspaper."

For Plunkett, it was essential to play the story fair and down the middle. He explained, "There's lots of ways you could sensationalize a shooting like that. It happened at the church. But it didn't have anything to do with the church. But you have to mention where it happened. You don't imply any blame that it was a 'church shooting.'"

Sands said, "It builds trust. They could have interviewed me—'What did you know about Dave and Mary?' Gossip stuff. I never got any of that."

Sands was born and raised in Salem, Illinois, a small country town about sixty miles north of Hillsboro. His father, Jimmie Dean Sands, was an Illinois

Gulf Central Railroad welder. His mother, Helen, was a homemaker. Sands's wife, Barbara, is from rural Flora, Illinois. They have two sons, Matt and Mark.

Sands attended nearby Greenville College, where he received his bachelor of arts degree in pastoral ministry in 1990. He had been an assistant youth pastor in Salem in 1987 when he got the higher calling to Hillsboro. Sands has led his church through tremendous growth. The Hillsboro Free Methodist Church dates back to 1890, when four women known as the Pentecostal Band arrived in Hillsboro. The original-frame church was on the opposite side of town from the present-day church—behind a Casey's, of course.

Empathy has been a guiding light for Sands. He said the median age of his church members is around thirty years old. He suggested there may be greater warmth in face-to-face conversation and tactile acts such as reading a physical book or newspaper. "Is there a lack of the human touch?" he asked. "I'm a teary guy and I'm passionate. But with teenagers, when you get the newspaper, or the media comes through your phone: so-and-so has just hung himself, and the guilt that sets in for our community—'What could I have done?' There is something about keeping a human touch. Right or wrong, I blame multimedia, texting. Giving somebody their fifteen minutes of fame because they make the newspaper? We make a big deal about it, and we should, but does another kid feel left out? It alarms me and it's not just kids. I have adults who are dealing with this. It is the toughest thing in ministry for me. And there's such a terrible ripple effect.

"We're blessed to have a small community. Everybody knows everybody. The curse of a small community? Everybody knows everybody. But I wouldn't trade it for the world. I'm a shepherd pastor. I'm marred with empathy. I'm marred with compassion. There's a thing called StrengthsFinder," he said, referencing a personal assessment tool developed by Gallup and outlined in books by Tom Rath. "Thirty-four different strengths a person has. Empathy is the top one. In my world, empathy is not feeling sorry for somebody, but feeling sorry with somebody. You're trying to walk in their shoes."

The bean supper is a strong tradition around Hillsboro. At least half a dozen area churches come together four times a year for the bean supper or a spaghetti dinner for fellowship and mutual support. "When one person hurts, we all hurt," Sands said. "When Dave shot Mary, the other pastors in town were praying for us."

In March of 2020, Sands was beginning to think about retirement. He wasn't sure if it would be five years or ten years. He enjoys fishing, going on cruises with his wife, and mowing. He push-mows and ride-mows his own lawn as well as the lawns of neighbors. "When I started here in 1987, my boss [Herbert H. Coates] looked at me in the eye," Sands said. "He just passed away a month ago. He was ninety years old. He said, 'Randy, there's no reason you shouldn't retire there, should God leave you there.'"

Sands was placing his trust in a larger truth. The political and social divisions in America have diminished the perception of truth in the media. In June 2021, the Reuters Institute for the Study of Journalism released a report that concluded the United States ranked last in media trust. A survey of ninety-two thousand consumers in forty-six countries landed the U.S. with a 29 percent trust factor. Local print and broadcast news fared better than national news. With media companies being splintered, you find your own tribe to trust.

But it has become increasingly difficult to discern the trustworthy from the imposters. During the 2016 election cycle, a series of newspapers in the far northwestern suburbs of Chicago were published by a political action committee. The *McHenry Times* was produced by the Liberty Principles political action committee, a Chicago-based PAC that supported Republican candidates in Illinois. The PAC was established by conservative radio host Dan Proft. According to a February 2016 *Northwest Herald* story, Liberty Principles was funded by Republican contributors, including another PAC supported by then–Illinois governor Bruce Rauner.

The *McHenry Times* included political advertising, stories about local events, and sports. Shaw Media's Peter Shaw said, "It is something that is being presented as real news that is not coming from any type of journalistic background, as opposed to the hashtag 'fake news,' where 'I don't agree with what you're saying, so I'm going to call it fake.' If I went to the editorial staff and started talking advertising, they would probably not very nicely ask me to leave. I would like to see our journalists be as public-facing as possible. I want them to be the stars. It's their content."

P. J. Browning, the award-winning publisher of the *Post and Courier* in

Charleston, South Carolina, said that her readers challenge the newspaper when it features articles that are not written locally. "I don't think we have a problem locally with trust," she said. "But certainly, if we run something from AP [Associated Press], sometimes the *New York Times*, the *Washington Post*, that's where we take a hit. Unless it is a story that has to be on the front page, we try not to run AP on the front page. We really scrutinize the amount of AP. We've had discussions of even doing away with it altogether. But we do have a lot of older readers who get all their news from the *Post and Courier*, even the national news. We tend to run what we think we need to run. Trust in journalism today is the difference between the national media and local media."

Hillsboro newspaper owner John Galer said, "One thing I'm proud of is that I can go to the Republican Lincoln Day Dinner and the JFK Dinner and I'm accepted in both places. And nobody thinks bad either way. I feel very strongly about the fact that I can do that. Because that's what you want to be. You have to carry the whole world because there's a whole bunch of different sides to community. You have to be able to represent them."

Curt Jacobs, the former sixth-generation publisher of Indiana's *Madison Courier,* said, "To me, the most currency you have as a newspaper is trust. It has gotten harder. People don't trust our institutions the way they used to. The only way I know how to do that is to have an honest relationship. That means if you make a mistake, you own it. When we changed delivery methods I wrote several columns about that. I'm not a writer by trade, but I tried hard to communicate with the readers and say, 'This is why this is happening.' We knew that many people weren't going to like the changes, but we tried to let them know. Transparency is kind of a buzzword, but it is about being genuine."

Independent family newspapers are also faced with many content options. As newspapers cut full-time staffs, publishers turn to bloggers, freelancers, interns, and "contract reporters." The content is delivered at a lower cost, and publishers don't have to pay for employee benefits, expenses, and office parking.

How are the motivations of these new contributors vetted?

Hillsboro *Journal-News* editor Mary Herschelman said, "When we talk to writers, we say we have the right to edit them. We don't do a ton of opinion-based things. It is very important for us to have no editorial comments in our reporting. Most of the stringer stuff we get comes for sports. We don't let them bag on referees for bad calls." She knocked on a wooden table and added, "We've been very lucky."

Herschelman attended a Southern Illinois Editorial Association meeting in 2018. A speaker asked the audience how many members had been tagged with the "fake news" title. "We don't get called 'fake news,'" Herschelman said. "People trust us. I don't try to pit one side against another. You can't always say that. People want to be hard on Facebook and hard on the media, but sometimes you have to take accountability. You have to say, 'Where am I getting my news from?' People come to us when it's important because they know we have a long reputation of doing things the right way. Mike [Plunkett, the publisher,] always says the greatest compliment is when people say it's 'our' newspaper."

In my long career, I've found that plain-speak works well. I do not have a college degree. I do not act like the smartest person in the room. I try to give my subjects room to talk, and I keep my mouth shut. I listen. Perhaps my style is a form of blue-collar journalism, but it has become a trusting thread with the communities I visit. I try to keep my opinions to myself.

The *Journal-News* in Hillsboro does not even have an editorial page. John Galer said he thought editorials no longer worked. "The world is such a polarized mess, you're causing more problems than you think," he said. "A community project editorial, yeah, but if you're talking policy or some major thing, you're going to immediately create sides. The world doesn't need to be polarized."

Social media has obviously played into this polarization.

Thanks to WordPress, Twitter, and countless other platforms, people can launch their own newsletters and newspapers, becoming citizen reporters or columnists without having to deal with meticulous editors or fact-checkers. And bonus points for the fact that news can be delivered immediately.

In October 2019, the *Lansing State Journal* revealed a network of nearly forty fake local news websites across Michigan. They had names like the *Ann Arbor Times*, *Novi Times*, and *Grand Rapids Reporter*. These were not family-run operations. The sites were a mash-up of news releases about local government and rewritten content from other sources like the Mackinac Center for Public Policy and the Heritage Foundation, two conservative think tanks in Michigan and Washington, DC. The outlets were under the umbrella of Locality Labs, LLC, which created similar sketchy websites in Illinois and Maryland. The sites didn't have mastheads or transparency of ownership. The *Lansing Sun* had an email address and an address in Dover, Delaware, for written correspondence. There were no names for contact information.

The mere physicalness of a printed newspaper gives the stories inside warmth and permanence. It's not unlike the divide between music on vinyl and streaming, except that with the news, polarization is amplified through Instagram, Twitter, and Facebook, where anyone can create their own narratives and false truths. The legacy of a family newspaper offers the kind of credibility that cannot be cultivated in short tweets.

"When it comes to trust, you have to prove yourself right," Galer said. "You have to do that yourself personally. It is something you earn over time by being straightforward so people know what you're saying is real. You have to be humble a little bit to pull that off. If you're really flamboyant and hanging out there, they're never going to trust you. If you have that stance where you're preaching down to the world, it doesn't gain a lot of respect. And if you are on that pedestal, you're going to fall off. Nobody can stay on a pedestal their whole life."

—

Political agendas have made the pedestal a hot moving target. During my mid-July 2019 visit, it was 105 degrees in the shade in Bakersfield, California. The *Bakersfield Californian* ran a front-page story that Bakersfield was the fourth-least-educated city in America, according to a survey of the 150 most populated U.S. metropolitan areas by the financial website WalletHub. Many residents here are looking for a lifeline.

"This is called the Appalachia of the West," columnist Robert Price said. "There's a lot of poverty here. It's a good thing for the colleges around here because they only have one way to go—which is up. There's always something going on here. We've had some great murders. That's a phrase only a journalist would use. This is the most conservative county in California. It used to be Kern and Orange County, but Orange County moved left. The almost–speaker of the house Kevin McCarthy is from here. The last two Republican leaders of the state senate are from Bakersfield."

McCarthy's district includes the city of Bakersfield and most of Kern and Tulare Counties south of Sacramento and north of Los Angeles. A life-long Bakersfield resident, McCarthy has stated that social media censors conservative politicians. In August 2018, he tweeted that then–Twitter CEO Jack Dorsey should testify before Congress with the hashtag #StopTheBias.

Iowa's Doug Burns said, "Look, if somebody was providing local news in a more affordable, more effective, and more penetrating way than me, I would just throw my hands up and say, 'You guys beat me fair and square'—be it a local website, a local radio station, a group of local bloggers. If they're out there reporting and investigating in more penetrating detail, then we are irrelevant."

And then he declared that is not happening.

Burns continued, "We have a generation of people that think anything they read in print that is presented in a certain font and a certain style of writing, they assume that has been vetted the way newspapers have been vetted most of their lives. So they don't know the difference. People nineteen or twenty know the difference. The problem is that people fifty and older grew up expecting a protocol in the way their information was presented. This isn't like TV news coming along and making radio obsolete, or a start-up free weekly alternative paper kicking the shit out of a lazy legacy paper. People are deciding they don't need facts anymore. And honestly, people don't see community whole cloth. They don't see the way elements are integrated the way regular newspaper readers used to or still do in some cases. As newspapers are diminished, it is almost a direct corollary: as we go down, so does our democracy.

"You're going to have this itemized existence where you have these roaring tribes that are out there throwing misinformation back and forth and seeing what catches and what doesn't. We are the last refuge for selective truth in our region. If we're gone, the value of the truth goes with us. In this very binary world where people line up on 'Team Blue' and 'Team Red'—here most people are on Team Red, the Republican-conservative team—media like us are just thrown in with MSNBC and CNN."

On Labor Day weekend 2019, a Carroll grade-school teacher driving with her mother crashed her John Deere Gator utility vehicle outside of Carroll. She was at nearly three times the legal alcohol limit to drive and was charged with first-offense OWI (operating while intoxicated). "The accident was so bad, her mother had to be airlifted to Des Moines," Burns said. "Nobody died. We ran the story about her being charged with OWI and we identified her as being a grade-school teacher. We had people threatening to boycott the paper, saying that we should be run out of town and that the newspaper should not be listing the occupation of somebody who got an OWI. 'You wouldn't list the occupation if she was working at the Pella window factory,' and yeah, there's a lot of jobs where we wouldn't. When I started in the business, people would have been angry at us if we didn't put that information in the story. The reaction would have been against the teacher for conducting herself like that, and 'Do I have something to be worried about with my child being in her classroom?' But now it has just turned.

"If somebody doesn't like the truth that we would have reported in the 1990s, now they go, 'That's fake news.' And 35 percent of the population will go along with it, whether the process is used by the president or someone else."

Chapter 12

Virus Crisis, 2020

On the quiet evening of March 11, 2020, the *Journal-News* staff in Hillsboro, Illinois, was putting together their March 12 print edition. This was the last run of normalcy for the *Journal-News* and thousands of other newspapers across America.

The front page featured a color picture of members from the Imagine Hillsboro Theater Group performing before a full house at the new Opera House Brewing Company, just a few doors away from the *Journal-News* office.

Above the fold was news about the Hillsboro City Council approving upcoming summer events. What a summer it was going to be. Rod Stewart— yes, that was his name—asked the council if the city would close Main Street for the Old Settlers Association annual car show on August 2. Tim and Sarah McConnell had renovated the restaurant at the Hillsboro Country Club and were preparing to open. The story featured a color picture of Tim and Sarah near a fence on Lake Hillsboro. Their dreams were as deep as the water.

There were no color pictures with Mary Herschelman's story. The headline read: "County Prepares for Coronavirus." At the time, there were nineteen confirmed cases of COVID-19 in Illinois. "The basic idea is to wash your hands," Herschelman said as she proofed the front page before it was sent to press. President Donald Trump was addressing the nation on the coronavirus pandemic as the six-person staff was assembling the paper in careful bits and

pieces. On March 10, 2020, President Trump had tweeted, "Best unemployment numbers in the history of our Country. Best unemployment number
EVER, almost 160 million people working right now. Vote Republican, unless you want to see those numbers obliterated!"

Deadline carryout for the newspaper office was from the Tacos & Nachos food truck across the street. Carryout would soon be the new normal.
Two proofreaders read paperback books, waiting for copy to come their way.
Mary Jo Hemken was reading a romance novel. "I'll read anything by the
beach," she said. Proofreader Louise Brown was reading J. D. Robb's *Golden
in Death*.

By the time the March 12 paper came out, life in America was reeling.
The World Health Organization declared COVID-19 a global pandemic.
The National Basketball Association postponed their season on the night of
March 11. On March 12, Illinois governor J. B. Pritzker canceled all events
with one thousand people or more. President Trump issued a national emergency on March 13. An April 24, 2020, *Wired* magazine story said that March
11 was a day that had "proved to be unlike any other in American history"
under the headline "An Oral History of the Day Everything Changed."

By March 20, all Illinois residents were ordered to shelter in place. The
Tacos & Nachos food truck went away for a very long time. The *Journal-News*
locked its front door, a necessity that stung congenial owner John Galer. The
staff began working from home via phone, email, and even fax machine.

People lost jobs. The stock market crashed. Newspapers lost advertising.
"We are adjusting to this crisis on a weekly and even daily basis," Galer said on
the evening of Sunday, March 22. "We've lost at least two-thirds of our insert
revenue. That totally supports our distribution of the newspaper and our shop-
pers. Time will tell on the total hit. We haven't cut any staff but have had two
employees who have decided to stay home. We were already in trouble. Here in
Illinois the new $15 minimum wage is going to hurt. The cost of doing business
is accelerating. You're in a flat market at best, and in some ways you're declining.
My whole career has been if you have a major cost problem, you need to expand,
you find another customer somewhere. It's really hard now.

"Our world is going to be vastly changed, but hopefully we will be able to
do our job and take care of the communities we serve. This industry will sur-

vive but it is going to change. We're not corporate and we don't have to show a quarterly profit somewhere along the line. I'm a glass-half-full guy, so we will thrive when we're through with all this. My grandfather made it through the Great Depression. He said to stay calm, carry through, and keep on going.

"We will do the same."

In 1974, Walter Jr. persuaded his father, Walter Hussman Sr., to buy the *Arkansas Democrat*, the afternoon daily newspaper in Little Rock. After a bloody newspaper war with the competing *Arkansas Gazette*, Walter Jr. emerged victorious in 1991 and created the present-day *Arkansas Democrat-Gazette*.

"This is the worst thing I've seen," he said in an April 24, 2020, interview. "It's not only the worst thing for newspapers, but it's the worst thing in the economy. This dwarfs 9/11 and the dot-com bust. It's worse than the financial crisis [2008–09]. We have 15 to 20 percent unemployment right now and it may go higher. The Great Depression peaked at 24.9 percent. I'm amazed the stock market is doing as well as it is. It's been devastating for us. Our ad revenue is probably down 50 percent from the same month a year ago. So many shops have closed and there's no sense for them to advertise. Dillard's is our largest advertiser. They were one of the last department stores to close all their stores."

In 2019, the *Democrat-Gazette* pioneered an all-iPad edition of its newspaper. During the pandemic, the paper began running interstitial ads between pages one and two on their iPad newspaper. An interstitial ad is an interactive, full-screen ad that covers the interface of the host app. Hussman explained, "People can click on the merchandise in the ad and go to a landing page where they can select the color, the size, and order a product right there on the page. I'm not sure how much it helped, but Dillard's told us their online sales had doubled companywide since they shut all their stores. We're just experimenting, trying to figure out ways to help our advertisers. We can do that for advertising, special news content, whatever."

Hussman, born in 1947, also came up to speed with the Zoom video-conferencing app. He was sheltering in place on April 24, 2020, and had spent the morning in one teleconference. "Then we had a couple Zoom meetings with people at the office trying to figure out how to reduce our costs with this huge drop in advertising. I didn't know much about these Zoom meetings six weeks ago," he said, laughing.

Like most newspapers in America, the *Democrat-Gazette* trimmed staff during COVID-19. "When this happened in 2008 and '09," Hussman explained, referring to the bear market when the S&P 500 lost about 50 percent of its value, "we told our employees we wanted to first consider something voluntary. We asked if they would apply for a furlough—one month, two months, three months. Or volunteer for a 20 percent salary reduction, or if you're hourly, a 20 percent reduction from forty to thirty-two hours a week. This time, out of nine hundred employees, we had ninety who came forward voluntarily to help the company. That was encouraging."

The *Post and Courier* in Charleston, South Carolina, actually expanded coverage into Greenville and Myrtle Beach during one of the peaks of the pandemic in May 2020. "We went to the board of directors and said, 'This is the amount of advertising we think we're going to lose, and by the way, you know that five-year plan of growing digital audience?" publisher P. J. Browning recalled in a July 2020 interview. "Like everybody else we had that five-year plan of what we thought traditional ad revenue was going to do." All projections for traditional advertising during COVID-19 declined.

Yet, monthly digital conversions were increasing by roughly 25 percent. "At that point we could hold back on expenses or go ahead and bet on [getting] the audience revenue we needed to expand," Browning said. "It was just a numbers play from all the things we learned from Google and Facebook and the number of digital subscribers we thought we could get. In times like this when most people fall back, we needed to get ahead."

Web traffic and conversion rates on the *Post and Courier* website from Greenville (pop. 68,000) and Myrtle Beach (pop. 34,000) readers revealed an appetite for digital content. In August 2020, a Myrtle Beach *Post and Courier* weekly newspaper and digital presence were launched, along with a digital-only Greenville platform. By March 2022, things were slowly moving forward. Browning said, "Greenville is definitely tracking. Myrtle Beach is behind. But the goal was within three years that each be supported by reader revenue. We won't give up on Myrtle Beach, but I think we're looking at four to five years."

The endgame is for the family-owned *Post and Courier* to become a statewide newspaper, not unlike the *Arkansas Democrat-Gazette*. "This is only my opinion, but I'm starting to hear from more people that are talking statewide brands and expansion," Browning said. "It's a combination of needing audience revenues but they're also seeing these news deserts start to form based on the ownerships of the newspapers around them. They also think they can make a statewide play for real strong content." The *Post and Courier* received $175,000 from the Facebook Journalism Project COVID-19 Local News Relief Fund that helped pay for new technology to manage the subscriber database and also paid for the hiring of a newsletter editor. By September 2021, Browning said the statewide initiative had moved to include the hiring of five reporters in Greenville, two in Myrtle Beach, two in Spartanburg, and two in Columbia, the state capitol.

"Pierre [Manigault] has always believed content is king," Browning said in February 2022, referring to the chairman of Evening Post Industries. "Without content and covering our communities, our democracy fails. He allowed us to hire reporters at the height of the pandemic when others were laying reporters off. In particular, with a focus on statewide reporting, we decided to add reporters. We were able to help seventeen community newspapers with a series called 'Uncovered' that focused on corruption in small towns, especially in those where newspapers have shuttered or become a shell of themselves."

During the pandemic, the 2021 "Uncovered" staff sifted through more than fifty-three thousand emails, invoices, and other public documents. They filed more than fifty Freedom of Information Act requests and interviewed more than 560 public officials, academics, and whistleblowers. Browning said, "Pierre has always been the family member that has been in touch with the newspaper side."

One benefit of a multigenerational independent family newspaper is the ability to draw on family lessons from the past. Walter Hussman Jr.'s parents, Walter and Betty, were married in 1931 during the depths of the Great Depression. "My mother's dad was in the newspaper business," he said. "My dad ended up working for the company. During the Depression, one of our papers in Hot Springs, Arkansas, had been taken over by the bank. It was in receivership. He told me how every day he would walk into the newspaper and there was the banker with his feet up on the desk. He had to approve any check that had to be signed. That made an impression on me. He got it out of receivership. He said, 'I'll give you some advice. As long as you have a lot of cash and a lot of credit, you'll never go broke. So when you go through one of these crises, it's really great.'"

—

Mary Pat Boian, the editor of the weekly *Eureka Springs Independent*, was also forward-looking during the early days of COVID-19, albeit in a more zen manner. "This is the best thing that ever happened to our culture," she said on April 3, 2020. "Cleaning up and shredding the unnecessary. People's lives are changing. They don't have any money. People aren't shopping as much. It's making people more contemplative and realistic, whether they like it or not. Everything is changing, but the people I've talked to are happy. I'm not on Facebook, but I've heard people on Facebook are not happy. Many letters to the editor are not happy. We're taking it day by day."

"Eureka Springs is a tourist town and there's no shops open. It's crippled but it's not dead. It's all a guessing game, trying to get something into people's hands that makes them think they need to think, let them know they can be entertained, informed, flummoxed, or enraged over two simple cups of coffee. For free. It's a mystery how everything will change, but we know it won't be the same. If we can just remain a reason for people to look forward to Wednesday's paper, I think we have value."

The rebirth of spring had kicked in throughout Eureka Springs. The redbuds and dogwoods were blooming. The lilac bushes were full. "I've been picking asparagus for days," said Boian, who lives twelve miles west of Eureka Springs. "I heard a mountain lion night before last. The turkeys are gobbling, and a fox runs through my yard every evening."

In early April 2020, the size of the *Independent* was cut from twelve to six pages. They were printing between 2,000 and 2,500 copies a week compared to 4,000 in peak tourist season. "People are still looking for something," she said. "Maybe it's the crossword puzzle. I wouldn't close the paper 'down-down.' I'd take a two-month break. We're staying far enough close to the edge that people think we're participating." Boian laughed. "We're wearing masks. We do alcohol if anyone dares come in. We keep the front door closed but there's not a sign. But they're not coming in. They're not going to the farmer's market. The farmers aren't going to the farmer's market. It's just affecting everybody. But we want to ride this out. We take our [vitamin] D₃. We're doing all we can to help our little lungs get through the mine.

"We want this all good."

Things were good up the road in tiny Eldon, Missouri, about twenty-five miles north of the Lake of the Ozarks. "The newspaper is in fine shape," said *Eldon Advertiser* publisher Trevor Vernon in an April 28, 2020, interview. "March of this year was better than March of last year, which is crazy to even say. I was just looking at the numbers." The *Advertiser*'s circulation stood firm at 3,500 in a town of 4,700. As the pandemic lingered on, in September 2021 Vernon even bought another newspaper. He liked the location and growth potential of the Camdenton *Lake Sun Leader* in the Lake of the Ozarks region and purchased it from the Gannett chain.

"Gannett is starting to sell their smaller properties," Vernon said. "I think they've figured out they have a hard time with them. It's because of the corporate structure. It takes longer to make decisions. The people at the top are only looking at bottom-line data and not what the community wants or is saying. Local ownership moves quicker and hears directly from the community at the grocery store, church, and everywhere in between."

By February 2022 the *Lake Sun Leader* numbers had doubled since the acquisition. The twice-weekly paper jumped from 700 to 1,450 paid subscribers. "That doesn't include rack sales or vendors," Vernon said. Vernon Publishing also gave new local blood to the former Gannett publications *Vacation News* (twice-monthly for locals and visitors), *Lake Lifestyles* (high-end magazine, published every other month), and *BOATS* magazine (once a month during boating season).

Vernon attributed much of his company's stability to his advertising representative, Benne Myers. "She's helped a lot of people through this," he said. "That builds a lot of trust." Vernon tells his employees they are working primarily for advertisers and readers. "Benne's bought into that. There's a person that owns a small car dealership and also has a small detailing business on the side. Part of their detailing business was a car wash. It quit working. They were having a hard time finding anybody who could work on it."

Myers's son worked for a company that repaired car washes. Vernon explained, "She said, 'This won't cost you anything on my side. Let me see if my son can work on it.' He did and it turned into a full-page ad every month for us. It's not only that she makes money, but she's going to build a relationship that later might help us in a different way.

"I thought 2020 was going to be huge for us. We were building on some things, doing some things outside the box, and it was starting to pay off in March. The last week of March was horrible. Economically we will be fine. Advertising this morning was one after another; one person doing a quarter-page, the next person doing a half-page, the chamber of commerce is going to partner with us. It was exciting to see things move again."

In early April 2020, the feisty *Carroll Times Herald* in western Iowa had lost two-thirds of its advertising due to COVID-19, according to co-owner Doug Burns. He credited his side company, Mercury Boost Media Marketing Solutions, for saving his newspaper. Founded in 2015, Mercury Boost is a digital marketing company and political advertising company based in Council Bluffs, Iowa. "I'm in a unique position probably in American journalism," Burns said after unloading groceries on a Sunday night in early April. "Not to self-aggrandize but I don't know anybody else who does what I do. I sell ads and represent all 270 newspapers in Iowa with presidential campaigns, senate campaigns, congressional campaigns. We had an extraordinary amount of political advertising that flowed into Iowa during the caucuses in early February [2020]. And that was also flowing during the summer and the fall. I sold all that individually with the Democratic and Republican consultants I work with. We brought in a significant amount of commission. If our newspaper was healthy and we were being able to cover expenses on our own, then that money would have just gone to me as a separate LLC. But I used that money to boost the newspaper and it put us in a great spot. We got our last commission check literally a week before the coronavirus started to hit."

—

It was an unseasonably cold and rainy Mother's Day in Carroll in 2020. Before going to his downtown office at the *Carroll Times Herald*, Doug Burns stopped by his mother's house. Burns dropped off some gifts, carefully placing them on a chair in her garage. He was practicing physical, if not social, distancing. "My mom is able-bodied and fine," Burns said in a conversation later that day.

Burns spent the Sunday afternoon working on two COVID-19 stories for the newspaper. One was about the charter bus company Windstar Lines, which had 152 buses based in Carroll. "They've lost 97 percent of their business," he said. "Congress and the stimulus plan have bailed out the airlines and Amtrak, but they've stranded smaller motor coach companies. It's a big business in Carroll. About 30 percent of their business is taking college teams around the country to events. So I'm writing about the family that operates that and what they're going through. If things don't change and they don't get any federal relief, they could be done. As a balance, there's also a home warranty company called American Home Shield that employs 453 people in Carroll. Their CEO was really fast on COVID. He sent people home right away. It's a call center and their business is performing well. They're still actually hiring in Carroll."

Burns sounded overwhelmed. Maybe it was the weather. Or maybe it was the stories he was trying to tell. "I was in my teenage years when I saw stories about family farmers killing themselves," Burns said. "I had a condescending attitude about it—just tough it out. 'So you can't farm anymore? Move to St. Louis.' It's what you would expect from a fourteen-year-old with the whole world in front of him and nothing built behind him to see.

"But now I've thought about killing myself. You can quote me on that. I haven't, of course, but I've spent thirty years of my life on this. We were best paper in the state [named by the Iowa Newspaper Association in 2013]. What for? Maybe I'll catch coronavirus. I've been flying around all over the country trying to find ideas and implementing dozens of them, working myself probably to an early grave trying to keep this paper from going to an early grave. It's not easy for me."

Burns was proud he did not furlough anyone through the early days of the COVID-19 crisis. He put his own money into the *Times Herald* to keep it afloat. "And we're still putting out a good product," he said. "All this coronavirus coverage is available for free. If we weren't here, there would be crazy people on the right and crazy people on the left fighting over inaccurate information."

On this Mother's Day, was Burns feeling the weight of family history?

"I've never said this to anybody, but I almost envy journalists at larger newspapers who are furloughed," he said. "It's just over for them. Even if I wanted to, I couldn't walk away. We don't have a massive amount of debt, a quarter of a million dollars, so it's not a terrific nut to crack. But we're losing money. We own the building. They could take that. Or they could come after my house or my mom's house. You have all these people counting on you, and you know you're probably playing a losing hand, and you're still trying to find ways to make it work. I've made the newspaper my life. Literally. I'm responsible for all the staff. I love journalism, I love our community and love our staff. There's the family legacy. So, yeah, it's a lot of weight.

"And if we did get knocked out, I'd walk away with nothing."

—

The scenario was even worse 410 miles east of Carroll at the storied *Chicago Reader*. The lifeline of *Reader* advertising—music clubs, bars, restaurants, movie theaters, and more—was cut off on March 20, 2020, when the city ordered all nonessential establishments closed. By March 27, 2020, publisher Tracy Baim said the alternative weekly *Reader* had lost 90 percent of its advertising.

The March 26 print issue of the *Reader* was distributed as PDF-only with a small press run to fulfill subscriber and library mailings. A limited-edition souvenir run of two hundred copies was available for $15 each. "Things are going to be massively different for local media the longer this goes," Baim said on March 27.

And then on June 22, 2020, Baim announced that the *Reader* was moving to a biweekly schedule. The print edition would have more than fifty thousand copies delivered to nearly 1,200 locations around the city. A renewed commitment to digital would come from more than six hundred thousand unique monthly visitors to the *Reader* website. There were no editorial layoffs or furloughs.

On April 10, 2020, the *New York Times* reported that their own analysis found that more than thirty-seven thousand news media employees in the United States had been subject to pay cuts, furloughs, or layoffs since COVID-19 began to spread around the country.

Among those were the employees of the suburban Chicago newspaper chain 22nd Century Media, which ceased operations on March 31, 2020, citing lack of advertising revenue. *Editor & Publisher* magazine wrote in 2014 that 22nd Century Media was the third-largest media company in Chicago, behind the *Tribune* and the *Sun-Times*. The hyperlocal publication company once produced fourteen Chicago-area weeklies from the north suburbs through the south suburbs. The company was founded in 2005 by former investment banker Jack Ryan. He was a candidate in the 2004 U.S. Senate race in Illinois, running as a Republican against Barack Obama. He left 22nd Century Media in 2015 to start a technology-based real estate company.

On March 19, 2020, the *Isthmus* in Madison, Wisconsin, stopped print publication after a forty-three-year run as the go-to alternative weekly in the Berkeley of the Midwest. "*Isthmus* financially depends on people coming together for concerts, food, drink, lectures, movies, and more," the staff wrote in a March 19 farewell post on its website. "And when it all goes away at once, we are left without options." In August 2021, *Isthmus* bounced back as a monthly publication. They also created the *Isthmus* Membership Program for exclusive access to newsletters and events.

On March 17, 2020, the *Sacramento News & Review* (*SN&R*) suspended publication, citing the loss of cultural and entertainment advertising. *SN&R* president and majority owner Jeff vonKaenel's farewell statement was transparent. He wrote, "It costs us roughly $45,000 a week to produce *SN&R*; that's a little more than 10 cents for each of our 433,000 readers. The bulk of that cost is labor. This week we have less than $20,000 in expected revenue to cover $45,000 of expenses. That is our problem."

The *Riverfront Times* in St. Louis, Missouri, temporarily laid off most of its staff and stopped its print edition. Seattle's *The Stranger* temporarily laid off eighteen of its employees.

On March 23, Baim wrote to her readers, "So now we 'shelter-in-place,' without much real understanding of what that can do now since the virus is out of the bag. We are building new routes in our social networks, rewiring our connections to one another through the internet and virtual concerts, book groups, dances, journalism, and more."

Carroll, Iowa's Doug Burns graduated from Northwestern University in Evanston, Illinois, and was familiar with the *Reader*. "The *Reader*'s equivalent in Des Moines is *Cityview*," he said. "They shut down within days of the virus breaking." The free monthly resumed publishing in July 2020, after a three-month hiatus. "Because we're in a rural area, we don't have that much entertainment and restaurant advertising. Secondly, we've already lost a lot of that. Third, and we might be a real outlier in the industry, but because we're rural and we're in the center of our own trade zone, we still have a pretty robust classified section. We have several hospitals in a forty-five-mile radius and they've stuck with us. One grocery store went out and came back. Another grocery store has been strong throughout with us. Our chamber of commerce has stepped up with a grant."

In April 2020, the home page of the Shaw Media website ("The Nation's 8th Largest Newspaper Publisher") promoted a community marketing grant. Shaw Media created a grant program of up to $1 million in matching advertising credits to assist locally owned businesses during the pandemic. The site read, "As a family-owned business, we are committed to supporting our local partners and helping them reach customers." Former trustee and sixth-generation newspaperperson Peter Shaw said, "It was a program specifically to work with advertisers through this time."

Is there any way a newspaper could have planned for something like a global pandemic? Could anyone have? After a long pause, Shaw answered, "The overall governance of our company, we're very focused on paying down debt. I would not say it's that we're planning for a rainy day. It's making sure we're not out over our skis—that a bump in the road doesn't tumble down and create an avalanche. The company is more similarly run to a professional shop than what would be traditionally thought of as a family newspaper."

The *Evanston RoundTable*, just north of Chicago, ceased their popular print edition on November 15, 2019, before the pandemic had an opportunity to wreak havoc on the business. "It was fortuitous that we stopped then," former *RoundTable* editor Larry Gavin said in a May 23, 2020, interview. "Many papers are down 70 percent of their advertising revenue in the last few months, and they don't know if they'll get it back. If we hadn't stopped then, we'd be dead in the water."

His wife, former publisher and manager Mary Helt Gavin, added, "And with COVID-19 we would not have been able to distribute our papers the way we did. I don't know anybody who would want to pick up a free paper. We didn't know if the delivery people would be safe. We didn't know if anybody wanted to open a box. The distribution of our paper would have been gone even if we had the money."

With the transition to a digital platform, the *RoundTable* laid off one designer and two salespeople. "The writers that stayed with us understood we didn't have any money," Mary said. "But they loved the idea of community newspapers. And visitors quadrupled on our website since we ceased publication." According to Google analytics, in November 2019 the *RoundTable* had about twelve thousand unique visitors per month. By April 2020 it spiked to eighty-two thousand monthly.

In Carroll, Iowa, Burns and his staff pivoted by launching a free dining and restaurant guide with online PDFs of carryout menus. "We're seeing record traffic on our website," Burns said. "And record engagement on social media." Burns quickly organized his priorities. Public health and community service shared the top spot on his journalistic agenda. He said, "Our local banker, Commercial Savings Bank, was able to get us information quickly. That's another advantage of being in a rural area. They were filing these Small Business Association [SBA] loans like two twenty-hour days in a row. That's the forgivable loan where if we continue to pay people for eight weeks, which I will, then the amount of money we get from the SBA will be forgiven. I jumped over from basically being a full-time reporter to the paperwork to make sure we have the revenue to stay open." His Herald Publishing Company was one of the first businesses in central Iowa to secure a PPP (Paycheck Protection Program) loan because of the newspaper's strong relationship with its local bank.

Burns admitted the 2020 pandemic brought urgency to his situation as a small family-owned newspaper, but hustling for money was old hat. He explained, "We're in a better spot than other businesses because we've been dealing with this for years. Now a lot of other people are on the same economic troubled waters. A lot of other businesses haven't experienced the kind of catastrophic hits we've had to endure for the better part of a decade.

"But this could clean me out, which would be heartbreaking."

———

The year 2020 was going to be big for the *Journal-News* and the Galer family.

The January 27, 2020, edition of Mary Herschelman's blog featured the story: "Galers Celebrate 75 Years in Hillsboro." Herschelman slyly wrote that she also had a milestone birthday coming up, "but we won't talk about that." In a separate interview, she said, "One of our favorite sayings is, 'If it's important to you, then it's important to us.' And we mean it. That's one of the great things about community newspapers. You won't find much national and international news in our paper, but you might discover who found the biggest mushroom."

There were humble glories around the *Journal-News* on the evening of March 11, 2020. A black-and-white photograph from the mid-1960s of a staff birthday party for Hillsboro newspaper legend Sam Little hung on a newsroom wall. Little was a Hillsboro newspaper lifer. Publisher Mike Plunkett said, "He started working at the paper as a high school kid in 1898. Forever. He never had children. The ownership of the paper transferred from Sam to Del and Phil Galer in 1966. After that, Sam was editor emeritus. He was a typical newspaper-person who stayed around until his last breath. He died in 1972."

Around 7:50 p.m. staff reporter Bethany Martin brought the "Agri-News" page proofs over to Herschelman for approval. Plunkett was proofing a "Meet the Candidates" page in preparation for the March 17 Illinois primary. At 7:55 Martin asked aloud, "Do you need any help on anything?" The office was quiet. At 8:05 the murmur of a police scanner indicated things were quiet in Montgomery County, at least for this moment in time. To no one in particular, Herschelman said, "We almost ran out of copy on Sunday night!" But she got through it. She always does.

Like fossils in rocks, distant burn marks were in the edge of every wooden desk in the newspaper office. These markers denote where Galer once put out his cigarettes. His kids nagged him to stop smoking. They finally succeeded. "He did it at age forty-seven," Herschelman said. "He had a big ceremony and threw all his cigarettes in a fire."

The old newspaper desks were salvaged from public auctions. Galer would cut corners for the common good. "Every time we needed something, we'd drive up to the state fairgrounds in Springfield," he said before the March 12 paper went to press. "Used to be you'd find that stuff in really good shape. Now if there is stuff out there, it's really beat up."

Due to the fallout of COVID-19, the March 12 edition of the

Journal-News would be the final robust version of the newspaper for a very long while. Their offices were finally closed to the community on March 16. On April 1, 2020, Galer said, "I'll be honest, our revenue is down 50, 60 percent, maybe more. We had a lot of our grocery stores, Dollar General, Aldi's, they pulled out for a while. But they'll be back. We're taking a huge hit adwise. Normally our paper is eighteen, twenty pages, sometimes twenty-two in each issue. Last Thursday we had a twelve-page paper and Monday we had a ten-page paper. You can do the math. But at the same time, I don't look at it as a permanent condition. We're going to keep putting out a paper. The one thing that scares me is that if we get someone on staff with the virus, then we're going to have to do some major stuff down here. Part of our stuff you can do from home, but the press work and the mail work here, that's our weak link."

As of January 2022, Galer reported that his company was holding steady. "Business revenue seems tougher," he said. "With the $12 minimum wage [that took effect in Illinois on January 1, 2022] we've had a lot of longtime regular customers wanting to change their ad budget—downward. Smaller businesses are really struggling."

After deadline nights, Plunkett heads straight home to unwind. "Sometimes I have a beer," he said. "But almost every time I have a cigar." He always thinks about the next edition of the newspaper. He can't help himself. "There's always the next morning when you review what you just did and when you see the mistakes you made in print," he reflected. "And even after thirty years, you still have that sinking feeling. Or there's a mistake that other people have called to let you know about. We always shoot for perfection, but when the readers call about it, that shows they are still paying attention. If you made a mistake and nobody knows it, then you've got a problem. Readers who also take responsibility and ownership is exactly what we shoot for."

On May 7, the state of Illinois was in its seventh week of a stay-at-home order. In a phone interview that day, Plunkett said, "Like anything else, when you're in a crisis, some days you see some rays of hope and some days you backpedal. Today was one of those days. John's an optimistic person. He reminds me of my dad. I heard it a million times when I was a kid: 'I don't mind problems, but I pray for God to make them fixable.' That's how John is. As long as he can see the solution, even though the sail is going to be rough, he's going to be okay. It's rough water but you can still see the lighthouse."

Plunkett agreed with Galer that the loss of advertising would not be a permanent condition. He was more concerned about the dent in community spirit. "The young entrepreneurs downtown have based their business on online sales anyway; it's still working out for them," Plunkett said. "One frustrating thing is that we as a newspaper had cooperated with the chamber and downtown groups to do an event a month. The first one was Mardi Gras, and it was an excuse to get people downtown to shop. We wanted to show how the newspaper can drive people in and let us help them stay in business. The first one, the Mardi Gras one, at the end of February was just spectacular. The second one was planned for the Orpheum [Theatre] one hundredth anniversary and that had to be canceled. We were working on a virtual Easter egg hunt for adults in stores. That never happened."

The *Journal-News* made a commitment to their community. The newspaper had a COVID story on the front page of every issue from March 2020 forward. "It's not good here," Mary Herschelman said in August 2021 as she reflected on the pandemic. "We're very much in Trump's rural America. When the governor mandated masks in schools, there's contingents in several of our communities fighting school boards, and there's movements not to vaccinate."

Plunkett was archiving the newspaper's coverage of the pandemic. "I'm saving our COVID-19 hard news stories, features, the letters, and everything so when we get through this we're going to make a souvenir edition," he said. "We'll have it ready to roll whenever we have something to be optimistic about again. I didn't realize how dramatic the change was until I started looking through those papers. One paper was a normal paper, talking about this celebration or that event. And overnight it went from that to everything is closed and every story has to do with COVID-19.

"From one issue to the next."

—

The historic *Madison Courier* in Madison, Indiana, was sold on February 28, 2020, roughly two weeks before most of America shut down. Sixth-generation publisher Curt Jacobs sold the family newspaper to the Paxton Media Group in Paducah, Kentucky.

His timing was more than perfect.

"I'm glad I don't have to deal with this right now," Jacobs understated in a March 24, 2020, interview. "In my situation there's a certain amount of irony. My great-great-great-grandfather bought this paper because the guy in Madison was afraid of the cholera pandemic. This pandemic didn't have anything to do with my decision to get out, but it is oddly coincidental that my family came in that way, and we go out in this time."

The day of our conversation was the last day of Jacobs's freedom around town. On March 25, 2020, the state of Indiana became subject to a stay-at-home order. "I was just down at the paper today talking to one of my former employees," Jacobs said. "I explained there's certainly a side of me where I'm glad because I don't have to deal with this. There's no doubt I would have had to lay people off, something I didn't want to do. On the other hand, you feel bad. I care about these people. I care about this community. I wouldn't mind being the one who helps take care of that. So it's a double-edged sword. I'm still rooting for the paper. If people come to me on the street, as they do sometimes, and they want to talk about it, I'm pretty careful not to talk about anything that they're doing now. I try to encourage people to support the paper. There's good people down there doing good work, and it is just so important to this community."

Jacobs knew that Paxton would immediately cut staff. "I wasn't naive about this deal," he said. "I know that's what they have to do so that they are still able to put out a newspaper. They immediately find deficiencies. That's good. I guarantee you there's no way that revenue is paying the freight the next couple months at least. It's going to cost them less money to run that paper right away than it cost me. Number one, they cut a lot of payroll. I don't know how much, and I don't want to speculate because it is their business. But they cut me and my brother [who ran the presses] and several other positions. Which I knew they would do. They're going to draw their scale more efficiently with less overhead. Thank goodness—because it is going to take that."

Did he want to stay?

"No," he answered. He would not elaborate.

The week after Jacobs sold, he networked with a few fellow small-newspaper owners. They talked about pre-pandemic advertising challenges. "Who knows how long this will go?" he said. "The timing for me was lucky.

Because it would be pretty ugly right now. The new owners are more passionate about it. There's no way you could operate that paper with the payroll I had. You'd be losing money. I mean, I was losing money a little bit at the end."

A similar scenario took place in rural Marfa, Texas, when Robert and Rosario Halpern sold the *Big Bend Sentinel* in April 2019. They had owned the paper for twenty-five years. "Rosario and I thank our lucky stars that we retired when we did," Robert said. "No one saw this coming. Our plan was to travel. Because if you run a weekly paper, you typically don't get to travel. When our daughter lived in Spain, we started taking two weeks off at Christmas, based on advertising. The minute we sold the paper we were in Spain for a month. We are glad we didn't have to try to run a small business in this climate. You have to remain upbeat and know you're going to get through it, but in the meantime it's a slog economy-wise. When you're this far out, you have to worry about printing, the internet, because the press is in Monahans, about an hour and forty-five minutes away by car. In the early days the drivers had to wait until we did the cut and paste so we could leave Marfa. Then when we had digital and internet, we would email the pages to the press.

"It's a tough time to be a small business; it's a tough time to be a big business."

COVID-19 also frayed tight connections in rural communities like Madison, Eureka Springs, and Hillsboro. People are tied into all neighbors, ranging from fast-food clerks to clergy to newspaper people. "Rural people are reliant on their neighbors and have more confidence and trust in their neighbors," said Ken Johnson, senior demographer at the Carsey School of Public Policy at the University of New Hampshire, in a March 2020 interview with the Associated Press.

In early April 2020, Hillsboro's Galer said, "There's young people and seniors all together where I live. We keep a distance. I'm not keeping a distance from my family. My preacher lives right behind my house. He's had a battle with cancer, so he's at high risk. He doesn't want to go anywhere. Most people here have more than one social relief person. If they need something, they usually have several people they go to. I know some seniors who are limited in their social world. My wife and I check in on people in our church. Every couple of days we call two or three people. Church groups are strong in rural areas. I'm sure there's people that slip through the cracks who don't have any-body. The main thing is to stay calm. I don't think the national news media is helping us. It's twenty-four hours. Some of it is news, but I guess they like the sound of their own voice. We'll be fine here."

I returned to Hillsboro in mid-July 2020. COVID-19 cases had spiked in Montgomery County, especially at a church in neighboring Litchfield. I had lunch at the Cozy Cafe, a tiny diner set back in a woody area off of Main Street. It's known for some of the best egg rolls in the Midwest. The Cozy Cafe was also a pro–Donald Trump establishment. The diner featured a life-sized cardboard cutout of the president and sold Trump 2020 baseball caps.

No one at the Cozy Cafe wore face masks, including the waitstaff.

When I next visited the *Journal-News* staff at their office, just several blocks away on Main Street, everyone wore face masks. "I'm a little disappoint-ed," editor Mary Herschelman said. "When everything shut down, we didn't even order takeout for a while. When some of the places opened up, some of the business owners weren't wearing masks. Part of that was people feeling like they were being told to do something. I don't understand the resistance to it."

Galer said the Hillsboro community was not vigilant in dealing with the pandemic. "Most people look at it as, 'It's not going to happen to me,'" he said. "Or, 'It's no big deal.' Or, 'Everybody's lying.' I'm worried now because you have people who don't want to take COVID as real. And that's sad. Because it is real, and it is killing people. You would think with a national catastrophe, this should be the time we're coming together. Usually, 9/11 and even the 2008 financial disaster, we came together."

Mary said it was important for the *Journal-News* to step up and assume a leadership role in the community. "Our paper has always been a leader," she said. "If we go out on assignment, we're wearing face masks. When you're out in the community, people associate you with the newspaper. We need to be that example."

Former Shaw Media trustee Peter Shaw agreed. "For a newspaper that is operating in today's world that is focused on a local market, I don't know how you can be passive in that regard. Companywide, we were very early on in shut-ting down offices and getting every person that could work from home to be working from home. Shaw Media handled the pandemic very well. It started very proactively, taking it serious. That's what we've also done in coverage. That's what I would expect from a newspaper. It is its own version of leadership."

Galer remained as optimistic about the future as he was three months earlier, although he spoke in more measured tones. "I don't see how we will get past day-by-day," he said. "Business-wise, what we are now is what we're going to be for a while. It will be a year or two."

The *Journal-News* received a Paycheck Protection Program loan, which helped smooth the rough waters. "We'd be in deep doo-doo without that," he said. "We've lost about 40 percent of our business. It's a very, very serious issue. The money to be made right now is probably technology like Amazon and Google. The big guys. The challenges we are going to face down the road are definitely real and definitely significant. It comes down to community. We want to make sure we're still here doing what we like to do for the world around us."

Chapter 13

Nonprofit Model

It didn't matter what community you were in; every newspaper took a hit after COVID-19 rolled through America in the spring of 2020. More publications began to seriously consider a nonprofit model to survive. In June 2021, the *NonProfit Times* reported that nonprofit news had recently grown at its fastest pace since the financial crisis of 2008. One-third of nonprofit news outlets in 2021 did not exist in 2016.

Mary and Larry Gavin of Evanston, Illinois, are two of those nonprofit newbies. When the Gavins started the biweekly *Evanston RoundTable* newspaper in February 1998, print journalism was already in a tailspin, but they had no way to anticipate the seismic shift in advertising that COVID-19 would create. Larry was fifty years old and Mary was forty-nine in 1998. They did not come from a long line of journalism families. In fact, neither of them had even taken a journalism course in college.

Mary and Larry took the perceived midlife crisis to a higher ground.

Larry practiced litigation law for thirty-six years in Chicago and retired at age sixty in 2007. Mary had already launched the *RoundTable*. She holds a doctorate in classical philology from Indiana University and taught part time at Illinois Institute of Technology and Loyola University.

Why in the world did she want to start a newspaper?

"Working on one that had failed," Mary Gavin answered during an

October 2019 conversation in the newspaper office. In 1994, Mary covered high schools for the now-defunct *Clarion* in Evanston, a lakefront suburb of seventy-five thousand just north of Chicago. She said, "I didn't like the *Evanston Review*," a weekly published by Pioneer Press, a division of Tribune Publishing. "It didn't seem like it was the same place I was living."

The Gavins had extra time and money on their hands. Their children were grown and out of college. "This was something worth trying," Mary said. "We didn't know how much work it was going to be. We formed our revenue liability company and put in some money." Their two children expressed no desire to take over the newspaper. "Maybe give it away to one of our grandkids," Mary said with a laugh. She was seventy and Larry was seventy-one in October 2019.

When asked about the future of the *RoundTable*, Mary answered, "I don't know. We don't have an answer." Larry echoed, "We don't have an answer right now."

But answers came fast for Mary and Larry.

Just a few weeks after I met them in Evanston, they stopped the print edition of the *RoundTable*. Then, in early 2020, they moved toward a non-profit model. Finally, in June 2021, the Gavins retired from their roles on the *RoundTable*. The retirement was planned as part of the transition to nonprofit. They continue to write and mentor young reporters.

"We were losing money," Larry said in a May 23, 2020, phone conversation. "Ad revenue had really gone down. Real estate ads were a big part of our revenue. We were the last local paper in Evanston to get real estate ads and one by one they dropped off. They did not look like they were coming back, at least to what we needed. We put out feelers in the community to see if anybody that had money would be interested in taking over the paper. There was no interest. People saw the losses of revenues. Also, Mary's and my salaries were averaging about $5,000 a year since we started. We actually had a lot of volunteers. It was not a financially viable business venture for anybody."

The Gavins found a friend in Mark Miller, the former editor of *Crain's Chicago Business* and Sunday editor of the *Chicago Sun-Times*. Miller had lived in Evanston since the mid-1980s. "I've always appreciated the *RoundTable*," said Miller, now an independent journalist specializing in coverage of retirement and aging. "It is a solid community newspaper. It is the go-to spot for what's going on in Evanston. I didn't know Mary and Larry terribly well."

Miller reached out to the Gavins in November 2019 after they stopped the print edition. He told them he had experience with publication management in editorial and business. As a community member, he wanted to help. "This is to make sure the *RoundTable* has a future going forward after they step out of the picture," Miller said. "It has been a labor of love for them. This is a unique circumstance in that the founders have been able to pour their heart and soul into this and not really get paid."

Miller learned more about their mom-and-pop operation. He asked the Gavins if they would consider converting to a nonprofit model. "It could be a perfect fit because of the strong reputation of the paper in the community and the kind of community Evanston is," Miller said. "Very civic-minded, and it is big enough where there are resources to support something like this and small enough that you can manage the task of networking and raising money. The *RoundTable* has always been a shoestring operation, which makes it easier. When you're looking to converting a big legacy operation—the *Chicago Sun-Times*, or pick who you want—that's a hard thing to do because there's so much built-in cost from the operation."

The Gavins talked to other people in the regional newspaper community and thought it over for a couple of months. They decided to make the transition in early March 2020, just before COVID-19 cut across America. They formed a nonprofit corporation and secured the Institute for Nonprofit News (INN) as a fiscal sponsor for donations before their paperwork for 501(c)(3) status (for donor tax deductions) was cleared with the IRS.

Mary Gavin explained, "You just can't be a non-for-profit newspaper. You have to choose a category that the IRS approves. So we are organized as an 'education institution.' That's what we've always considered ourselves as."

Larry added, "A lot of newspapers get denied 501(c)(3) status because they're not regarded as institutional. We're following the format of the Salt Lake City *Tribune*. We always regarded ourselves as educating the community. If we do something on affordable housing, we might do an in-depth article at the start and then five or six more articles on affordable housing, tying them together. In-depth journalism. Salt Lake City was able to get by on that."

In November 2019, the *Salt Lake Tribune* became the first legacy paper (not a start-up) to be granted nonprofit status by the IRS. The *Tribune* pivoted to nonprofit after 148 years in business, telling the community that if they still want a newspaper, they have to support it. Free news isn't free. The *Tribune* is the primary beneficiary of the Utah Journalism Foundation, a stand-alone entity.

INN has become a steady resource for newspapers making a commitment to watchdog, public service journalism. The Los Angeles–based institute formed in 2009 when twenty-seven nonpartisan, nonprofit news organizations met to examine the future of investigative journalism.

By 2020, INN had grown to include 250 nonprofit organizations in North America. And by spring 2022, that number had skyrocketed to 350. "I don't know if they're moving [to the nonprofit model] as much as starting new newsrooms," INN communications director Sharene Azimi said in a June 2020 interview. "There's been some conversions. The Salt Lake City *Tribune* is the classic example. It's not as much about changing your tax status as an organization as it is when the newsroom decides whether they want to be in the business of mission-driven public service journalism."

Independent, small-town family newspapers are starting to sniff around the nonprofit model, according to Jonathan Kealing, chief network officer of INN. "We're seeing more look at it," he said in March 2022. "We're not seeing a rush to embrace it. For some family-owned papers that are looking for a way out and make sure it remains community-centered, nonprofit is a good option. But the longtime family businesses are proud of the profits they have made, the businesses they built, and they want to stay for-profit in the future.

"We've seen a trickle of conversions [as opposed to start-ups]. Growing Community Media [in Oak Park, a near west suburb of Chicago] was a conversion, *Salt Lake Tribune* was a well-known conversion. I do think we will see the number increase over the next few years."

Kealing was a reporter and online editor for the multigenerational family-owned *Lawrence Journal-World* in Kansas between 2006 and 2011. "Coming to build the digital nonprofit future of media is what attracted me to INN," he said. "That's what I was working on in Lawrence—building digital journalism."

Approximately 40 percent of INN publishing members cover local news. The organization does not break down by suburban, rural, or urban demographics, only by local, state/regional, and national or international. INN also breaks out who covers specific topics versus who provides general news coverage. For instance, a handful of INN members have established singular news services in small communities that no longer had a newspaper or for subjects they were passionate about.

INN assists start-ups by providing services like fiscal sponsorship. "The collapse of the stock market and financial crisis in 2008 and '09, in a weird way, increased opportunities because you had a lot of traditional newsrooms shutting down," Azimi explained. "And a lot of that money went elsewhere."

INN members must adhere to certain standards, such as:

- **Editorial quality.** Members must regularly publish original reporting that is investigative or public service by nature, such as community, civic, and public affairs coverage. INN generally does not accept publications that primarily publish opinion, analysis, arts/cultural/community events, reviews, and literary writing.

- **Editorial and organizational independence.** INN members do not operate in a way that promotes any legislation, policies, government actions, or outcomes. Members avoid conflicts of interest that could compromise the integrity of the work.

- **Transparency.** Members must disclose where their funding is coming from to prevent undue influence and identify all donors that give more than $5,000 a year by publicly listing them on the publication's site. And no more than 15 percent of the member's total annual budget can be derived from anonymous donations.

Mike Jenner, faculty group chair at the University of Missouri School of Journalism, has worked at four independent, family-owned newspapers. "I'm not optimistic about the nonprofit model," he said. "It sounds great because it's like, 'Wow! You don't have to make a profit.' The problem is you have to make money. You can't operate a nonprofit if you can't pay salaries. The model is broken. As print circulation dwindles, the print piece of it is still expensive. Advertisers are less interested in publishing their ads in a local printed product. They think they can do better on the internet or Facebook. That continues to erode newspapers. The print edition is always the most profitable piece of the operation. It's twenty-five years on now and they're still trying to figure out how to make money on the internet. Nonprofit sounds great. The execution is difficult. You have to get contributors to write big checks to pay the bills and fund your operation. If the advertising is not there in a for-profit way, it's not going to be there in a nonprofit way."

Phil Murray, formerly of the newspaper merger and acquisition firm Dirks, Van Essen, Murray & April, added, "Certainly more people are talking about nonprofit. It's tricky. Because nonprofit doesn't mean they can afford to lose money indefinitely. It still doesn't change the business structure for a single, standalone small daily to have good economics going forward."

In February 2022, Walter Hussman, publisher of the *Arkansas Democrat-Gazette*, said, "Nonprofit is a tax status. It is not a business plan. Even if you're a nonprofit you have to take in more revenues than expenses. In my opinion, the greatest economic model ever created for sustainability is for an entity to show a profit. As long as it is profitable, someone will want to own and operate it."

INN's Kealing said that nonprofit goes beyond tax status into exploring the core of community. "Of course you still have to be a viable business," he said. "The differences between for-profit and nonprofit are twofold. Number one, as a nonprofit, you are a community asset. Your profit, your return, your operating balance exists to serve your mission and your community. It doesn't exist to enrich a particular owner or shareholder. The money in a for-profit exists for the owners.

"And as a nonprofit, you have the ability to attract philanthropic support because of the importance of community-enabling work you are doing. You can do work that may not be the biggest click or drive the most pickups, but it may be what's going to keep your city government in line."

Nancy Lane, CEO of the Local Media Association, said, "We're encouraged by the nonprofit model, and we think there's a place for it. We don't think it's for everyone, but it's an option in a lot of communities. Especially when it is a family-owned organization and the next generation doesn't want to be involved. The current owner, to make sure the newspaper survives, working with the community to become a nonprofit, can be a powerful thing. We're keeping an eye on it."

—

Before the weekly *Evanston RoundTable* moved to nonprofit status, the *Chicago Reader* alternative newspaper was also shifting to the nonprofit model. In a January 2020 conversation, publisher Tracy Baim said, "It's been a very heavy lift. We're sixteen months or so in. Our accountants and lawyers, who I love working with, are not really from the media space. Then I got the material. It was very dry and very narrow. We all had seen the Salt Lake City *Tribune* application. Our team was playing off that. First, I didn't think we should. Second, I didn't think we could. And then, why would we want to? So over the holidays I took two weeks and wrote eleven thousand, twelve thousand words of 'Who is the *Reader*?' and 'Who is local media?' I got ninety-five footnoted sources of various studies and *New York Times* articles. I tried to give a range of things to the IRS."

Up in Evanston, Mark Miller helped the *RoundTable* form a diverse group of voices for an eight-person board of directors and an Evanston-based advisory committee of up to forty-two people from the community. The board of directors is responsible for oversight and management of the business. Miller became vice president of the board. Tracy Quattrocki, the *RoundTable*'s president and executive editor, serves on the board. From 2013 to 2016 she was president of the Evanston–Skokie District 65 school board. The advisory committee consisted of community leaders, representatives from Evanston nonprofits, school board members, and five members affiliated with Northwestern University (the journalism and business schools). It included former Emmy-winning Chicago television news reporter Derrick Blakley, former *Chicago Sun-Times* metro editor Mark Jacob, and Pam Cytrynbaum, former executive director of the Chicago Innocence Center and a former legman for famed Chicago newspaper columnist Mike Royko. The advisory committee gives input to the board and editorial staff.

"That's important," Mary Gavin said. "It's pretty provincial. If you're not from Evanston, and you're putting out news about Evanston and working for a non-for-profit in Evanston, you're not regarded as legitimate."

Miller helped start a *RoundTable* podcast—the *Evanston RoundCast*. He hosted an episode on retirement and racial inequity, which touched on Evanston's reparations issues, and reporter Bob Seidenberg interviewed primary election candidates.

The *RoundTable* began to highlight photography as part of the new digital platform. That's unusual for an online publication. Regular photography features are contributed by former *Chicago Sun-Times* photo editor Richard Cahan and School of the Art Institute of Chicago graduate Joerg Metzner. The *RoundTable* also established a gallery where readers contribute photographs. "We think it's a great medium for involving the community and providing a mirror of it," Miller said in March 2022.

While the nonprofit organization exists to publish the news, Miller believes the company can also become a significant community organization. "We're hopeful we can develop educational programs with the schools around journalism and writing," he said.

In April 2022, journalism professor and former *Chicago Sun-Times* reporter Susy Schultz was named editor of the *RoundTable*. Her father was *Chicago Daily News* columnist and editor Robert G. Schultz.

The Gavins remain as part of the *RoundTable* operation, serving on the board. They are planning a three-hundred-page book of Evanston history that will feature updated stories that appeared in some of the twenty-five magazines the *RoundTable* published over the years. Mary Gavin said, "For example, Larry wrote a story a couple years ago called 'Developing a Segregated Town.' The city has used that as a basis for their reparations movement. A lot of the stories are about things that are difficult in our community."

In the fall of 2021, the *RoundTable* also struck an agreement with the Medill School of Journalism at Northwestern University in Evanston to fund an annual Medill fellowship in reporting on racial justice, to be awarded each year to a Medill graduate.

Miller explained, "By changing the structure to nonprofit, it goes from being a closely held LLC to something we hope the entire community feels invested in. That's going to take time. The initial job is to stabilize the operation. Another goal is to get back to the printed edition. The resources are available in Evanston. So we can adjust on the fly."

While the *RoundTable* nonprofit model was built around networking with community leaders, the *Reader* took a slightly different approach. Baim networked with sixty-two Chicago independent media outlets through a project called Chicago Independent Media Alliance (CIMA). The alliance included for-profit and nonprofit organizations. Baim explained, "We released a report in November [2019] to funders about the precariousness of the local media landscape of independent community and ethnic media—everything from *La Raza* [Chicago's Hispanic newspaper] to the *Crusader* [a weekly Black newspaper that publishes in Chicago and Gary, Indiana]. Even the *Sun-Times* participated in the survey. About fifty out of one hundred or so responded.

"The alliance we're building in part is obviously to save a lot of papers at once by working together. But it also shows the *Reader* has an ability to be a connector and to be a filter for additional online entities to have more impact and visibility. It amplifies all at once to the foundation world."

During the early days of the coronavirus crisis, CIMA helped secure advertising buys, worked on grants, and held an online fundraising drive between May 8 and June 5, 2020. The general fund was split between all sixty-two outlets, partly matched by a variety of foundations. CIMA raised $160,000—close to $60,000 from foundations and $100,000 from individuals, according to Baim. In February 2021, when the *Chicago Tribune* was taken over by Alden Global Capital, there were pleas from staffers and the community to take the *Tribune* nonprofit. Baim was not concerned that charitable pockets would be drained. "The more nonprofits, the better in this space," she said in February 2021. "It shows the need."

While *Tribune* staffers in Chicago pleaded for nonprofit status, dreams did come true for staffers of the *Chicago Sun-Times*, their longtime tabloid rival. In January 2022 the *Sun-Times* merged with the radio station WBEZ Chicago to go nonprofit and create one of the largest news organizations in the country, with the potential to reach more than two million Chicagoans a week.

Chicago Public Media (CPM) raised $61 million in philanthropic support to cover a five-year period. CPM is the nonprofit company that owns WBEZ. The move saved the struggling *Sun-Times*. In 2017, my feisty alma mater was sold for $1 to a coalition of Chicago unions and former Chicago alderman Edwin Eisendrath.

INN works with thirteen media organizations in the metro Chicago area. How is the donor pie divided among so many groups? "Think about how many hospitals there are in a community," answered Kealing. "Think about how many museums there are. There is more than enough philanthropy to support nonprofit news organizations in a community. Chicago is a great example. You've got the BGA [Better Government Association] that is focused on government accountability. You've got *Block Club Chicago* that's really focused on neighborhoods [like small-town newspapers]. You've got the *Chicago Reader* that has the alt-weekly background. You've got *Borderless* magazine [a weekly newsletter on immigrant voices]. They each have a distinct role in the Chicago journalism ecosystem. The way you split it up is by making the case for the essential distinction of your work and the community that you're serving as being essential to that community."

Then, with so many foundations and donors involved, how does a nonprofit newspaper maintain editorial independence? What happens if a foundation member pitches a story that will benefit their foundation? "It's a great question," Miller said. "It's not that different than advertising pressures. We have to be on our toes and make sure we don't get pushed around. The best defense against that is diversity of funding. You can always say, 'Take your money and leave if you're not happy' to any one person. Another important component is to develop a membership model not unlike what WBEZ has. We hope to get members of the community to be members of the *RoundTable* for whatever we decide it will be, fifty bucks a year or whatever.

"The more diversity in the funding you have, the better."

When a newspaper applies for an INN membership, they are required to sign up for the organization's "Editorial Independence Policy." The *RoundTable* immediately added the policy to its masthead, stating in part, "We maintain a firewall between news coverage decisions and sources of all revenue. Acceptance of financial support does not constitute implied or actual endorsement of donors or their products, services or opinions."

Mary Gavin said, "The editorial decisions at the newspaper are separate from anybody on the board or the advisory committee."

Lack of diversity in funding sources is another potential problem with the nonprofit model. In October 2019, *Inside Philanthropy* (*IP*) cited a

Harvard–Northeastern University study on foundations and nonprofit media. *IP* reported, "One of the key problems they noted was a tendency of such funding to be lavished on a small number of prestigious outlets, such as ProPublica. And as *IP*'s Mike Scutari explained at the time of the study's release, its results suggested a case of 'elites supporting elites,' with funded media feeding the geographic, demographic, and ideological bubbles that many believe have led to rising populism and political dysfunction in the U.S. and abroad."

—

Meanwhile, one state over in Iowa, *Carroll Times Herald* co-owner Doug Burns started networking with the Local Media Association (LMA).

LMA was founded in 1971 in Chicago by the area's suburban newspapers. Early members included the Paddocks outside of Chicago, Shaw Media in Dixon, Illinois, and Larry Randle of Suburban Life Media. The organization has grown to more than three thousand newspapers, broadcasters, digital news sites, and research and development partners. LMA unites these groups to collaborate and learn.

"About 40 percent of the members are newspapers and maybe 50 percent of them are family newspapers," said Nancy Lane, CEO of LMA. "The big ones are members as well, like the Gannetts. We're focused on reinventing business models for news. That's all we think about every day. We're heavily focused on the digital side, but not just digital. Anything that will be a sustainable model for the future. We work with companies in all kinds of different ways, but a lot of our focus is on reader revenue, whether it is digital subscriptions, memberships, or contributions. Journalism funded by philanthropy is one of our pillars. It certainly overlaps with content because the walls are down. The silos aren't there anymore. Newsrooms are very involved with business affairs now in a way they never have been before. That's actually a very good thing."

In April 2020, Burns said, "I want to make sure we're branded as public service and using all our resources to getting information out on public health issues. The Local Media Association has a nonprofit component, and they're allowing small independent-owned newspapers like mine and several others to use their nonprofit. We'll put something out in our website, that this coverage is important and we've made it free. But it is not free to produce.

"Regardless whether we get a cent or not, we will continue to make the coverage free. There's hundreds of newspapers in North America doing this [nonprofit model]. To be honest, one of the reasons we've struggled, and several other newspapers that are family owned have struggled, is because we've made up for losses by putting family money into the paper. And going to all sorts of lengths to keep our operations going instead of selling to a chain, which, arguably, from a financial point of view, any family in our situation, just looking at it from a pure bottom line—it's almost economically suicidal to stay in this business. It's been a miserable business for the past five to eight years."

Back in Chicago, the revenue at the *Reader* grew almost 50 percent between the time new ownership took over in 2018 and January 2020. Dorothy Leavell, publisher of the Chicago and Gary *Crusader* newspapers, led a group to purchase the *Reader* in June 2018. The paper had previously been owned by the *Chicago Sun-Times*. "One sales rep said, 'The *Sun-Times* was the dog and the *Reader* was the fish,'" Tracy Baim recalled in January 2020. "When the *Sun-Times* owned both, and not out of any intentional neglect, they gave all the attention to the dog. Because every single day that dog needed to be fed and walked a couple times a day. The fish, you could go feed once a week and it would be fine. The *Reader* didn't have nourishment. And by the time we got them, they had no business side and no sales side. It was embedded with the *Sun-Times*. And the digital had been very neglected. It almost was impossible not to grow it, because it was dying."

After about a year on the job, Baim told the owners that they did not want to be the "bad guys" who shut down the *Reader*, and the company needed to find a path to a smooth transition. The owners who saved the paper were Chicago real estate developer Elzie Higginbottom and Chicago criminal defense attorney Leonard Goodman. Baim said, "I'm not comfortable trying to save this paper by finding new owners. So the only path left is foundation, philanthropic, and individual donor money. It absolutely needed more than advertising revenue. But it is not enough to sustain the *Reader* at the level it wants to be as an entity and as a footprint in Chicago. You cannot cut your way to a successful *Reader*. You may be able to do that at smaller papers. The *Reader* is different. I knew it from the outside, but I know it much better now.

"We're learning all the time. Shutting down print would be a ridiculous approach. Print is a great equalizer, especially free print. Many people don't have a way to use the internet and don't have smartphones. The people that produce this newspaper is almost half the cost. So the printing and delivery is another, maybe, 15 percent. But the ability to get revenue is always print. The amount of money you can make on an online website is ridiculously small.

"So philanthropic is the way to go."

Higginbottom and Goodman purchased the *Reader* for a dollar. "They were not going to endlessly fund it, so they agreed to sell it to a nonprofit once it gets established," Baim said.

The blurred lines of editorial independence played out a year later for the *Reader*. It's never a good sign when a newspaper's family affairs become bigger than the stories it covers, but in November 2021 the *Reader* found itself in that position.

Goodman wrote a November 2021 column that raised doubts about vaccinating children against COVID-19. There was pushback from readers and staff due to inaccuracies and misleading statements in the article. The *Reader* team had cycled the article through editing and fact-checking before publication. After the backlash, the *Reader* hired an external fact-checker to review the article. Baim then told Goodman the column would remain in its original form.

Once the *Reader*'s board members caught wind of the conflict, a resolution was introduced to delay the sale. A second resolution in January 2022 demanded that the board be allowed to appoint three additional seats to the nonprofit board, a review of the column's fact-checking methods, a financial audit, and Baim's resignation as president and co-treasurer of the nonprofit. In a February 28, 2022, Poynter Institute article, Goodman said, "There's so few spaces for dissent or nonconforming opinions in the press. That's one of the reasons I invested in the *Reader* because it's always had a place where you could say things that were unpopular and say things that would make people in power uncomfortable. We want to make sure that the not-for-profit will respect that tradition."

The anticipated January 1, 2022, transition of assets to the new nonprofit did not happen. The newspaper stopped fundraising. In April 2022, the unionized *Reader* staff and other Chicago union members took to the streets and protested outside of Goodman's North Side home. On April 26, 2022, Goodman announced he would give up control of the *Reader* and approve the transfer to nonprofit status. Three members of the nonprofit board resigned, including newspaper publisher Leavell. Higginbottom remained. Baim told the *Sun-Times* that the paper had fallen four and a half months behind its financial plans because of the disagreements. The *Reader* finally completed its transition to a nonprofit organization on May 16, 2022, ending many months of dissension and drama. The newspaper was sold to the nonprofit Reader Institute for Community Journalism.

The dustup is an example of what can go wrong in nonprofit journalism.

"Conversions are tricky," said INN's Kealing in a February 2022 conversation. "When you have powerful people involved and you're trying to keep the old while building the new, things can get confused. I'm following the story. It's a sad situation. The *Reader* has some exciting things going on, but they have to get their house in order. Everyone has to go back to why they did this in the first place.

"Conversions are not as common as start-ups. But we are seeing more conversions. *Salt Lake Tribune* did it successfully [in 2019]. The *Reader*? The book is still being written. Part of the challenge is how long the *Reader*'s process has gone on because of its own circumstances. The *Salt Lake Tribune* happened very quickly. In fact, quicker than they were prepared for it."

John Reed, the former publisher at the Champaign *News-Gazette* and the Danville *Commercial-News* (both in Illinois), said he spent up to three years researching nonprofit models. While sitting in his soon-to-be-vacated *News-Gazette* office, Reed said, "You try to figure out what the model might be, and I haven't seen anybody land on the answer. But certainly you cannot produce the product we were producing a year ago in a market like Champaign-Urbana and do so profitably. You have to rightsize the expenses, what the revenue streams are. And unfortunately, not just here, but at every newspaper, those revenue streams are trending down."

In some corners, pitching the need for nonprofit media could seem like a daunting task in the tribal America of the 2020s. Tracy Baim countered, "This is the perfect time to be doing this work with philanthropists in Chicago. Now, that may not be the case in other cities, and it may not be the case with philanthropists I'm not approaching. I'm approaching the kind of foundations that give to criminal justice reform, environmental issues. These are the foundations that fund homelessness issues and know that journalism amplifies the work."

As another example, the nonprofit *Daily Memphian* news site was founded in 2018 in Memphis, Tennessee. It raised $8.2 million in donations, also known as "philanthropic venture capital," to take on the *Commercial Appeal*, founded in 1841 and owned by Gannett. In 2021, Politico called the *Daily Memphian* "one of the best local news sites in the country." It reported that in 2000, the *Commercial Appeal* landed at 238,000 Sunday print copies and around 184,000 daily. In 2021, the numbers had dropped to 52,000 on Sunday and 29,000 daily. Several *Daily Memphian* reporters are former *Commercial Appeal* employees. In 2021, the *Daily Memphian* had almost 14,000 subscribers, who were paying an average of $9.25 a month for content.

John Galer is vice chairman of the board of the National Newspaper Association (NNA), founded in 1885. "We deal with this on a lot of levels," Galer said. "I don't see how nonprofit would work in Hillsboro per se, but that's because I'm so crazily independent. I think it's a neat idea. But it goes back to the worry of control. If you get money from somebody, does that color who you are or give you the appearance that maybe you're not as open-minded and non-biased as the world might think you are? You do have several things going on with several foundations. Here in Illinois, one of the biggest is the McCormick Foundation, who have put a bunch of money into the Illinois Press Foundation. We have set up *Capitol News Illinois*. It is basically free, dedicated journalists that work the state capitol. Because even the Springfield *State Journal* [*Register*] doesn't have a full-time reporter at the statehouse anymore. The *Tribune*, the *Sun-Times*, nobody's there full time. So we set this up where there's independent, professional journalism coming out of Springfield. We make those stories available. Because we're a foundation that is nonprofit, we can't charge for it. Newspapers, radio stations, TV stations—they all pick up these stories. That's all been through donations. Illinois publishers have put significant dollars into the whole thing, and that's on a nonprofit basis, too. It's a totally viable function."

In 2020, *Capitol News Illinois* added two reporters through a grant that was awarded by Report for America, which is a national service program that places emerging journalists into local news organizations for one or two years to focus on under-covered issues.

Galer remarked, "It could be as we figure the world out, reporting could be done on another scale. It's not an impossible task. But the main thing with local newspapers is you gotta have somebody local. If somebody is a hundred miles away, they don't know the names of the people in town and they don't know the community. We got our kids in school here. We know the world here and that's such a big deal. And if you're here and people trust you, you have a thousand different sources for what you need. If you're from somewhere else and they might not know you, well, they might not be too open with information."

Over in Iowa, Doug Burns said, "Local owners like myself that have a long track record in the community of a certain editorial voice and civic-mindedness, our readers will see if we're consistent. It relies on my integrity to continue to do the kind of journalism and not compromise our organization to where we don't have that trust."

Ethics call for nonprofit donors to have no influence over a newspaper's editorial content. "Look, is it perfect?" Burns asked. "No. But we got hit by a fucking duopoly known as Facebook and Amazon. They wiped out the fourth leg of the table of democracy in the fourth estate. We can't have the independent, unattainable model. I used to be the guy in the room that could pretty much tell anybody they were wrong. I don't have that leverage anymore. It's tragic. Because the one person in the room that could tell people in positions of power to do that in smaller rural areas was the newspaper owner. He or she had the credibility of being a big community booster, and also, it's our job. Can we still do that? Yeah, but not as much. The question is, do you want a news desert or a news organization that may have to go after donors?"

In February 2021, the Western Iowa Journalism Foundation was approved for nonprofit status by the IRS. The foundation was the brainchild of Burns. He formed an alliance with five other independent, family-owned newspapers in western Iowa. The foundation is separate from the newspaper operations. *Des Moines Register* columnist Kyle Munson left his newspaper after twenty-four years to become founding board president. The *Register* had been owned for eighty-two years by the Cowles Media Company, until 1985 when the Cowles family sold to Gannett.

Burns said, "Generally that type of nonprofit support is found in more urban areas. I can't stress enough how much we all loved this business when we weren't facing an existential financial threat every day. It was enjoyable to be able to come in every day and make a difference in people's lives. To do the kind of government accountability work we want to do and the regional reporting we want to do, we need three more positions and a couple part-time positions. That should be funded through nonprofit. We can prove we've been losing money and that the market won't stand us up, yet this is essential public service. If that doesn't work, we could be done. If we weren't here right now, it would be anarchy of misinformation and recrimination."

Burns took a sip of his bottle of water. The solution for the co-owner of the *Carroll Times Herald* was clear: a bifurcation of a profit/nonprofit model. Bifurcation happens when one company splits into two new companies that can each sell shares to stockholders.

"We like that model," said LMA's Nancy Lane in a summer 2020 conversation. "I don't know that anyone has done it. You put the journalism on the nonprofit side, and if you have something like digital marketing services, you can make that on the for-profit side. The other thing is on the nonprofit side, you can't endorse political candidates. You have to be willing to give up a few things. But the restrictions are not that great."

Burns said, "If it doesn't work, I'll have to gut the newspaper. I'd have to cut half my staff. At this point we've been breakeven or losing money for the better part of a decade now. We're almost like a nonprofit. There is no money to be made in the kind of journalism that we do. I've been working for less than $40,000 a year for three years. I'm a Northwestern graduate who is fifty years old and done about everything I can in my community. First-place column writing in the INA [Iowa Newspaper Association] ten out of fourteen years. Being [Carroll's] Citizen of the Year this year. I've worked fifty- to seventy-hour weeks. I'm fifty. I just can't keep doing that for $37,000 a year. I'm doing it through the coronavirus because that's what I have to do. But it's just not right.

"I could pop over to Mercury Boost," he said, mentioning his side marketing company, "and go after the banks and some political clients and work in

Council Bluffs or Omaha. I'd have a nice office there, and I have no doubt with a staff of myself and two other people could bring in $1 to $2 million in revenue in the first year. It costs me money staying in the newspaper business. I love it and feel a responsibility to the community. So I'll try nonprofit, but I want to make sure the journalists who work for me are compensated reasonably.

"Look, we're four generations and we love it. I see this as being part of a cultural war that we're in, and I don't want to walk off the battlefield. But if I'm having trouble staying on that battlefield, how in the hell are you going to recruit new people into it? Tell me the career trajectory for somebody who is twenty-two and has $32,000 in student loan debt—how do I get them to come work for me at a starting salary of $31,000 and where I probably won't ever be able to give them a raise? The mid-level papers like the *Des Moines Register* and the *Sioux City Journal* are being wiped out. So where do they go? We're trying everything you can think of, but at the end of the day, if people don't see community as community and if they want to lead these individualized, itemized, narcissistic lives, then what's our role?"

Profits are not the top priority for many of these legacy community newspapers. There are no shareholders riding roughshod. But they still need to find ways to sustain. As newspapers confront diminished readership and lack of trust, the service journalism model is one logical path: sending readers brief texts once or twice a day while monitoring the needs of residents. The outreach can include breaking news, road construction updates, and store closings. A newspaper can become a vehicle to build bridges within the community, and with that connection, the community can better understand journalism.

Chapter 14

The Future

How do community papers secure their future? The answers are bold and imaginative because boundaries have yet to be shaped for tomorrow. The best community newspapers build trust and value in their towns, embrace technology, honor their staffs, explore nonprofit models, and more. In addition, some have found the future may lie in diversification and staying nimble, as well as promoting civic engagement and education to inspire the next generation.

Max Kabat and his wife, Maisie Crow, are two freethinking Texas newspaper slingers who met journalism's future at high noon.

They did not blink.

In 2019, Kabat and Crow purchased the *Big Bend Sentinel*, a weekly newspaper in Marfa, Texas (pop. 1,700) that has served the region since 1926. They expanded the operation to open The Sentinel—a bar, coffee shop, and restaurant next door to the newspaper office.

The future of independent family newspapers can blossom from daring models like this. The Sentinel became an inviting component of the community. The newspaper had a face.

Crow is co-owner and editor-in-chief. Kabat is publisher and co-owner of the West Texan Media Group, which includes the *Big Bend Sentinel* and its smaller bilingual publication, *Presidio International*. They were in their late thirties when they bought the paper from Robert and Rosario Halpern.

"To make local, independent journalism thrive instead of just survive, the idea was to build a community gathering space around the idea of a newspaper," Kabat said in a June 20, 2020, interview, the one-year anniversary of opening The Sentinel. "What would happen if you brought people into a space to talk and exchange information instead of yelling at each other on Facebook? How would you make people comfortable? Serve them coffee, cocktails, and something to eat. You'd have programming. And all of that would be in service of investing more money into journalism.

"That was our wacky idea. And even in these COVID times we're figuring out how to make it work."

Kabat and Crow published their first edition on July 4, 2019. Subscriptions have gone up. Digital traffic has gone up. The Sentinel has hosted weddings, a New Year's Eve party, and a DJ collective from Mexico City. "We partnered with the local NPR station and did a town hall on aging and dying in the Big Bend," Kabat said. "It's a multipurpose space with the idea of having it for multi-factions of Marfa. The economic challenges here are the 'haves' and folks that don't have as much. There's that tension of the needs of a community that is always being worked on here.

"We're constantly evolving and trying to figure out the best way to serve the community while running a profitable business. Coffee, breakfast, cocktails, and a place to relax and congregate seven days a week is a constant. Food is constantly changing as we try to figure out the market fit and the right staff."

Robert Halpern also maintained a welcoming connection with the community during the years he owned the paper. "It was an open-door policy," he said. "It's in the middle of downtown. On election night, before the internet, we would post the results on paper in the front window. There would be a gathering on the sidewalk. I would have coffee. Somebody would bring donuts. Sometimes the results wouldn't come in until the morning and then everybody would filter out and go home. That's the point of a community weekly. Everybody is entitled to bring in a letter to the editor, an organization, or an idea, to bitch and moan. We practiced true community, collaborative journalism, so our readers, politicians, artists, musicians, activists, and the area's eccentrics dropped in on us. There was never a dull moment."

The Sentinel community space was subsidizing the newspaper until

COVID-19 hit. The new owners were pivoting to implement an expansion plan on covering the entire Big Bend region. "We're nimble now," Kabat said. "So now it's about reimagining our reimagination. We have a bunch of ideas and they're all focused on alternative revenue streams."

By July 2021, Kabat had established the Broadsheet ad network, a national advertising platform based on values instead of clicks. Most national online ads have been devalued because of Google. Kabat's thinking with Broadsheet is that advertisers would rather be seen on quality, local websites. To that end, he was targeting newspapers in Telluride, the Hamptons, Jackson Hole, and other edgy tourist destinations—like Marfa. Kabat created the network as a partnership with The goodDog, his advertising agency that he started in New York.

"Broadsheet is rocking and rolling," Kabat said in January 2022. "We have more than two hundred publishers and counting." Broadsheet's pitch deck points out that 73 percent of Americans across the political spectrum have "a great deal" or "a fair amount" of trust in local newspapers, versus 59 percent in national newspapers, according to a 2018 Poynter Media Trust Survey.

Broadsheet's 2022 advertising net had grown to include the *Chattanooga Times Free Press*, the *Crested Butte News*, and Black-owned publications such as the *St. Louis American* and Washington DC's woman-owned *Washington Informer*.

Kabat and Crow lived in the Navy Yard section of Brooklyn, New York, in 2013 when they first visited Marfa. In July 2016, they bought a house in Marfa and got married three months later. Kabat is a strategy consultant. Crow is a social justice documentary filmmaker who also was a photojournalist at the *Boston Globe*. She is from Corpus Christi, Texas, and as a child she would visit family ranchers in the area. "When we wanted to get out of New York City, I was trying to push us up to the Hudson Valley," Kabat said. "Maisie kept saying, 'Why don't we go to Texas? Let's check out this place Marfa.' Every time we got outside of the city, there was opportunity to think. We became disenfranchised with city living in the sense that there was no way we could afford to live in New York the way we wanted to live.

"We also wanted to be part of a community. And there was no more community in New York. We were living in an echo chamber. My wife makes films about change. She's said, 'Let's go do something. What do we do with our lives?'"

Like Trevor Vernon did in Eldon, Missouri, Kabat jumped into the local political scene in Marfa. He became the Presidio County Democratic Party chairman mainly because no one else wanted to assume the role. He helped run the election cycle in 2018 and met a lot of people in the county. He resigned before taking over the *Sentinel*. Kabat said, "We did a candidate's forum and Robert and Rosario [Halpern] asked the questions."

Robert and Rosario were in their sixties at the time of the forum. They had owned the *Big Bend Sentinel* for twenty-five years. After Max and Maisie got to know them better, they invited the Halperns to their house for dinner. The couples started talking about visions, past and present. Robert and Rosario raised three children in Marfa, and all three kids worked at the newspaper. "Marfa and far west Texas has been very good to us," Robert said.

Robert is from nearby Alpine, Texas, and Rosario is from Presidio, a border town along the Rio Grande in Presidio County. "Two days after Robert and Rosario left our house, we got an email from them," Kabat said. "They asked if we wanted to buy the newspaper when they retired. They said, 'You're the perfect couple: a marketing and brand person and a journalist.'

"And we said, 'No way. It's a dying business.' Then we were like, 'Well, why is it a dying business?' That's what I do in my consultancy and that's what Maisie does as a human being. 'Why is it like this?' and 'What if?' are questions we both ask in our professions."

Max and Maisie saw themselves in Robert and Rosario.

Kabat thought about that mirror image. He fell silent for a long time and elaborated, "It takes a certain kind of person to run a newspaper. You're trying to abide by certain criteria, facts, and information. You constantly try to do what's right. But you live in a small town, and people love you and people hate you at the same time. You see them every day. How does that work? Rosario is a strong-willed, strong-minded individual. Maisie is a strong-willed, strong-minded individual. We're leveraging her. Let me be clear about that. She's the brains, I'm the brawn.

"Robert and Rosario have this balance of a relationship where they talk about everything. They're super excitable. They believe in community. We saw them and looked at ourselves thirty years from now. Contributing and being part of the community is something we really wanted to do when we talked about getting married and spending our lives together."

In a separate interview, I asked Robert if he and Rosario saw Max and Maisie as their younger selves. "If they saw us that way, we saw them that way too," he said. "I had the journalism degree. Maisie had the journalism degree and was an Emmy-winning documentarian. Max is a marketing guy, Rosario has an accounting degree, so there's the business side. When we started in 1994, we already had a family, but in meeting them they said they would want to have a family someday. When you own your own business, you can facilitate kids. We were lucky to have a big office as a newsroom, a big old building downtown.

"At one time, we had a playpen in the newsroom when our youngest son was born," he recalled. "The school bus would drop our school-age kids at the office in the afternoon. We once had to store our piano at the office while we built our house because the place we had to move in the meantime was too small.

"All our kids worked at the paper. Our daughter became a very good photographer and darkroom tech. Our son became a good photographer— not so much darkroom because by then it was all digital. The beauty is that the kids worked at the paper. You explained the issues, and they saw the paper as a community center."

—

There is a Buddha quote that says, "The past is already gone, the future is not here yet. There's only one moment for you to live." The trouble is that those moments can be so fleeting in the newspaper business.

Mary Herschelman sat at a long table in the kitchen of her family's office at the *Journal-News* in Hillsboro, Illinois. She looked out a window as she considered the future.

"It keeps me up at night," she admitted. "I hope it keeps going. I don't have a clear answer. I hope the investments we have made in our community continue. My parents let us carve our own paths in life and I want my daughter to be able to do that too. She may have no interest in anything like this. I don't know. I worry a lot about something happening to my parents and something happening to the paper on my watch. But I try to keep my same philosophy that you just keep rolling. The paper celebrated its 150th anniversary when I was in college, and it is certainly one of the oldest long-standing businesses in this area."

Herschelman attended the University of Missouri in Columbia, and Mike Jenner, the present-day Missouri School of Journalism faculty group chair of journalism professions, said the school was still attracting students some twenty years after Herschelman attended. "They're smarter than I ever was," he said. "They're true believers in the power and promise of journalism. They believe that it is vital to a democracy. The news today is so overwhelming. There's so much stuff. It's like a soffit from a fire hose.

"The job market is better on the television side than print right now, and I worry about it. It's not that hard, at least for our students, to get entry-level jobs. But there used to be one hundred jobs in the newsroom and now there's twenty-four. When I graduated from Missouri, I went to a little paper in Mississippi and worked there for two years. Every two years I could go get a new job. I moved up in market size and moved up in responsibility and pay. I worry that ladder is missing now or at least a few rungs are gone. I worry about how it is going to work for students graduating today. But they still want to do it. They still believe in its importance to our country and our society. That's heartening to me."

—

Eliza Gaines is a young fourth-generation newspaperperson.

She was named managing editor of the *Arkansas Democrat-Gazette* on January 27, 2020. Her father, Walter Hussman Jr., made the announcement in the *Democrat-Gazette* newsroom. Pride ran river-deep in his eyes. Gaines succeeded retiring managing editor David Bailey.

Her first day on the job was March 17, 2020. Her first task was to send home the staff because of COVID-19.

Her second day on the job was her thirty-third birthday.

"I came in at the height of all that," Gaines said in 2020. "Illness spreads very quickly in the newsroom. People are always congregating in groups, there's a lot of meetings. So I was like, 'I'd rather have everybody home safely rather than everybody getting sick at once—and then we can't put the paper out.' We got the hang of it really fast. But yeah, it was my first day working on my tiny desk from home."

In 2012, Gaines earned a master's degree in journalism from the University of North Carolina, the same school that her father attended. Before becoming managing editor, she was vice president of audience development at the *Democrat-Gazette* and other papers operated by her father's privately owned WEHCO Media.

She brought a contemporary business sensibility to her paper's future. "I'd worked at the paper growing up, interning, learning about each department," she said. "In graduate school my focus was on business media. I always saw myself as a reporter or an editor. When I was thinking about my future, I considered the business side a little more. I told my dad that if I went into the business side, I'd be worried I would not be able to be creative. He said, 'You have no idea how creative you'll have to be in business.' And he was right."

On January 10, 2022, Eliza Gaines was promoted to executive editor. Longtime staffer Alyson Hoge was promoted to managing editor.

Between 2009 and 2010 Eliza was an intern and staff writer in the *San Francisco Chronicle* travel department. She returned to Arkansas in 2012 to become assistant publisher at the *Democrat-Gazette*. She told her father she wanted to move the paper into the fourth generation. In a separate conversation, Hussman recalled, "I told her, 'Newspapers are really struggling. There's declining ad revenues all over. Are you sure you want to go in this business?' She said, 'Absolutely.'" So Eliza worked hand in hand with her father and visited each newspaper under the *Democrat-Gazette* umbrella. She was executive editor of the *Sentinel-Record* (a WEHCO holding) in Hot Springs, Arkansas, in 2013–14 before taking time off to have her first child. Eliza and her husband, Alec, a Little Rock attorney, have three children.

On January 27, 2020, her father told the newsroom how proud he was of Eliza. "This job wasn't given to her," he said. "She's earned it. We try to operate a meritocracy around here even though we're a family business. This has been a family business since 1909 and it's going to continue to be a family business. There's a lot of big benefits to that.

"Too many newspapers in America have been sold to corporations. Some of them went public and they answer to their shareholders first instead of readers first. Now we have private equity groups who come in and take over newspapers and try to get everything they can out of them as long as they are around. And I don't think they have a long-term plan for being around. We have a different set of priorities and Eliza embraces those priorities."

In a May 2020 interview, Gaines said that her youth will be an asset to the *Democrat-Gazette*. "I hope that it gives some faith towards the future of our company if I'm this vested and coming in as a younger person," she said. "This will be a lifelong career, I hope. Also, as a younger person, our generation's reading habits are very different than my dad's. We have a real issue with not having younger people subscribing to the newspaper. It frightens me, not only for people who aren't getting the right news, but getting news through Facebook and the internet. If people only visit the website or get our newsletters, they're not loyal subscribers."

Eliza remembers her childhood home being saturated with newspapers and magazines. "It's absolutely part of my DNA," she said. "I remember walking around the newsroom as a child, and I thought it was the coolest thing. I remember the newsroom being so noisy. Now you walk through the newsroom and it's so quiet. Everybody is sitting at their computers with emails, where back in the early '90s, everybody was on their phone, the TVs were on. It was a lot of movement and that's changed. I kind of miss that."

A spirited newsroom leads to a vital future. In Dixon, Illinois, the sixth-generation publisher Peter Shaw said the key to negotiating the future is to stay vital. "Our non-involved family members, regardless of generation, are skeptical of the future, as they should be," said the former family trustee. "The future centers around consumer-driven revenue, mainly in the form of digital subscriptions. We talk about the retail apocalypse. All that stuff has gone away, even the suburban concept of America. And what some of the large non-metro newspapers were working off of were the expansive retail areas, the advertising, and everything that came with it. That's gone. Look at Reddit. I don't have a user tag, but I'm on it several times a day."

The world is breaking down into niche interests. Independent family newspapers understand local news is an essential niche. Shaw said, "Niche is for people who live in communities like ours and who care about their community. It is a niche of interest. We're focused not only on that, but we're working on a way to connect that regionally [in] our reach of northern Illinois that goes from outside of Cook County coming west, except for Rockford and Freeport. We have *Pro Football Weekly*, which is really focused on the Bears. We have *Starved Rock Country* [quarterly magazine], which is focused on Starved Rock State Park, and a couple other niche things like that."

Niche thinking can lead to the bigger picture of diversification. A cutting-edge idea can cross over to cultivate new audiences.

In February 2021, the Haymarket Beer Company in Chicago rolled out a limited-edition line of "Don't Stop the Presses" lager that directly benefitted the *Chicago Reader*, *Block Club Chicago*, and the *Daily Line*. *Reader* publisher Tracy Baim said, "We have diversified revenue to include merchandise, memberships, donations, grants, and still do ads—hopefully those will come back after COVID-19 business closings end."

John Barnwell, the former CEO of Evening Post Industries (EPI) in Charleston, South Carolina, is no stranger to diversification. He credited his newspaper's heartbeat to its once-largest subsidiary, Cordillera Communications, a successful operator of network-affiliated broadcast television stations. "Television over the last twenty years overtook our newspaper business as far as revenue and operating profit," Barnwell said in a December 2019 interview. "That was a pretty mature business, and we needed to get bigger or get out. We decided to get out about a year ago [in 2018]."

EPI sold fifteen of its sixteen television stations to the E.W. Scripps Company for a whopping $521 million. The remaining station in Tucson, Arizona, was sold to Quincy Media of Illinois at an undisclosed price. EPI had been in the television business since 1974. Barnwell said, "So we are no longer in the media diversification business with television, but in the meantime, we diversified into health care and a few other areas to sustain the company.

"Just thinking back to a board retreat we had a few years ago, a question was, 'Is it more important to stay in our legacy newspaper business or more important to sustain the overall business?' It was a draw. We have never subsidized our newspaper business by diversification. It's always stood on its own two feet. It has been profitable. And it is still profitable. But we do see the ability to sustain the company, and it's a better bet on the shoulders of health care and some of the other things we got involved in, specifically the hospice business, which we got into five years ago and where we're probably into double digits as far as acquisitions go. We invested in a pharmaceutical sales company a few years ago. That's dermatological products, and that's growing as well."

Barnwell continued, "Five or six years ago we hired someone specifically to look at noncorrelated investments. We approached it in an opportunistic way. We looked at a lot of things and if something stuck, we would go with it. That's how the hospice operation came about. We've grown that to be a fairly substantial business."

In October 2021, the company sold off its hospice business as Evening Post Industries split into three companies: a newspaper division, a health and hospice division, and a real estate group. "In lots of families, especially in the newspaper business, somewhere along the way the passion for the business is compromised by the challenges of economics, especially in the last ten, fifteen years," Barnwell said in September 2021. "Here, you had some family members who wanted to push ahead on the business, and other parts of the family didn't want to do that. The sale of our hospice operation with the television money allowed us to have enough money to structure the split for the part of the family that wanted to stay in the newspaper business. This allowed that family member to break off with the newspaper and [to have] cash to invest in newspapers and other things."

That family member is Pierre Manigault, chairman of EPI. His newspaper division includes the newspapers, Evening Post Books, and White Oak Forestry, a forest and land management company. Barnwell said seven fourth-generation family members were in play. "If we had stayed together, there would have been a continuation of competition for capital," he explained. "More and more the board was unwilling to continue to support the newspaper business the way Pierre wanted to. The forestry business is kind of neutral. It's valuable, it's a lot of acres, but it doesn't produce much in cash flow. We continue to have the pharmaceutical sales company. This allows each of these groups to focus on what they're interested in without being distracted competing for capital as a bigger company."

Evening Post Industries (then Evening Post Publishing) also helped launch the award-winning *Garden & Gun* culture and food magazine in 2007 but divested itself of the publication at the end of 2008. The *Post and Courier* still owns a "minority passive interest," according to Barnwell.

Barnwell retired in September 2021 at age sixty-five. He said the sale had nothing to do with him moving on. What were the benefits and drawbacks of being a non-family CEO? "The family decided to have independent management twenty-five years ago," he answered. "It provided a lot of value. There's jealousies and squabbles when you have family members running the company day-to-day. I suppose it's been a process of peacemaking. It's a big advantage to have somebody they trust. And the most important thing is to find someone you can trust."

"Charleston is a great example of a company that has diversified themselves," said Nancy Lane, CEO of the Local Media Association. "Selling the broadcast division gives them a lot of runway on the newspaper side. They can experiment and figure it out over the next few years. They have the ownership that will allow that. And most papers do not. We spent time in Charleston. We know the leadership there very well. It's a brilliant strategy. You have to diversify. Right now a lot of newspapers are putting all their eggs into digital subscriptions. But digital subscriptions alone is never going to save the business. Unless you're the *New York Times*. And local media companies are not that. Advertising is not the savior. There's nobody out there who thinks that will be going up. Journalism funded by philanthropy is probably what we're most excited about at this moment in time. But we continue to look for other opportunity areas. Funders are finally realizing that funding local news is as important as funding the arts and health care. Once local news goes away— bye-bye democracy. Everything starts to collapse."

Dixon, Illinois's, Peter Shaw said, "Diversification is important as a future addendum. We never went outside the media field, but we have seen value in that. We looked at car washes. A community theater. We almost bought a movie theater in McHenry. We just didn't have the expertise. Our bank was leery of us getting into a field we didn't understand, but at the same time they were very encouraging for us to find more opportunities.

"But the focus for existing company leadership is not to do anything outside of what their core competencies are. Right now, with the change in the industry, it is head down and focus on that."

Former newspaper broker Phil Murray mentioned that Ogden Newspapers (based out of Wheeling, West Virginia) is one of the top twenty largest newspaper companies, owning forty dailies in the spring of 2020. "But they also own ski resorts and the Pittsburgh Pirates," Murray said. "Divesting like that is relatively rare. Sometimes diversification took the form of other media like radio and TV, but usually not manufacturing business or hospice business." Ogden CEO Robert Nutting is principal owner of the Pirates and formet owner of Seven Springs Mountain Resort in Seven Springs, Pennsylvania. Long-suffering Pirates fans have tagged Nutting with the unfortunate saying, "Spend Nutting, Win Nutting." In the summer of 2020, the Poynter institute said Ogden had layoffs and furloughs companywide due to COVID-19.

In addition to the newspaper, the late *News-Gazette* publisher Marajen Stevick Chinigo owned Champaign radio stations WDWS-AM and WHMS-FM, as well as the Prairie Production Group, an audiovisual production company, and Direct Impressions, a direct-mail company.

Former *News-Gazette* publisher John Reed said, "These things are gray areas. Charleston got into the hospice thing, and they did see that as a way. The family has done a lot of the right things. They had a war chest. This entity never had a war chest. We had a little bit of reserves, which we invested into new production facilities at the absolute worst time. We poured a bunch of money into a state-of-the-art printing and packing facility. The press we had wasn't worn out. Then the world really changed [with the recession]. Things weren't great the first part of that decade. But everybody was still profitable. But there was change coming. By the end of 2008, the change accelerated. So others, like us, who made major capital investments at that point were never able to recoup it."

—

The tiny but mighty *Carroll Times Herald* has tried to diversify in its modest corner of western Iowa. In the winter of 2020, co-owner Doug Burns said, "We're fighting like hell to keep it independently owned. We started doing search engine optimizations seven or eight years ago. We put up digital billboards. We started our own digital marketing company. I run a political advertising operation on the side that sells and places ads into all 270 newspapers across Iowa. We have a commission arrangement with *La Prensa*, a Spanish-language paper [in Denison, Iowa]."

The *Times Herald* did take stabs at buying other small family newspapers in the region. The most notable example was the historic *Adair County Free Press* in Greenfield, about forty-five miles south of Carroll near the Missouri border.

The *Free Press* was in the Sidey family for 125 years. Hugh Sidey (1927–2005) was best known for writing "The Presidency" column for *Time* magazine and hosted the PBS series *The American Presidents*.

"Hugh and his brother ran the family paper after their father died," said *Times Herald* publisher Ann Wilson. "When he died his wife kept it together for a few years, then a mutual friend came to us and asked if we would buy it. It was an interesting community."

The *Times Herald* purchased the *Adair County Free Press* in 2014 and sold it in 2017. Wilson explained, "Rural communities want the person to live in the community and be a part of the community. We were viewed as a 'chain' in Adair. We tried to work on their economic development, which is something we do best. But we weren't accepted. Financially it became something we couldn't continue. So we sold it to a real chain. And they hate it."

Through a broker, the paper was sold to Shaw Media out of Dixon, Illinois.

"It didn't feel right for us," Wilson continued. "We had known the Sidey family for years. We knew that wasn't what they wanted. But there was really no other option. Linda Sidey [Hugh's sister-in-law] was still in the community. She had some ideas on how we should do things. It wasn't our way. It didn't mean she was wrong. But it's a smaller community than this. We just needed to get out."

Doug Burns said, "The same thing happened in Guthrie County [*Guthrie County Times*] and Panora [*Lake Panorama Times*]. Our county borders Guthrie County. But people in that county wanted a local owner. We didn't go in there like some hedge fund, slash and burn. The alternative was: if it's not us, it's going to be a chain or no paper. Immediately I went into these places and served on local economic development boards."

Wilson added, "The towns are seven miles apart. I combined the papers because it was not economically feasible to print two of the same thing. We got rid of the paper in the summer of 2019. The current owner does not put anything in the paper that happens outside the county."

In 2020, the *Times Herald* still owned the *Jefferson Bee & Herald* in Jefferson, about forty-five miles southeast of Carroll. In 2012, *Jefferson Bee* owner Rick Morain wanted to retire for health reasons. He asked Ann Wilson to buy it. She did. She changed the format and asked Morain to stay to write columns.

Doug Burns diversified into economic development and helped bring the Wild Rose Casino & Resort to Jefferson in 2015. He also worked with Democratic congressman Ro Khanna in bringing Silicon Valley jobs to the area. Wilson said, "That was very important. We've all been involved. Doug mainly in economic development, but Tom and I have done things in that community. And it's all worked well."

Burns then changed lanes and looked at fin tech (financial technology) in the future. "The founder of Square has an idea to create a massive cooperative where every newspaper that signs up gets micropayments," Burns said with a sigh. "I've heard, 'Let's go all-digital.' I've heard to cut our staff as much as we can. You talk about building an airplane as it's flying? I've built a fucking squadron of airplanes in the air. At this point anybody who will criticize a newspaper owner that is still open can go fuck themselves. You can use the f-bomb and I'll be disappointed if you don't quote me accurately with the f-bomb."

Fine.

Crain's Chicago Business reported in 2013 that Shaw Media in Dixon, Illinois, was valued at $25.4 million in 2009. "Somebody would have to come close to offering double the market value for selling to be a real consideration," former trustee Peter Shaw said in November 2019. "Because the market values on newspapers are so low. You can continue to make more money or sell it. That's not guaranteeing the value is going to be at the same level it is now. But the ongoing operational value of the company is much greater than the return you can get on the market.

"Even for a family that does not all live and work here, we take great pride in the legacy we have. We wouldn't want someone like Gannett coming into our town and doing what we know they would do to the property. We've had to cut expenses, but we still feel we are stewards of the community."

Former Champaign *News-Gazette* publisher John Reed is unsure about the future. He helped navigate the sale of his newspaper in August 2019, which was followed by layoffs in November 2019. "For me, there's a little distance now," Reed said in a March 2020 interview. "I've been out of the thick of it since November. I wish I had an answer. I don't think the industry is going to go extinct in the foreseeable future, but it's really hard. Right now you can still extract profit by managing the expense side and doing everything you can to try to bring back some of the top-line stuff. The latter, though, is a really hard sell."

Mary Schenk has been a *News-Gazette* reporter since 1983. She sat across the room from Reed and said, "The bottom line is that we have a lot of people working for free around here. I put in routinely fifty-five-hour weeks. They didn't offer me any more money to stay. They cut my pay. I cover things other people did—babies, engagements—in between murder trials. I call it 'The Cradle to Grave' beat. I cover cops. I do whatever my boss tells me to do: rewrite this. It's painful. There's things I'd like to be able to have the time to dig into and I don't. It's just grueling. And what we're doing is not sustainable from a human standpoint."

So why does she continue?

"Because I'm so close to retirement," she answered. "I'll be sixty-two this year. I have a child in college. This is all I've known. Why do I stay? Because I love it. It's my family. I was the last president of the union here. I knew I was going to lose most of my membership. The people who stayed were clearly the ones who had been the heavy lifters for years. They're like me. They're devoted to this place, and they already have their homes paid for, and they don't want to pick up and move for what might be seven more years of a career. I'm thirty-six years in. We have long-term people here."

A year later, in the summer of 2021, Schenk was still at the *News-Gazette*. "The pandemic caused a 15 percent cut in pay paper-wide in 2020 that lasted several months," she wrote in an email. "Our editorial staff has not grown at all, but we continue to pack a punch in output. A paper six days a week, two quarterly magazines, and numerous special sections.

"However, we are tired, really tired."

—

One day of the year stands apart from all others for Vernon Publishing president Trevor Vernon. It is a day of promise and renewal. "Democracy Day" is held every spring in Eldon, Missouri, at Eldon Upper Elementary School, just a couple blocks from the newspaper offices. Vernon said that launching Democracy Day is the type of gamble newspapers need to take to remain vital in the future. Small papers are looking at greater civic engagement to educate kids about journalism and accountability.

Vernon Publishing hosts the event, which features nearly seventy-five community leaders. All fourth, fifth, and sixth graders attend Democracy Day, which adds up to 450 kids along with a couple dozen students from smaller rural schools in the area.

A mini press corps roams the halls while snapping photographs and interviewing attendees. Vernon creates a "town forum" where student council members ask hard questions to area legislators. After the event, a school newspaper section is produced and printed in the *Eldon Advertiser*.

Vernon came up with the idea in 2005 when he was twenty-four years old. "I was at a National Newspaper Association meeting in Milwaukee," he recalled in a May 2020 interview. "The Newspapers in Education coordinator from Missouri was there as a presenter. We talked a lot about civics, struggles in schools, and getting kids involved in the community. She said we had to figure out a way to reach kids. I agreed. Taking chances like this is how we get better. We can survive on a 1 percent profit margin for a couple years. Big corporations cannot do that, they would no longer have investors."

Vernon is investing in the future.

Democracy Day leaders move between classrooms explaining what they do for the community and how their organizations operate. A private vote selects two reporters from each fifth-grade class. "It has changed into something where political leaders show up and they [kid reporters] grill them," Trevor said. "It's hard sometimes for them to answer to a kid. They're a little more direct with me normally, but for them they want to make sure they're politically correct. Reporters can go into whichever classroom they want to. The interest outside the school is huge. Politicians call: 'When is it going to be this year?'"

Reporter Lily Henley, eleven, was a witness to the spiritual cycle of a newspaper in 2020. Her first career byline was in the March 26, 2020, edition of the *Advertiser*. The Eldon native wrote two stories: one on the three generations of Vernon Publishing, and the other on Aflac Insurance in Eldon. Each story ran about five paragraphs.

Her stories appeared in the same newspaper that carried the obituary of her grandfather, Graham Terrance Grimes. He died on March 20, 2020, after a ten-year battle with bone and lung cancer. He was sixty-five years old.

Lily said she reads the print version of the *Advertiser* when there's "important things, like my grandpa's obituary." On an early summer day in 2020, Lily sat in the *Advertiser*'s conference room with her mom, Kyle. The walls are covered with cases of bound issues of the *Advertiser* from the 1950s forward. Lily looked around the room and said, "Sometimes when the newspaper is at my grandparents' house, I'll read it, but not very often. I like history books."

Vernon Publishing gives the kid journalists the "reporter's notebook" that adult journalists use, and the kids carry pencils to take notes. Lily faced a challenge because she was writing her story as COVID-19 broke out. Vernon said, "Her deadline was on March 13, when everything was exploding. School was halfway going at that point. She wrote hers at home and brought it in later."

Lily added, "It was definitely difficult. I left my notebook at school, so I had to remember all the facts. I had to research a little more, which is how I found more information. They didn't really tell us everything. When I got it back from school, I put more detail into it. It's good for older adults in the community to hear from younger kids because you don't hear that very often."

Lily was proud when she saw her stories in black and white. She said, "When I saw it in the newspaper, it was real."

Her mother understood how the paper can make things real. Kyle thought of her father's passing and the obituary and said, "It was a paper we didn't quite want to look at, but I also came and grabbed five copies. We mailed it to all our families in Chicago and they were quite happy to see it."

What was Lily's greatest discovery about the newspaper business?

"I learned that in the olden days they made hats out of newspapers," she answered. "When they got their hands in ink, they would wipe it on their hat." Vernon Publishing distributes the classic newspaper hats to the two reporters from each fifth-grade class.

Democracy Day has won many state and national awards. The National Newspaper Association gave the *Advertiser* a 2018 first-place honor for "Education Support & Civic Literacy, Daily and Non-Daily Division." Democracy Day is different from the Career Day that is popular in junior high and high schools. Vernon explained, "Many of the people are from service groups, volunteer organizations, and are political figures. The focus is on community and what they do to make the community better. We try to make it about civics and life lessons. For example, the bankers talk about why it is important to invest locally and save money. The insurance people talk about why insurance is important." A May 22, 2019, tornado tore through downtown Eldon, causing severe damage to many businesses and homes in the community. Students listened carefully to the insurance folks.

"We don't have a property tax in Eldon, so we make sure the kids know if they buy something in Eldon, they are taxpayers and should have a voice in their community," Vernon said.

Lily's father, Michael, is plant manager at Adient automotive seating in Eldon. Kyle is a stay-at-home mom. Lily has a brother, Graham, who is two years younger than she is. She declined to comment on Graham.

The family's roots are in the Chicago area. For more than twenty-seven years, Kyle's father managed the King Nissan dealership in Niles, just north of Chicago. Every summer he would take his family for a four-week vacation to the Tan-Tar-A at Lake of the Ozarks (now Jimmy Buffett's Margaritaville Lake Resort). Graham Terrance Grimes enjoyed the area so much he moved his family to Eldon in 1996. Kyle said, "I love it here. You get the small-community feel from everyone. My father had cancer for ten years and everyone rallied around us."

Back in the Chicago area, Kyle's family was close friends with the family of Dennis FitzSimons, former general manager of WGN-TV in Chicago and then-president/CEO of Tribune Broadcasting. He is now chairman of the board of directors of the Robert R. McCormick Foundation in Chicago. "We knew the big media, big newspaper thing forever," Kyle said. "It was interesting to go from that to see the small town of this. We read the *Sun-Times* and *Tribune*. They were delivered to our house."

In order to understand any community newspaper, you need to understand community.

What does community mean to Lily?

"Family," she answered. "Everybody here knows everybody, and everybody here is welcome for anybody."

News-O-Matic is a national version of Vernon's vision for children.

Established in 2013, the News-O-Matic site delivers news, sports, fashion stories, and more to kids on a daily basis. By 2021 more than two thousand schools across America were reading News-O-Matic. The New York–based company partnered with Amazon Unlimited to present stories on Audible or podcasts through the Echo Dot Kids Edition.

Like Trevor Vernon, *Chicago Reader* publisher Tracy Baim sees civic engagement and education as essential components to independent journalism's future. She said, "We're missing civic education and part of that is understanding journalism. The campaign I want to do annually would be around 'I Am Chicago Journalism.' We pick a journalist in every media outlet that's part of the campaign. We get an ad agency to do a tremendous visual effort around each of them—two-minute videos. High-powered stuff. Then we all get driven to one website where you can get to any of these community outlets. And then the fund matches it."

Such a campaign has the potential to raise new money sources and educate the community on the role of journalists. Just as important, it puts a face on journalists. "That is what's missing," Baim said. "What you see on TV, most of those are talking heads that are not journalists. They're compromised. We need people who are true journalists. That's my big dream. I don't think we're that far from it."

The future should always contain dreams. When I began my newspaper career, nothing was impossible, and I tried to maintain that boundless spirit. Think outside the box. The future contains fun and fellowship. As I became a seasoned (and hopefully not too cynical) journalist, I used Randle McMurphy from *One Flew Over the Cuckoo's Nest* as a metaphor with younger, frustrated writers. There is a scene in the film where McMurphy (Jack Nicholson) attempts to lift a watercooler. He cannot do it. His fellow repressed patients view the struggle in disbelief. He asks, "Giving up? I'm just warming up." McMurphy ultimately fails. Drenched in sweat, he tells the room that at least he tried. The future is bright when you take risks with a sense of adventure and awareness. The next generation of journalists knows this. They are just warming up.

Coda

My journey on the road of long-standing, independent community newspapers began in Hillsboro, Illinois. I watched the *Journal-News* and its staff navigate change through personal tribulations, a long global pandemic, and social unrest in America. I visited other small-town newspapers going through the gristle and shank of the newspaper business. They tried to deliver clarity and justice in a world that can be confusing and crooked. They continued to search for a better self along a humble path.

I reflected on my own triumphs and failures in my fifty years of journalism. I could have discussed this more in my writing, but that would have been selfish. I wanted my words to honor these papers' work and their place in time. I wanted to listen and learn. I recalled a quote from Martin Luther King Jr. I had heard while researching a previous book. "If I cannot do great things," he once said, "I can do small things in a great way." Despite immense challenges, men and women across America's small-town newspapers were doing just that. They understand that small things matter.

Debates about community exploded across the country in 2020. America turned into an uptight place, engulfed by fear, racial strife, and cancel culture. Questions were tossed about in newspapers, and heated debates defined social media. But there was no debating that democracy is wounded without community voices.

This chorus of declaration grows from a generous family tree and branches into all walks of daily life. Carroll, Iowa's, Doug Burns spoke of a fiercely proud journalism world that is shaped by the American work ethic of character and persistence. You truly are in it all together. Readers have a responsibility. It is an investment of analysis, time, and money. A free press is not free. I heard that many times in my newsroom visits. One editor told me that community is a circle over a circle over a circle. The truth is found in the center.

Hillsboro's John Galer said, "We're the first stop in history. In twenty, thirty years, people are going to look at what happened here. So it is important you get everything right. I tell my staff, you have to do this right, but don't expect a lot of pats on the back because I'm not sure, unless it is a controversial issue, that it will be that well read. That's what we are here for. Community journalism is reporting in an honest, fair, and open manner about the events that happen in your world. If you do that, then that's how communities drive and go."

These newspaper mavericks grew up in a world void of hedge funds and corporate management. The truth is easier to hear without all that static. And then, we discover the humanity in each other. It is the hopeful song of a bird that travels from house to house. As *Journal-News* publisher Mike Plunkett said in one of my first visits to Hillsboro, the highest praise he receives is when a reader says the *Journal-News* isn't *the* paper. They tell him, "It is *our* paper."

A community is only as strong as its community paper. This is not an elegy. The visions of these foot soldiers give newspapers hope for tomorrow. This is our world. Pay attention. We can determine how the future is written.

Acknowledgments

Thank you: Doug Seibold for the opportunity, Lisa Reardon for the empathetic editing, Amanda Gibson for the production editing, Jane Seibold for the production effort, Jacqueline Jarik for the publicity effort, Morgan Krehbiel for the cover design, and Patrick Embry for the guidance.

Sources

NEWSPAPERS

Arkansas
Arkansas Democrat-Gazette
Eureka Springs Independent

California
Bakersfield Californian

Florida
Miami Times

Illinois
Champaign *News-Gazette*
Chicago Reader
Evanston RoundTable
Hillsboro *Journal-News*
Paddock Publications
Pana News-Palladium
Shaw Media

Indiana
Madison Courier

Iowa
Carroll Times Herald

Missouri
Eldon Advertiser

South Carolina
Post and Courier

Tennessee
Tri-State Defender

Texas
Big Bend Sentinel

INTRODUCTION

Friedman, Thomas L. "Finding the 'Common Good' in a Pandemic." *New York Times*. March 25, 2020.

PEN America. "Losing the News: The Decimation of Local Journalism and the Search for Solutions." November 20, 2019.

Rodriguez, Richard. "Final Edition: Twilight of the American Newspaper." *Harper's Magazine*. November 2009.

CHAPTER ONE: THE COMMITMENT

Blow, Charles M. "As the Press Weakens, So Does Democracy." *New York Times*. July 19, 2021.

Dylan, Bob. "Q&A with Bill Flanagan." *Bob Dylan*. April 2009.

Jackson, David and Gary Marx. "Will the *Chicago Tribune* Be the Next Newspaper Picked to the Bone?" *New York Times*. January 21, 2020.

Tracy, Marc. "Gannett, Now Largest U.S. Newspaper Chain, Targets 'Inefficiencies.'" *New York Times*. November 20, 2019.

CHAPTER TWO: THE PRICE OF COMMUNITY

Boian, Mary Pat. "ISawArkansas." *Eureka Springs Independent*. July 3, 2019.

Butcher, Sterry. "Long Live the 'Big Bend Sentinel.' Viva 'El Internacional.'" *Texas Monthly*. October 2019.

CHAPTER THREE: SERVING HISTORY

Ebert, Roger. *Life Itself: A Memoir*. Grand Central Publishing, 2011.

"N-G Publisher Dies—Life's Work Spanned Radio, Arts, Charity." *News-Gazette*. December 23, 2002.

Wood, Paul. "Friends Remember *News-Gazette* Owner—Mrs. Chinigo Knew Magnates, Surgeons, Stars." *News-Gazette*. December 24, 2002.

Works Progress Administration. *WPA Guide to Illinois*. New York: Pantheon Books, 1939/1983, p. 596.

CHAPTER FOUR: STOP THE PRESSES! TECHNOLOGY HAS COME TO TOWN

Mateos, Evelyn. "A Whole New World." *Editor & Publisher*. September 2019.

Sasse, Ben. *Them: Why We Hate Each Other—and How to Heal*. St. Martin's Press, 2018.

CHAPTER SIX: OLD-SCHOOL FAMILY BUSINESS

Beaujon, Andrew. "Study Says Civic Participation Fell in Denver and Seattle After Newspapers Closed." Poynter. February 18, 2014.

Bennett, Jessica. "Kamala Harris Will Make History. So Will Her 'Big, Blended' Family." *New York Times*. January 17, 2021.

Fitzgerald, Mark. "'E&P' Names Moorhouse 'Publisher of the Year.'" *Editor & Publisher*. April 28, 2003.

Marek, Lynne. "Shaw Media Family Settles; Suit Against Northern Trust Goes to Trial." *Crain's Chicago Business*. January 8, 2014.

O'Dell, Tori. "A Column Written to Myself." *Journal-News* (Hillsboro, Il.). June 15, 2020.

Bakke, Dave. "Grace Is Among Good People of Montgomery County." *State Journal-Register* (Springfield, Il.). January 9, 2016.

"Shaw Media Family Lawsuit Ready for Trial." *Family Business*. December 3, 2013.

CHAPTER SEVEN: SEEDS OF CHANGE

Baim, Tracy. "The Child Consumer." *Chicago Defender*. February 27, 1975.

Borden, Jeff. "Uneasy Reader: A Quest for Youth." *Crain's Chicago Business*. September 30, 1996.

Dixon, Lance. "He Fought for Civil Rights for Almost a Century. Now a Street Has Been Named After Him." *Miami Herald*. November 3, 2017.

Michaeli, Ethan. *The Defender: How the Legendary Black Newspaper Changed America*. Houghton Mifflin Harcourt, 2016.

CHAPTER EIGHT: SELLING A FAMILY NEWSPAPER

Abernathy, Penelope Muse. "News Deserts and Ghost Newspapers: Will Local News Survive?" University of North Carolina Hussman School of Journalism and Media. June 2020.

CHAPTER NINE: OUTSOURCING AND RURAL AMERICA

Smith, Doug. "Hostilities Again in Eureka Media." *Arkansas Times*. July 18, 2012.

CHAPTER TEN: INSOURCING SPIRIT

McKinsey, Rebecca. "I've Known Men Like You, Donald Trump." *Daily Times Herald* (Carroll, Ia.). October 11, 2016.

CHAPTER ELEVEN: THE TRUTH ABOUT FAKE NEWS

Bowden, Bill. "*Times Free Press* Publisher Walter Hussman and Family Making $25 million Donation to UNC School of Journalism." *Arkansas Democrat-Gazette*. September 10, 2019.

Edmonds, Rick. "US Ranks Last Among 46 Countries in Trust in Media, Reuters Institute Report Finds." Poynter. June 22, 2021.

Flynn, Meagan. "A Small-Town Iowa Newspaper Brought Down a Cop. His Failed Lawsuit Has Now Put the Paper in Financial Peril." *Washington Post*. October 10, 2019.

Thompson, Carol. "Dozens of New Websites Appear to Be Michigan Local News Outlets, but with Political Bent." *Lansing State Journal*. October 20, 2019.

CHAPTER TWELVE: VIRUS CRISIS, 2020

Flaccus, Gillian. "Rural America Watches Pandemic Erupt in Cities as Fear Grows." Associated Press. March 25, 2020.

Graff, Garrett M.. "An Oral History of the Day Everything Changed." *Wired*. April 24, 2020.

"Survival Plan." *Isthmus*. March 19, 2020.

Tracy, Marc. "News Media Outlets Have Been Ravaged by the Pandemic." *New York Times*. April 10, 2020.

CHAPTER THIRTEEN: NONPROFIT MODEL

D'Amato, Erik. "Hard News for Nonprofit Media: 23 Pitfalls Facing Donor funded Journalism Initiatives." *Inside Philanthropy*. October 31, 2019.

"Nonprofit News Media Pace Picking Up." *NonProfit Times*. June 28, 2021.

Shafer, Jack. "Why Has Local News Collapsed? Blame Readers." *Politico*. June 12, 2021.

About the Author

Dave Hoekstra was a *Chicago Sun-Times* staff writer between 1985 and 2014; before that he spent three years on the staff of the *Suburban Sun-Times*. He was a 2013 recipient of the Studs Terkel Community Media Award and received a 2012 Peter Lisagor Award for Best Arts Reporting and Criticism. He has contributed pieces to *Chicago* magazine, the *Chicago Reader*, *Newcity*, and *Raw Vision* and has written books about Midwest supper clubs, soul food, the civil rights movement, van camping across America, Farm Aid, and minor league baseball. He has written and coproduced two documentaries, *The Staple Singers and the Civil Rights Movement* and *The Center of Nowhere: The Spirit and Sounds of Springfield, Missouri*. He lives outside of Chicago.